# Competence to Consent

**CENTER FOR BIOETHICS**
University of Pennsylvania
3401 Market Street - Ste 320
Philadelphia, PA 19104-3308
(215) 898-7136

# Competence to Consent

Becky Cox White

GEORGETOWN UNIVERSITY PRESS / WASHINGTON, D.C.

Georgetown University Press, Washington, D.C.   20007
© 1994 by Georgetown University Press. All rights reserved.
Printed in the United States of America.
10   9   8   7   6   5   4   3   2   1      1994
THIS VOLUME IS PRINTED ON ACID-FREE OFFSET BOOKPAPER.


Library of Congress Cataloging-in-Publication Data

White, Becky.
    Competence to consent / Becky Cox White.
        p.      c.m.   --   (Clinical medical ethics)
    Includes bibliographical references and index.
        1. Medical ethics.   2. Capacity and disability.   3. Informed
    consent (Medical law)   I. Title.   II. Series: Clinical medical
    ethics (Washington, D.C.)
        [DNLM:   1. Mental Competency.   2. Patient Acceptance of Health
    care.   3. Informed Consent.      W 85 1994]
    R724.W47   1994
    174'.2--dc20
    ISBN 0-87840-559-3 (cloth).   --   ISBN 0-87840-560-7 (paper)   94-9917

*To Viola L. Cox*
*my mother*
*without whom nothing would have been possible.*

# Contents

# Acknowledgments

Numerous people contributed to this work. For their indispensable advice, guidance, and meticulous review of various drafts of this work, I owe much to George J. Agich, Ph.D.; Baruch A. Brody, Ph.D.; H. Tristram Engelhardt, Jr., M.D., Ph.D.; Edmund L. Erde, Ph.D.; Stuart F. Spicker, Ph.D.; Laurence Tancredi, J.D., M.D.; Stephen A. Wear, Ph.D.; and Kevin Wm. Wildes S.J., Ph.D. Thanks, too, to the editorial staff at Georgetown University Press for their invaluable assistance with the entire manuscript.

I am also indebted to Joyce Schmidt, M.D.; S. Kay Toombs, Ph.D.; and Joel Zimbelman, Ph.D.; for their many conversations about health care and the meaning of competence to consent and why both competence and consent are morally fundamental.

Earlier versions of this work were presented in 1988 and 1991 at national meetings of the Society for Health and Human Values. The suggestions that resulted improved the work significantly. Thanks, too, to California State University, Chico, for granting me leave with pay, January through May, 1990.

My special thanks to Manuel M. Davenport, Ph.D., teacher and friend, for convincing me that I could do philosophy; to Baruch Brody for making me want to and teaching me how; to Tris Engelhardt, without whose many efforts of all sorts this book would never have been born; and to my husband and daughter, Kelly and Kathy White, my mother, Viola Cox, and An's ears, without whose love and support I would never have survived the birthing process.

# Introduction

Questions of competence arise within the health care setting when persons must decide whether to (1) consent to recommended therapy; (2) forgo the recommended treatment, but pursue a therapeutic alternative; or (3) refuse health care entirely. This volume addresses the question of who is competent to make these decisions. In its entirety, it identifies and justifies both the structure of and the capacities that define competence to give a free and informed consent.

This work is not the first word about competence. Its starting point is a rich body of literature in which clinicians and philosophers alike have toiled to clarify the meaning of competence to consent and how to determine which patients possess it. In fact, practicing health care professionals, the intended audience for this work, may take the issue to have been settled long ago, especially since most experienced clinicians have a good intuitive grasp of which patients are competent, which are not, and which require further investigation. Nevertheless, since health care interventions have the potential to alter patients' lives in momentous ways, whether or not a patient is competent should not be left to "gut-level" feelings.

Some professionals will claim that nothing beyond experienced intuition is required. Why, they wonder, is a new analysis of competence needed? This question has both practical and theoretical answers. Practically speaking, the current approach to competence analysis is often found wanting. In many cases, a patient's competence cannot be determined with certainty. Chapter One considers cases in which competence assessments are crucial, identifies patient conditions and behaviors that trigger health professionals' concerns about their patients' competence, examines the strengths and weaknesses of relying on professional intuitions, and reveals why the law is unable to resolve cases of contested competence.

Theoretically speaking, the answer is more complex. To begin, competence is the cornerstone for one of the most widespread practices of modern health care—free and informed consent. Informed consent cannot move forward without a competent consenter because an informed consent is neither morally nor legally valid unless the person giving it is competent. Because a competent patient is the sole source of decisional authority for diagnostic or therapeutic interventions, competence must be determined in order to ascertain whether the health care provider has legitimate authority to diagnose or treat.

Moreover, this requirement cannot be omitted; without competence, informed consent cannot guarantee the goals for which it was established: respecting patient autonomy and promoting patient welfare. First, autonomous patients construct sets of values, interests, goals, and beliefs (which jointly comprise a patient's value structure) in terms of which they organize their lives. They are the best sources about the content of these value structures, and their autonomous choices take these factors into account. Respect for autonomy depends on facilitating and supporting such autonomous choices. And, as Chapter Two demonstrates, autonomy depends on competence.

Second, a patient's value structure provides the basis for the second goal of informed consent—promoting beneficent patient care—because what will count as beneficent, that is, what actually will promote a patient's welfare, depends on what the patient values. Here, again, competence is central because only competent patients can reliably report their own settled views about what interventions will be best for them. In short, competence is an essential feature of free and informed consent, and free and informed consent is a key mechanism by which to respect autonomy and provide beneficent patient care. As established, the practice of free and informed consent strives to promote and protect patient autonomy and welfare by making the patient a partner in the health care decision-making process. Chapter Two examines the relationship between the practice of informed consent, the principles of respect for autonomy and beneficence, and competence to give (or withhold) consent.

In spite of the discussion competence has provoked, no universally (or even widely) accepted definition of competence exists. Agreement is widespread that competence ought to be assessed in terms of capacities (abilities). That is, one is competent to do a task if one possesses the particular capacities that doing the task requires. For example, cardiovascular surgeons are competent if they have (among others) the capacities to diagnose surgically correctable cardiovascular pathology, perform operative procedures that remedy these disorders, and recognize and respond to postoperative distress. Likewise bioethicists are competent if they have particular abilities: they can diagnose moral dilemmas that arise in the biological sciences, understand moral theory and principles and apply them to the resolution of moral dilemmas, and recognize and respond to the distress that attends moral decision making. Examples could be multiplied here, but the point is clear: persons are competent to do particular tasks when they have the abilities required for their successful completion.

Likewise, persons are competent to consent if they possess certain capacities—those required for decision making in health care settings. Various suggestions have been made as to what these capacities might be. Confusion has arisen because some or all of the suggested capacities may not be present in some persons who seem to be generally capable of managing their affairs. Or these capabilities may be present in some persons who do not seem capable of managing their affairs. Or the abilities may be present in varying degrees in different persons or within one person at different times. Currently no consensus exists about what capacities—and in what number or to what degree—constitute competence to consent.

Confusion also exists regarding the important distinction between *defining* competence and *measuring* it. To pick an example from bioethics, it is one thing to decide on a definition of death (e.g., loss of the brain functions necessary for minimal sensory-motor functions, for minimal consciousness, or for the individual to function as an integrated human person). It is quite a different thing to decide how to measure the loss of these functions to determine when death has occurred (e.g., clinical observations of brainstem-mediated reflexes, CT scans that depict widespread cerebral damage, or cerebral angiography that demonstrates absence of cerebral blood flow).

Chapter Three looks at these two closely interwoven aspects of competence. After a discussion of the task-oriented nature of decision making in general and competence to consent in particular, problems with previous efforts to define competence are considered. The analyses of the nature of decision making and of past definitional difficulties point toward a preliminary definition of both the capacities and the structure required for competence.

Chapter Four extends this discussion by defining, justifying, and applying the structure of competence. This structure provides an understanding of competence as occurring within a specific, rather than general, context; as occurring in degrees rather than as precisely specified by a threshold; as independent of consequential appeals; and as incorporating both cognitive and affective capacities.

Chapter Five completes the task of defining competence by not only identifying the characteristics, that is, the capacities, that competent persons possess, but also by justifying them and examining their implications. Chapter Six considers the implications of this definition in a broader context and anticipates a few criticisms of the new definition.

My task in this book is to provide a conceptual analysis of competence. As a result, certain important issues will not be examined other than tangentially. For example, I do not develop a test for competence. However, since the choice of a test will depend on how competence is defined, this volume will provide the necessary conceptual starting point without which tests for competence are impossible.

Similarly, I do not address competence within a legal context. Nor is any discussion included within the book intended to pass for legal advice. Competence has long been a concern of the courts, which must often determine whether persons are competent to participate in their defense proceedings, manage funds, and so forth. This volume limits its focus to the problems of defining competence within clinical practice, and completely eschews consideration of any particular laws in light of which actual cases are adjudicated.

Lastly, I do not attempt to justify the nature or the use of the doctrine of informed consent as that practice is currently understood. (For such a justification, see Stephen Wear, 1993.) Nor will this volume address how competence may be applied to particular patient populations (e.g., children, the developmentally disabled). These concerns are interesting and important, but their analysis exceeds the scope of this work.

My goal in exploring the bioethical issues that surround competence and its role in the practice of free and informed consent is to introduce health care professionals and bioethicists to the key practical, philosophical, and moral issues involved in assessing competence. The concepts developed here are unlikely to be the last word on competence. To make such a claim would be presumptuous. More likely the concepts developed here will be an early stage in an evolutionary process that will, in time, produce an even richer and more nuanced theory of competence to consent. If the book stimulates others to think about this concept in new and exciting ways, I will count it a success.

# 1

# Competence in the Health Care Setting

## WHEN COMPETENCE IS AN ISSUE

Health care professionals (HCPs) face the question of competence every time they solicit a patient's consent. In most cases the issue is not problematic because there is no reason to question the patient's competence. Just as the law assumes people are innocent until proven guilty, clinicians presume patients are competent until their incompetence is proven or until there are good reasons to suspect it. Nonetheless, every HCP has had occasion to wonder if a particular presumption of competence was appropriate. Consider the following case:

> Mr. W, a businessman from a distant state, was admitted last night to ICU with massive head trauma following an automobile accident. He is not expected to live. His wife, who is 38 weeks pregnant, arrived this morning to be with her husband. Late this afternoon Mrs. W went into labor and began bleeding vaginally. Sonography revealed a complete placenta previa. Dr. X, a complete stranger to Mrs. W just hours before, explains that she needs a Cesarean Section immediately, that without it the baby has a 99 percent and she has a 50 percent chance of dying. Family and friends are unavailable for consultation. Mrs. W, sobbing, refuses the surgery. When asked to explain her decision, Mrs. W. only shakes her head, cries, "No! No!" and continues to weep.

Would most HCPs assume that Mrs. W's refusal ends the matter? Should Dr. X wash his hands of the case? Of course not. Two lives are at stake. But if concerted efforts fail to persuade Mrs. W to consent, what options remain? In all likelihood the question of Mrs. W's competence would be raised at this point. Why? Because clinicians recognize that many factors—all commonly part of a patient's environment—can

impair decision making. Stress, fear, pain, drugs, and pathophysiology
(especially that which alters mental status—e.g., hypoxemia, hypercal-
cemia, hypoglycemia) can interfere with decisional ability. Since Mrs.
W is affected by stress, pain, and fear, most HCPs would not be surprised to hear Dr. X suggest that Mrs. W's refusal is not competent and
should be ignored. But should we ignore her choice? Was her refusal
competent? How do we know? Can we be sure? Since stress, pain, and
fear do not always eliminate decision-making ability, what aspect of
Mrs. W's refusal raises the issue of incompetence?

Undoubtedly a major stimulus for questioning Mrs. W's competence is that she has refused to undergo an established and effective
treatment for an easily and reliably identifiable condition that threatens her life and the life of her baby.[1] Her choice appears to sacrifice
not only her child's well-being, but her own as well; thus, it seems
irrational. Mrs. W's competence would most likely not have been
questioned (though perhaps it should be) had she agreed with her
doctor's recommendation. In fact, even if she had agreed, we would
probably not be surprised to hear Dr. X mutter, "I hope she really
understands."

Or consider the case of Ms. Y:

> Ms. Y has just undergone a lumpectomy for breast malignancy. Axil-
> lary lymph node biopsy was negative. Her oncologist, Dr. Z, recom-
> mends follow-up radiation and chemotherapy. He informs Ms. Y
> that he has recommended follow-up radiation for several years, but
> has only recently begun to recommend chemotherapy as well. His
> new recommendation is based on studies suggesting mortality rates
> decrease when both adjunctive therapies are used. In addition,
> because Ms. Y is anemic, Dr. Z wishes to give her a blood transfu-
> sion and begin iron supplements prior to beginning adjunctive treat-
> ment. Ms. Y appears disinterested in Dr. Z's comments; after he
> finishes speaking she says, "I don't care. Do what you want."

Here we might begin by asking whether Ms. Y did consent. Is her
off-hand remark, "Do what you want," a genuine permission to treat?
If we think Ms. Y has given consent, was that consent competent?
How do we know? Are we sure? Do the conditions of her illness significantly impede her decision-making capacities? Would we be surprised to hear Dr. Z state, "Maybe I should discuss this with her
again?"

## WHY COMPETENCE IS AN ISSUE

Competence is an issue for HCPs because it is the foundation of one of the central practices in the provision of health care: informed consent. Morally and legally, health care cannot be provided until an informed consent has been given by a competent patient. As a result, assessing competence is the necessary first step in the process of obtaining informed consent. If the patient is not competent, he is not the appropriate decision maker. If the patient is not the appropriate decision maker, the information must be provided to and consent solicited from someone else. In short, the process of informing the patient cannot begin until the patient's competence has been established. Thus, HCPs must be able to determine which patients are, and which are not, competent decision makers. Unless determinations of patient competence are possible, the validity of consents cannot be assured.

## THE PRESUMPTION OF COMPETENCE AND PROFESSIONAL EXPERTISE

Doctors X and Z are not certain their patients are competent to consent. Their uncertainty stems from the fact that competence is an extraordinarily complex concept that has not been well defined. The combination of complexity and the lack of an explicit definition gives rise to uncertainty about the competence of particular patients. Before examining the causes of such ambiguities, however, we should recognize three important areas about which there is widespread agreement: (1) Patients are assumed to be competent until there is good reason to think otherwise; (2) Some patients are obviously competent and some patients are obviously incompetent; and (3) HCPs have a good intuitive grasp of which patients are competent and which are not.

### Why patients are assumed to be competent

There are two good reasons to assume, absent evidence to the contrary, that patients are competent. The first is practical. Most persons enter the health care system from real lives that they manage successfully. Patients are persons first and patients second. They are motivated to seek help so that they can get back to doing what they usually do. The stockbroker who visits a doctor for right lower quadrant pain intends to return to her world of investments as soon as she recovers from her appendectomy. The football player who consults a physical therapist for an exercise regime following a knee injury seeks to reduce both temporary and permanent damage so he can quickly return to his success on the playing field and enjoy a long career. Patients with chronic illnesses have similar pragmatic motivations. The architect consults a diabetes nurse specialist in order to be as free as possible from symptoms that interfere with her personal and professional life. The housewife with emphysema seeks to minimize the exertional dyspnea that impedes her ability to complete her daily chores. Indeed, the vast majority of patients intend their encounters with HCPs to be brief but necessary interludes in their "real" lives. HCPs share this perspective and work to promote quick and full restoration of health or to minimize disability so patients can resume those lives. Since most patients give little or no evidence that they are incompetent to manage decisions in their ordinary lives, there is no reason to assume they are incompetent to manage health care decisions.

The observation that most patients competently manage their lives is practically important for three reasons. First, routinely assuming incompetence would be an onerous imposition on practitioners. Each patient would have to have his competence assessed prior to each health care decision. The commitment of professional time and effort required to perform such assessments would be enormous at best, impossible at worst; and those resources would be much better spent in diagnostic and treatment efforts. Second, no reliable test for competence currently exists. Thus, even if HCPs had time to test for competence, they lack the tools necessary to do so. Third, even if professionals had the time and a reliable test for competence, the delay in treatment caused by routine and repeated competence assessment would jeopardize patient health and well-being. In sum, devoting professional resources to a non-problem is time-consuming, wasteful, impossible, and threatening to patient welfare—or, impractical. Thus, in the absence of evidence of incompetence, the better approach is to assume competence and devote professional attention to treating patients so they can resume their lives.

Of course some patients do a better job of running their lives than others. Moreover, some persons engage in unusual, bizarre, or unpopular lifestyles or behavior that most of us would shun. HCPs may be unsympathetic to the patient who is injured while bungee jumping, or who continues to contract sexually transmitted diseases as a result of promiscuity. The second reason to assume that patients are competent is that the assumption of competence helps protect an important moral and social value: freedom.

The freedom to run one's own life is an important value. Many governments explicitly recognize its importance for their citizens. Some, such as the United States, adopt it as the foundation for their structure and as a constraint against governmental interference in the lives of their citizens. Residents of free countries cannot be forced to do things they do not wish to do. Such communities commonly recognize that many citizens will engage in activities of which other citizens disapprove. Nonetheless, Jones's disapproval of abortion does not allow her to keep Smith from terminating a pregnancy. Just because Green does not approve of cosmetic surgery does not permit him to interfere with Brown's rhinoplasty. The importance of freedom as a value supports one's right to be wrong (where "wrong" is defined by other people in terms of their own values). So long as other persons are not directly harmed, competent persons are free to pursue their lives according to their own goals and values. They can bungee jump, engage in casual sexual encounters, have abortions, skydive, overeat, and so forth. Incompetent persons are not accorded such freedom. However, given the importance and centrality of freedom in many societies, the burden of proof is on those who would curtail it—and disapproval of a person's choice is not by itself sufficient reason to intervene.

The importance of freedom in the consent setting is acknowledged in the requirement that legally and morally valid consents must be freely given; and, once given, must be respected. In society generally and in health care derivatively, allowing competent persons to take charge of their lives is the best mechanism for protecting their freedom. In fact, the purpose of the practice of informed consent is to protect this freedom within the health care setting.

### Patients who are obviously competent or incompetent

Why do HCPs assume that people are competent to take charge of their lives? The best evidence for this is that they are successfully doing so. People make decisions each day about how to manage their lives. They identify problems, weigh the pros and cons of different solutions, and decide what to do. While HCPs have little access to the majority of their patients' day-to-day decisions, they do have some evidence of competent decision making: the person is considering treatment for a specified problem. Patients solicit (or, in cases of unplanned encounters with the health care system, do not refuse to consider) health care advice because they appreciate that disease and disability threaten their general well-being. They turn to HCPs to help minimize this threat. Patients bring their decision-making abilities with them to the health care setting, and there is usually no reason to doubt these abilities merely because the occasion for their use is a health care problem. If patients continue to demonstrate decent problem-solving techniques, their competence is not questioned.

On the other hand, some patients clearly possess no decision-making ability. Patients whose decision-making capacities are intractably absent or impaired are obviously incompetent. The patient who is permanently confused, profoundly intellectually disabled, or permanently comatose is in no position to recognize the problem at hand—let alone to understand or resolve it. Moreover, some patients are simply too sick to participate in health care choices. The patient who is obtunded by posttraumatic hypovolemic shock is physically incapable of making decisions. Full-blown acute paranoiacs who suspect everyone's motives are psychologically incapable of taking part in choices.

### Professional expertise and competence determinations

HCPs are generally quite adept at recognizing which patients are competent and which are not. This skill results from frequent encounters with persons in decision-making situations. HCPs routinely observe how people manage information, consider therapeutic options, and weigh the burdens and benefits of various treatments. HCPs have helped countless patients decide whether to undergo coronary bypass grafting, have surgery or chemotherapy and radiation for breast cancer, use exercise and diet or antihypertensives to lower blood pressure. They can recognize when the process is running smoothly and when it is in danger of being derailed. Moreover, HCPs are familiar with the conditions that can impair decision-making facility. They can anticipate and often prevent or reduce the stress, pain, or fear that impedes mental acuity. Their routine participation in patient decision making leads to professional expertise in determining how well it is going.

To recap, society in general and HCPs in particular routinely and rightly assume that persons are competent. There are clear-cut cases of both competence and incompetence, and HCPs are expert in identifying both. Nonetheless, even experienced HCPs occasionally have doubts about their patients' competence. Mrs. W and Ms. Y exemplify cases in which doubts about patient competence may arise. In such cases HCPs are uncertain how to proceed. This uncertainty is problematic because the practice of obtaining free and informed consent from patients requires that persons giving consent be competent. Valid consents depend on knowing when patients are and are not competent.

## WHEN COMPETENCE IS IN QUESTION

Even if most patients are competent, some are not. Numerous conditions trigger suspicions about patients' competence. The most common cause for questioning a patient's competence is the patient's refusal of a recommended therapy. Patients who are even minimally involved in the decision-making process are usually given the benefit of the doubt—until they disagree with their providers. The patient who, following a cerebellar CVA, agrees to the ventricular shunt, agrees to physical therapy, agrees to the medication regime, and agrees to attend "stop smoking" classes will be fully supported in all these ventures. However, were the same patient to refuse those interventions, her competence may be questioned. The patient who refuses these therapies may be incompetent. If, however, the explanation for the alleged incompetence is cerebral hypoxia, it is worth noting that cerebral hypoxia is quite likely present even if the patient agrees to the shunt and physical therapy and so forth. Competence does not vanish just because professional decisions are contested, nor does compliance guarantee its presence. The point is that refusing therapies that will most likely restore health or minimize disability triggers the suspicion that patient decision-making abilities are impaired. That is, the patient's competence is suspect.

More generally, patients may rouse suspicions about their competence if they behave oddly in other ways. One example of odd behavior is a patient's failure to participate in her health care choices. This failure may be explicit, as in the case of Ms. Y who says, "I don't care. Do what you want." It may be subtle, as when patients pay no attention to discussions about their therapeutic alternatives. The patient newly diagnosed with multiple sclerosis who stares vacantly out the window while his doctors are attempting to plan a treatment regimen triggers suspicion that he may not be competent to participate in these decisions.

Historically, patients were neither expected nor encouraged to participate in decisions regarding their care. They were assumed to be incapable of or uninterested in doing so. Of course, the doctor would do what he wanted; he knew best. This approach is no longer the norm. Patients are expected to participate actively in their care, and their failure to do so evokes concern. At the very least nonparticipation raises questions about whether patients appreciate the gravity of the situation.

Concerns also arise when patients are trying to participate in health care choices, but exhibit difficulty doing so. A patient may be willing, but unable, to acquire relevant facts. I am not referring here to obvious cases, such as head-injured patients who are stuporous, or Alzheimer's patients who cannot assimilate or remember anything. Rather, I refer to more subtle symptoms, for example, a patient who does not demonstrate decreased level of consciousness or general memory deficit but who must repeatedly be given information about differing morbidity and mortality between simple vs. radical mastectomy because she repeatedly forgets it. After her HCPs make several attempts to provide the relevant information, she finally says, "Look. I can't remember this stuff anyway. Let's just do that radical one." Should her surgery be scheduled? Was her decision competent? How do we know? The lack of informability suggests she may not be competent.

Other patients cannot meaningfully consider data. They lack the ability to appreciate relevant facts or to apply them to themselves. Consider a couple undergoing natural childbirth. Prenatal classes extensively educate couples about the discomfort of labor and techniques to manage it. Yet, some couples who intend to forgo analgesics find that they have underestimated either the pain or their ability to control it. The anticipated relatively comfortable labor has not occurred. But the couple, now weary and in a great deal of psychological and physical pain, are unable to appreciate that they are among those for whom analgesia is recommended or required. They continue steadfastly to refuse analgesia. Is the couple's continued rejection of medication competent? Should the HCPs, who recognize that analgesia is indicated, override their refusal? If HCPs do override the refusal, have they done something wrong? The couple's inability to appreciate their current circumstances raises the possibility of incompetence.

Another trigger of concern about patient competence is the inability to come to a decision. Patients may be able to understand facts and even appreciate their importance, yet be unable to decide on an option. What should be done about the patient with nasopharyngeal carcinoma who really does understand that the mortality and morbidity rates are virtually the same following local radiation with chemotherapy and surgical removal, but who cannot decide which to undergo? Since the morbidity takes different forms without altering mortality, therapy really is a matter of personal preference. Of course, some time can be taken for patients to get a sense of their preferences, but delaying the decision too long increases the risk of metastasis. Does indecision ever become incompetence? Certainly at some point it can lead HCPs to suspect the patient's decision-making ability.

Many people who behave oddly are not incompetent but only eccentric. From the perspective of consent, however, odd behavior may indicate an inability to participate competently in decisions about one's care. When patients withdraw from health care decisions, or attempt unsuccessfully to participate, their odd behavior leads HCPs to question their competence.

These triggers of suspicion focus on behavior, on something patients do or fail to do. Additional suspicions arise on the basis of what patients are. That is, the general status of certain patients may cause anxiety. Stephen Wear, for example, notes that patients with histories of mental illness, dementia, or stroke raise worries about competence (1993, p. 49).[2] A psychiatric diagnosis traditionally provokes worry that patients may not be competent to consent. Likewise, head injuries, CNS pathology, multisystem disease, advanced age, and developmental disabilities may also cause HCPs to question patient competence. As previously noted, common clinical conditions—pain, fear, stress, drugs, pathophysiology—spark concern.

There are, then, numerous factors in clinical settings that make HCPs uneasy about accepting patients' consents or refusals. The question is, what should be done in such cases? If we knew with certainty who among our worrisome patients is competent and who is not, we would at least know when to redirect decision-making authority from the patient to someone else. But, in hard cases, we do not know with certainty whether patients are competent—that is why they are hard cases. A precise definition of competence would identify the characteristics necessary to be competent to consent. If our patients possessed these characteristics—that is, if they can meet the definition— they are competent. We do not have this sort of definition. That is why we have tough cases.

## WHY THE LAW IS NO HELP

Many have suggested that in tough cases where competence is in question the law should be involved. If HCPs cannot determine a patient's competence, the courts should decide. There are two reasons why this approach will not work.

The first reason the law cannot help is a practical one. If HCPs must turn to the courts every time a patient's competence is in doubt, it will be difficult if not impossible to provide health care. The courts are known for thorough, not quick, consideration of problems. Even if the courts were speedier, the time taken to involve the courts (e.g., making certain that all parties have competent legal counsel) is much too unwieldy and expensive to be of use in managing day-to-day patient care. Many—perhaps even most—patients would suffer increased disability and suffering while awaiting determinations of their competence. Some would die.

The second reason the law is of little use is that law, like medicine, has no operational definition of competence. That is, the law does not specify how competence is to be assessed. In 1941, Milton Green noted that "judicial tests of incompetence . . . remain purely subjective" (Green, 1941, p. 145). More crucially, he notes that even appealing to cases that have been adjudicated cannot provide a suitable definition:

> . . . no verbal formulation of a test can be made which will fit the standards laid down by the courts. So diverse is the phraseology of the test[s] by courts in different jurisdictions, and even by various opinions within the same jurisdiction, that no single statement of a rule can be constructed (p. 147).

This flaw has not been remedied since Green voiced this complaint fifty years ago. Loren Roth notes: "There are today no universally accepted criteria for adjudicating a patient's competency to consent to or refuse treatment" (Roth, 1979, p. 1122); and as recently as 1991 psychiatrist Mark Perl remarked: "There are no unanimous standards for competency" (Perl, 1991, p. 179).

Oddly, this void has not deterred courts from adjudicating the competence of particular persons. However, to support their findings, courts generally rely on physicians (particularly on psychiatrists) to instruct them regarding the person's capacities, decisional and other.

As Kenneth Schaffner indicates:

Though a determination of 'incompetency' in its strict sense is a *legal* determination and is made by a judge, the determination typically rests on information and an interpretation of that information provided by medical personnel and in particular by psychiatrists (Schaffner, 1991, p. 253).

Relying on HCPs is understandable, given their familiarity with complex decision making and their ability to recognize when it proceeds with less proficiency than normal. However, HCPs themselves continue to debate the standards and tests that best define and determine competence. In their seminal 1977 article, "Tests for Competency to Consent to Treatment," Roth et al. list five different standards or tests for competence. That the issue has yet to be resolved is attested to by leading physicians and philosophers who continue to puzzle about this problem.[3] Physicians themselves are often puzzled about whether particular patients are competent. Since these are just the cases that courts are called on to address, HCPs are unable to help the law *and* the law is unable to help HCPs.

Suppose, however, that the law decided to construct a definition of competence to resolve future hard cases. Legal scholars would still quite likely consult the experts, that is, the health professionals. In fact, if the law failed to consult medicine, medicine would—and should—insist on being involved. Any attempt to construct a definition without information from the group who knows the most about it and will be largely responsible for its implementation would certainly be ill-advised. However, the use of such information will be limited unless HCPs themselves can provide an unambiguous operational definition of competence. To date they have not been able to do so.

Clinicians and bioethicists need a clear understanding of competence to consent. Without it, they cannot determine the appropriate person from whom to solicit consent or decide which principle—beneficence or autonomy—should govern decision making. Because the capacities that define competence have not been specified, the moral and legal authority of current consents is in doubt.

## SUMMARY

The health care environment is loaded with conditions that can impair patients' decision-making abilities. As a result, HCPs face tough cases in which the decision-making competence of patients is in question. In such cases HCPs' normal expertise at evaluating competence fails. Yet because of the central role competence plays in decision-making authority and informed consent, its moral importance cannot be ignored. An explicit definition of competence is needed against which particular patients may be compared. The law has not, and cannot, provide such a definition. It is up to others to do so. This volume is a step in that direction.

## NOTES

1. Health care has a long tradition of suggesting that patients who make "wrong" choices are incompetent. As a general rule, patients who accept their clinicians' recommendations do not have their competence questioned. However, if the patient disagrees with suggested therapies, the question of competence is often raised. The thought is that "no sane patient" would choose contrary to the recommended regimen. For discussions of this asymmetry, see Abernethy, 1984, 1991; Appelbaum et al., 1987; Appelbaum and Roth, 1981; Baumgarten, 1980; Buchanan, 1985; Buchanan and Brock, 1986, 1989; Morreim, 1991; Pellegrino, 1991; Perl, 1991; Wear, 1991; and Weinstock et al., 1984.

2. See Wear, 1993, pp. 46–50, for a good summary of conditions that trigger suspicions of incompetence.

3. See Wear, 1993, Chapter Seven; and the Cutter-Shelp volume generally.

# 2

# Ethical Foundations of Competence to Consent

A patient's consent for or refusal of health care is not morally valid unless that consent is competent. This claim needs to be defended, so this chapter will examine the relationship of ethical principles to informed consent in general and competence in particular. Here we will address three issues: the relation of competence to the ethical principles of (1) respect for autonomy and (2) beneficence, and (3) the nature of practices. Understanding the relationship of competence to ethical principles demonstrates that competence is an important moral issue. Understanding competence as an example of a practice demonstrates how health care acknowledges its moral responsibility to patients, and helps explain why competence cannot be ignored when its assessment is inconvenient or difficult.

## COMPETENCE AND THE PRINCIPLE OF RESPECT FOR AUTONOMY

The word "autonomy" comes from the Greek words for "self" (*autos*) and "government," "rule," or "law" (*nomos*). Autonomy means self-government, self-rule, or self-legislation. Autonomous self-rule must be distinguished from mere capricious choice. To be autonomous is to base decisions on principles or laws, not on whimsy.

### The Moral Importance of Autonomy

The moral importance of autonomy was demonstrated by the great eighteenth century German philosopher, Immanuel Kant. Kant was so firmly committed to morality based on laws that he proposed a single, exceptionless principle of morality (the Categorical Imperative) which states "Act so that you can at the same time will that it should become a universal law" (Kant, *Foundations of the Metaphysics of Morals*, p. 44=[421], trans. Beck). According to the Categorical Imperative, persons act morally only if their behavior would be universally appropriate; that is, if they are not making exceptions in their own cases. For example, Jones can lie only if he is prepared to allow others to lie (i.e., if lying is universally appropriate).

Kant based his Categorical Imperative on the capacity for rational thought. He believed that morality comes from reason, that any rational being can understand—without relying on others, for example, parents, clergy, or moral philosophers—what behaviors are morally required and morally forbidden. With reason, persons could formulate, appreciate, and choose to abide by moral laws. Without reason, people are like animals—unable to be moral or immoral. In sum, the ability to reason is the foundation of morality.

As bearers of reason, persons are also inherently valuable.[1] This belief does not mean that, having determined the nature of morally appropriate behavior, rational persons necessarily do the right thing. Rather, reason means that persons are capable of determining for themselves what is right and wrong, capable of "instructing themselves" to do the right thing, and capable of understanding why, depending on what they choose to do, they are morally praiseworthy or blameworthy. This constellation of capacities is what is meant by "autonomy." To be capable of autonomy is to be capable of independently (1) developing principles of behavior, (2) recognizing that these principles should guide one's own behavior, and (3) evaluating one's own and others' behavior with reference to those principles. This trio of capacities identifies autonomous persons.

### The Morally Neutral Importance of Autonomy

Autonomy is morally important because autonomous persons develop moral principles to guide and evaluate behavior. But autonomy also has value outside the moral realm. Individuals engage in autonomous behavior in two morally neutral ways.

#### Choosing a Value Structure

First, the same abilities that allow persons to be autonomous moral agents also allow them to develop morally neutral principles with which to guide and evaluate behavior. Using these abilities, persons construct unique lives that have special value for themselves. People pick and choose from a plethora of values, goals, beliefs, and interests those that they believe are most important. The products of such choices are individual value structures on which people then base their lives. The possibilities are endless. For example, one person might value a life of excitement. Her goal might be to see as much of the world as is possible because she believes that life is short and there is no afterlife or reincarnation. She therefore has an interest in getting as much excitement from this life as possible. This month she is off to Tanzania for a photographic safari; next month she is off to scale Mt. McKinley. Another person who believes in a Judeo-Christian God may value a life ordered by the Ten Commandments. Her goal is a life that is as Christ-like as possible; she has an interest in preparing herself for an eternal life in Heaven. This year she is off to Somalia to help distribute food to the starving; next year she will devote her energies to assisting Mother Theresa.

The world is full of values, goals, beliefs, and interests. Different people make different choices, choices that provide them with value structures that define their personalities and provide the basis for principled action. Based on their chosen value structures, persons may choose to live alone or in community, to marry or remain single, to have children or not to have children, to join a religion and embrace its beliefs and rules or to forswear all organized systems of value and develop their own codes of conduct, to value education or to drop out of school, to devote their lives to serving others or to be self-centered. Value structures, as collections of values, long-term goals, and beliefs, are an indication of an individual's best interests. Individual value structures define for persons the best intermediate goals and the best (for them) means for achieving the outcomes that are in their own best interests. This dynamic raises the second morally neutral realm in which autonomy plays an important role: decision making.

### Choosing in Terms of a Value Structure

Persons use their value structures to guide their behavior throughout their lives, though many people will, of course, continue to scrutinize them. New information and changing circumstances will often lead them to reconsider their values, goals, beliefs, or interests. Value structures may be revised periodically. As moral principles guide behavior in the moral realm, so value structures guide behavior in the personal realm. Persons who treat these values as principles for personal decision making are said to act with integrity. For example, the vegetarian who values animal welfare consistently chooses not to eat meat.

Autonomy is important to decision making because choices are opportunities to act on values. Since autonomy has to do with principled decision making, autonomous choices have three characteristics: They are *informed* (i.e., the choice is made by someone who possesses the material data); *made with understanding* (i.e., the choice is made after the material data have been considered and their import appreciated); and *uncoerced* (i.e., the choice is freely made rather than being forced on the decision maker). These characteristics are important because without full information and freedom to act, principled choice cannot be assured.

In short, there are two morally neutral opportunities for exercising autonomy: (1) consideration and selection of various goals, interests, beliefs, and values so as to erect a personal value structure; and (2) choosing in terms of that value structure. Choices based on ethical principles are ethically principled; choices based on one's value structure are personally principled.

**Respecting Autonomy**

Since autonomy is the source of moral principles, morality requires that autonomy be respected. But what does it mean to respect autonomy? Practically speaking, what must one do? First, because "autonomy" refers to making choices in concert with one's value structure, respecting autonomy forbids one to thwart another's autonomous choices. If a patient autonomously chooses a therapeutic alternative that the HCP considers less than optimal, the HCP must not interfere when the patient acts on that choice. For example, HCPs should not forcibly administer blood to autonomous Jehovah's Witnesses. Second, respecting autonomy requires that one foster the conditions (e.g., being informed) necessary for making and acting on autonomous choices. In what follows I will focus on the implications of autonomy for free and informed consent.

In the context of informed consent, autonomy is respected when patients are recognized as the appropriate decision-making authorities and as the best and most reliable sources about what best accords with their own value structures. This recognition requires that HCPs (1) provide their patients with full information about the situation in which a choice must be made; (2) work to maximize the patient's ability to understand that information; (3) take care not to coerce patients' choices; and (4) implement autonomously chosen therapies. A brief discussion should clarify these claims.

Autonomy has to do with making principled choices. For health care choices to reliably promote patients' values, patients need full information regarding their options. Persons who do not have such information are at risk for making choices that will not promote—and may even sabotage—their values. Thus, respect for autonomy dictates that decision makers be given all the facts. (Wear (1993) offers an approach that provides relevant data without inundating—and thus overwhelming—patients.) Of course, merely providing information is useless unless the facts are given to someone with the capacity for their careful consideration—that is, to someone who is competent. To give data to those who are unable to assess them is, again, to put persons at risk for inappropriate choices that work against their values and interests. Lastly, respect for autonomy requires freedom from inhibitions that impede decision-making ability and authority. Inhibitions can be internal (e.g., fear, pain, altered mental status) or external (e.g., pressure from family, friends, or HCPs to choose a particular option). Autonomy requires that patients not be forced to make particular choices (though they may be encouraged to do so).

A word of caution. HCPs may be tempted to reason thusly: I will find out what the patient's values, goals, and interests are; then I will respect them by choosing the medical regimen that will most likely enhance or protect these values. This reasoning is problematic for a number of reasons. Most basically, the approach is inappropriate because HCPs are almost always operating with an information deficit about the patient's full set of values, interests, and goals. But, what is more important, part of respecting autonomy is respecting decisional authority. This respect requires that the patient be given the opportunity to make all important choices, not simply the choice about which aspects of his value structure to share with his providers.

In sum, the principle of respect for autonomy springs from patients' abilities to assemble their own value structures and make choices in light of them. The permutations and combinations of values, goals, beliefs, and interests and their applications in definite circumstances are probably infinite in number. Two people rarely, perhaps never, choose identically throughout an entire life. Each person's unique value structure supports differing conceptions of what constitutes appropriate action.[2] Informed, uncoerced patients who understand their circumstances are capable of on-going self-legislation and, when adequately informed, will surely be the best authorities on how best to promote their own values. Competent decision makers are best able to (1) be informed, (2) fully understand their circumstances, (3) relate their circumstances to their value structures, and (4) make principled choices to promote chosen values. Since only competent persons can make autonomous choices, competence is a necessary condition for autonomy, and respecting autonomy requires the promotion and preservation of competence.[3]

## COMPETENCE AND THE PRINCIPLE OF BENEFICENCE

The word "beneficence" comes from the Latin words for "well" (*bene*) and "doing" (*ficus*). Beneficence means doing well or well-being. Moral behavior has the welfare of persons as its goal. The ethical principle of beneficence states that we must never act to thwart and that we must actively promote and protect the well-being of others.

### The Moral Importance of Beneficence

Why morality requires promoting others' well-being is unclear. Unlike autonomy, beneficence is not a necessary condition for morality. Nonetheless, morality is thought to exist, at least in part, to promote the welfare of persons; and moral rules (e.g., don't lie) generally do benefit persons. Moreover, as Baruch A. Brody (1988, p. 18) notes, in the world at large there seems to be a "general moral fact . . . that actions which have good consequences are better to perform than actions that have bad consequences." Most of us would agree with this statement. We think that it is better when things go well for people than when things go ill for them, and we often appeal to consequences in everyday life. We frequently issue consequence-based warnings: If you batter your children, they will grow up to batter their children; if you embezzle funds, you will be caught and punished; or if you conceal the truth from patients, they will find out and lose their trust in you. The thrust of such remarks is that if a particular action is performed, bad results will occur.[4] The goal of the principle of beneficence is to forestall bad and promote good consequences. Beneficent HCPs will strive to promote good outcomes for their patients.[5] As clear as this statement appears on its surface, its implications bear further investigation.

Many scholars suggest that there are limits to the extent to which we are obliged to exert ourselves on behalf of others. The belief is widespread that we have strong obligations to refrain from hurting others, but only weak obligations to take positive steps to help them.[6] The mandate not to harm others (which may be termed the principle of nonmaleficence) requires only that we leave them alone. It is easily met, and few exceptions are permitted. On the other hand, helping others (which may be termed the principle of positive beneficence) takes resources (time, effort, possibly money). These impositions suggest that, while it is morally praiseworthy actively to assist others, we need not always do so. There are many exceptions to, and we may often be excused from, the duty of helping others.

## The Professional Importance of Beneficence

Regardless of the position one takes on the general question of beneficent obligations to persons in the world at large, HCPs have a role-specific obligation to positively promote and protect the well-being of their patients. HCPs are "in the business" to benefit others. In the preamble to its "Principles of Medical Ethics," the American Medical Association announces: "The medical profession has long subscribed to a body of ethical statements developed primarily for *the benefit of the patient*" (AMA, 1989, p. ix, emphasis added). Likewise, the preamble to the American Nurses' Association Code of Ethics notes: "Since clients themselves are the primary decision makers in matters concerning their own health, treatment, and *well-being*, the goal of nursing actions is to support and enhance the client's . . . self-determination to the greatest extent possible" (ANA, 1985, p. i, emphasis added).

Put another way, part of what it *means* to be a health professional is to work actively to benefit patients. So the question before us is what does the principle of beneficence require of morally responsible clinicians? We saw in the preceding section that morality requires us to respect autonomous choices. But is respecting persons' autonomy the same thing as promoting their welfare?

## Defining Beneficial

As important as it is for guiding behavior, the principle of respect for autonomy is sometimes accused of failing to promote the well-being of decision makers. Worries arise when families, friends, clinicians, or bioethicists suspect that an autonomous patient either has chosen incorrectly in light of her own value structure or has an inappropriate value structure.

Choices that are clearly at odds with a patient's value structure are relatively easy to address (at least in theory). If the patient is competent, he can be asked to explain the disparity. Often what appears to be an incongruous choice can be justified by publicizing facts or values of which the patient alone is aware. (Recall, however, that competent patients can change their minds, even about their value structures—a not uncommon experience in the face of serious illness.) Of course, if the unsuitable choice is made by an incompetent patient, its discrepancy with the patient's value structure provides a reason to override it. In such cases therapy should be directed at restoring the patient's competence, if that is possible. If that is not possible, treatment that honors the patient's known values should be provided.

The second source of alarm is the belief that there are certain interests that *all persons necessarily share* and that interests that conflict with these are illegitimate. Thus, we are led to ask if there is something that really does benefit all persons. This question is not about what particular people define as good or even good for them (though that is an important aspect of the question). Rather, it is a question about whether certain things are objectively and universally beneficial. Put another way, are there some things that each and every person should incorporate into her or his own value structure? If so, such things would always be in a person's best interests and ought always to be promoted. Can we determine whether such things exist and if so, what they are?

Presumably something is universally good if it always has value for persons, whether or not they appreciate that value. Some ethicists and theologians have argued that human life always has value for its possessor. Others have argued that human life is only sometimes good, that it is good only when qualified by other criteria (e.g., when a person also has the capacity for rational thought, psychosocial activity, or some such). If there are no universal goods, but only goods that individuals choose for themselves, then the patient's choice (assuming it will promote what she calls good) must stand. If, on the other hand, there is some universal good (e.g., human life) that applies to all persons at all times, such a thing would always benefit patients, and clinicians would be obligated to seek that good when providing care. If life is always a benefit, life-sustaining treatment is always required. If life is only sometimes valuable, life-sustaining treatment may sometimes be forgone. Thus, the question: is there anything that is universally good?

Philosophers and others have widely divergent theories of what is universally good for persons. Although there are many candidates for the good, we will limit our discussion to three major contenders: hedonism, desire satisfaction, and objective goodness. Hedonism argues that pleasure is always good (and pain is always bad). Having to assert the goodness of pleasure may seem silly, since most people generally do prefer pleasure to pain, and do seek the former and eschew the latter. The theorist, however, is not asserting merely that people do seek pleasure and do avoid pain, but that they should do so. The hedonist argues that what is really good for human beings (and what they really should desire, even if they themselves think otherwise) is pleasure.[7]

The second theoretical position asserts that the good for persons is the satisfaction of their desires or preferences. Some of these preferences are for acquiring pleasure and averting pain, but other desires are equally important. The desire satisfaction theorist notes that people sometimes desire things that cause pain or prevent pleasure. Some people choose to promote the interests of others, even at the expense of their own pleasure. Others go to war to serve their countries, subject themselves to arduous programs of education, join the Peace Corps to serve humankind, donate their bone marrow or kidneys to strangers, are martyred for ideals, and so forth. Realization of desires, whatever their content, is the good for persons according to the desire satisfaction theorist.

Third, some theorists claim that some things really are objectively and universally good or bad, whether they give us pleasure or pain and whether or not anyone desires them. For example, sadistic acts are desired by and give pleasure to some people, but might plausibly be claimed really to be objectively bad. Likewise, telling the truth might be really (objectively) good whether or not anyone ever wants to hear the truth, and even if some people prefer to hear (or tell) lies. We recall that some people think that human life is objectively good, even lives that are full of pain and suffering and even if the people living those lives desire to end them. If human life is universally good, then it is good even when full of pain and even when its end, rather than its continuation, is desired.

Of these contenders, the desire satisfaction theory seems preferable for both theoretical and pragmatic reasons. First, hedonism seems implausible. Although only empirical evidence can be cited, nearly all people do pursue things besides pleasure, and even at its expense. Moreover, many other things that people prefer do make their lives go better, independently of their production of pleasure.[8] For example, one might desire to be the best physician possible and work to fulfill this desire, even though its realization demands long, arduous hours of work and study that are often deficient in pleasure.

Well, then, are there any objective goods? The answer is: No one knows. First, objectivists have been unable to produce any universally *shared* plausible list of things that are objectively good or evil. Suggested lists invariably meet with one of two criticisms: the list is too long (i.e., contains items that others think are not objectively good); or the list is too short (i.e., fails to contain items that others think are objectively good).[9] After centuries of effort, there still is no widely accepted list of what is universally good. Second, things that enhance or diminish the quality of persons' lives clearly do so quite independently of any particular approved list. No matter how long the list of objective goods might be, there will be things not on the list that are good for individuals.

In addition, the absence of a single list of objective goods leads to certain practical difficulties with which clinicians and bioethicists are all too familiar. To pursue the earlier question, the objective value of human biological existence is the subject of continuing debate. (The controversies on abortion and on withdrawing or withholding care from the terminally or irreversibly ill come quickly to mind.) If human life has universal value, it must be preserved (so long as its preservation is not overridden by other universal values). If, on the other hand, life is not on this list, its preservation would not be required (though it might be allowed, for other reasons). The absence of a universally accepted list of good(s) leaves patients and clinicians trying to devise a therapeutic regimen without clear guidance as to how best to proceed. Ought they always try to preserve biological existence? Or may they (indeed, ought they?) abandon intervention when only biological (but not rational or pleasurable) existence is possible? Without an objective list, this question is objectively unanswerable.

We should note, however, that the health care professions have their own list of objective goods: life, health, and absence of pain or suffering. These goods, sometimes referred to as "the big three," are values shared by and goals inherent to the profession. Since the purpose of health care professions is to promote these goals, HCPs should, other things being equal, work to promote and protect life, health, and minimal suffering. However, not everyone shares even these fairly uncontroversial values. Patients with terminal illnesses may choose to die; persons daily jeopardize their health by continuing to smoke, drive without seat belts, and eat fatty foods; and many people willingly suffer pain en route to a larger goal.

In short, objective good theorists have not been able to construct a list of what is really good for people, independent of their own assessments of what is good for them. Nor has anyone produced a list of what all (or even most) people actually desire (regardless of whether our desires are for what is really good). Left without a list of what is universally good, people have to compose their own lists.[10]

That neither hedonists nor objective good theorists have been able to make a conclusive argument for their positions does not settle the matter, but it does allow us to entertain the desire satisfaction theory. Theoretically this approach is not better or worse than its two opponents. Just as the truth of hedonism and the truth of objective good theories have not been proven, neither has it been proven that the satisfaction of particular desires is the good. Thus, the desire satisfaction theory is no worse than the other options. If that were the only reason for choosing it, the choice would be completely arbitrary; however, it is a better choice than its two competitors for a wholly other reason: Empirically, the desire satisfaction strategy fits much better with our observations. First, people do desire other things than pleasure and the goods that different objective good theorists advocate. Second, most people agree that having their desires satisfied makes their lives go better than having their desires thwarted. That is, most people agree that desire satisfaction is a good (if not the good). These observations rightly seem to give this theory the edge over its competitors.[11]

Moreover, while it has proven impossible to identify an objective list of goods or the goods that would yield the greatest amount of pleasure or least amount of pain, it is usually possible to determine a patient's desires—just ask her what they are. On the preference satisfaction theory, guidance is more readily available than it is with other theories.[12]

Finally, informed consent makes the most sense on this particular theory of the good. In consent settings, clinicians are not asking people to tell them what would maximize pleasure or minimize pain (although pain and its avoidance or control surely inform many consents). Nor are we displaying a list of objective goods and pointing out which therapeutic options would best promote the items on that list (although HCPs certainly have opinions about which outcomes would be, clinically or generally speaking, better for their patients). Thus, the desire satisfaction theory provides the best fit within the practice of informed consent.[13] Within a context of free and informed consent, the good for persons is the satisfaction of their autonomous desires.

## BENEFICENCE THROUGH AUTONOMY

We determined in Section I that personal welfare was defined in terms of one's autonomously chosen value structure. We determined in Section II that actions that satisfy individuals' desires are preferable to those that thwart them. Since the principle of beneficence requires promotion of well-being, and since patient well-being is promoted through the satisfaction of their autonomous desires, the principle of beneficence requires that morally conscientious practitioners try to satisfy their patients' autonomous desires regarding their health care options. Let us look at this claim in greater detail.

Beneficence is a cornerstone of the patient-practitioner alliance because, as noted above, health professions are substantially defined in terms of promoting patients' welfare. HCPs have many opportunities to honor or thwart desires, and much of what clinicians do for patients has the potential to change patients' lives in significant ways. The plan is, of course, to change them for the better; but positive results are never guaranteed. For example, a patient who takes medication to control his hypertension may suffer noxious side effects (e.g., impotence). Occasionally these effects can be disastrous (e.g., death following anaphylactic shock).

Patients engage clinicians as one way of satisfying their desires. Those who desire to preserve or improve their health consult HCPs for advice and other assistance. This approach is most likely to succeed if HCPs understand their patients' desires. Clinicians need to appreciate both immediate and long-term desires so that, in cases of conflict, action can be taken to promote the patient's most substantial preferences.

Understanding precisely what acting beneficently requires is crucial because disagreement about a patient's best interests is always possible. First, some desires may be satisfied only through experiences that are not themselves desired. The recovery that follows months of rehabilitation for severe burns surely includes many undesired events, such as painful debridement. Although the patient desires to avoid the pain, she desires her recovery more. Second, patients can be mistaken about what will actually satisfy their desires. For example, the patient who requests Laetrile because he thinks it will cure his cancer is mistaken. In such cases, clinicians need to ferret out the true desire (cure of the cancer), rather than simply accept a patient's misinformed choice. Third, patients and clinicians can agree on a patient's goal, but be diametrically opposed in their estimates of what must to be done to attain it. A busy, sedentary executive with essential hypertension may insist that medications are the best way to lower his blood pressure, while his physician recommends weight loss and exercise. Although the patient and the professional share the goal of lowering the patient's blood pressure, the physician defines the best approach in terms of a "healthier" lifestyle and non-exposure to the side effects of powerful antihypertensives. The patient, on the other hand, prefers medication to a low sodium, low fat diet combined with regular exercise. He desires to continue his present lifestyle and is willing to risk (while hoping, of course, to be spared) the medication's side effects.

Many people would cluck their tongues at the executive's choice, insisting that objectively his health is the most important interest at stake and that it can be better guaranteed by changing his lifestyle than by swallowing medicine. (Their claim is that health is objectively good and ought to be desired. We have seen, however, the problems with appealing to objective goods.) Others would insist that good health is only one of many things people desire. Having different desires helps to make people unique and forms the basis of particular value structures.

Sometimes such disparities can be adjudicated by appealing to the patient's more powerful desires. It appears that the executive prefers medication to changing his diet and exercise habits; in fact, these preferences spring from the desire to be as professionally productive as possible. Diet and exercise are seen as interfering with that stronger preference. Perhaps the clinician can make the case that the desire for medication is a "false" desire—one that the executive will not have once he has considered his options more fully. Once he realizes that controlling his blood pressure is (probably) possible through diet and exercise and, moreover, that these do not expose him to a different set of risks that may themselves impair his professional performance, the executive may embrace the desires that the clinicians think he ought to have, especially in view of his own preferences for a long, productive career. The HCP's argument, here, is that the patient is confused about how best to achieve his own goals. This scenario represents many patient-professional encounters, where professionals attempt to show patients why they are "really" making the wrong choices. Sometimes patients are persuaded to change their minds, but sometimes they persist in their choices. When patients are adamant, must their choices must be honored? Yes, if the choices are autonomous, because autonomous choices are reliable statements of their own preferences.

Two points need elaboration here. First, it is crucial to distinguish between being the best judge of one's goals, and being the best judge of how to achieve them. The best judge of the former is not necessarily the best judge of the latter. Persons may be the best judges of their goals while someone else (e.g., HCPs) may be the best judge of the means to those goals. Persons might want something, even quite badly, and be completely at a loss about how to attain it. Patients need advice on how to best conquer or control pathophysiology, and those who fail to solicit such input may actually thwart their self-determined projects.

Second, HCPs often assert that patients literally have no idea what it will be like to live with particular afflictions and, hence, how their goals or values will be affected. This assertion is, in one sense, trivially true. Until I have diabetes, I do not know what it means for me to be a diabetic. This point is often made to buttress claims that HCPs are better able than patients to make decisions, because the HCPs have seen many diabetics and can generalize from that experience. These claims, while also true, are somewhat beside the point because the HCPs' knowledge of diabetes generally need not reliably extend to my diabetes. Put another way, HCPs know nothing of my subjective experience of diabetes.

HCPs can draw on a wide range of individuals with diabetes. On that basis they can make predictions and recommendations that are statistically respectable for diabetics in general. But I can draw on a wide range of my individual experiences (e.g., how I manage stress or disability, or what I take to be legitimate causes for revising my goals and values). HCPs' statistically significant $n$ comes from a large number of particular different experiences—those of their patients. My statistically significant $n$ also comes from a large number of particular different experiences—mine. The former qualifies HCPs to give advice; the latter qualifies me to accept or ignore it, in my case. They know more about diabetes; I know more about me. Who knows more about my diabetes is surely open to discussion.[14]

The upshot is that being a beneficent professional may require the clinician to help satisfy patients' desires that the clinician genuinely believes are inappropriate (especially in terms of "the big three"). Nonetheless if professionals are committed, as their codes of ethics promise, to helping their patients achieve the good, they are committed to satisfying their patients' autonomous desires. Two qualifiers are worth noting, however. First, in the absence of information about what is beneficent for a particular patient (i.e., what goods the patient has autonomously chosen), the beneficent professional appropriately promotes the big three. We may refer to this nonspecific (as opposed to patient-specific) approach as "general" beneficence. Second, neither the principle of beneficence nor the HCPs' codes of ethics requires clinicians to ignore their own *personal* value structures. Professionals whose own consciences prohibit participation in certain activities must be allowed to withdraw from the care of patients requesting those activities. Otherwise professionals would either have to give up practicing altogether, foist their own values on their patients, or themselves be held hostage to their patients' values. The principles of autonomy and beneficence also apply to HCPs. They can promote their own welfare as well as their patients' because they, too, are valuable autonomous agents. What HCPs may not do is promote their own well-being at the expense of their patients' welfare.

The principle of beneficence, then, plays a large role in the patient-professional encounter. Its importance within the practice of consent follows from the fact that a person's good lies in the satisfaction of her autonomous desires. HCPs play a key role in helping to determine the means to satisfy patients' desires; but their role in forming these desires is limited. Patients quite often desire things that clinicians find foolish and inappropriate. Nevertheless, their professional role is to help patients achieve their desires, not to dictate what desires their patients should have.

## COMPETENCE AND THE PRACTICE OF INFORMED CONSENT

Health care professionals and bioethicists are familiar with the goals and procedures of the practice of free and informed consent. Its goals are (1) to provide opportunities for persons to be self-determining, and (2) to provide care that will promote the well-being of their patients. The procedures for informed consent include assessing patients' competence; providing competent patients with the information they need to understand and discuss their diagnoses and treatment alternatives (risks, benefits, and prognosis of each option, including the option of no treatment at all), and the answers to any questions they raise about this data; and ameliorating any coercive influences on patients. Once patients are determined to be competent, they are given the information and a chance to digest it, ask questions, and relate it to their own value structures. Patients then choose the alternatives they prefer. Following their decisions, clinicians provide the requested care (or continue, if there is concern that the choice is somehow inappropriate, to offer further information to persuade patients to change their minds). These actions are commonplace in the day-to-day care of patients, and professionals are thoroughly acquainted with them. They may be less knowledgeable about the fact that these goals and procedures constitute a practice. As such, they regulate (rather than simply organize) behavior. What, then, are practices and why are they adopted?

### The Nature of a Practice

Actions within a practice are regulated to achieve the goals that the practice was established to promote. Behavior within the practice is governed by precise rules. Both the goals and the rules help define the practice. Consider Alasdair MacIntyre's definition:

> By a 'practice' I . . . mean any coherent and complex form of socially established cooperative human activity through which goods internal to that form of activity are realised [sic] in the course of trying to achieve those standards of excellence which are appropriate to, and partially definitive of that form of activity, with the result that human powers to achieve excellence, and human conceptions of the ends and goods involved, are systematically extended (1981, p. 175).

What does this have to do with free and informed consent? If we dissect the definition we get some understanding of this particular practice. Free and informed consent is an "established cooperative human activity through which goods internal to that form of activity are realised [sic]." This means that free and informed consent is a strategy adopted to reach mutually agreed upon goals. The goals are to enhance patients' self-determination and to promote their well-being. These goals are "internal to that form of activity" because they provide a reason for the practice. An example may clarify this issue.

A clinician may reason about free and informed consent in one of two ways. She may think that getting consent from patients is a bothersome task, but if she does not ask the patient's permission, she will probably be sued. Thus, she seeks consent. Another clinician may think that getting consent from patients is an important way of respecting their self-determination and of promoting their well-being. The first clinician is motivated by a goal *external* to the practice—that of protecting herself from liability. The second practitioner is motivated by goals *internal* to the practice—patients' autonomy and welfare. The internal goals are *foundations* of the practice, goals without which there would be no reason for the practice to have been established. External goals may be closely related to a practice (e.g., HCPs are legally liable if harm befalls patients from whom they fail to obtain an informed consent), but they do not help to define it (that is, informed consent was not instituted as a method by which to avoid legal liability, though it may do so).

The "standards of excellence which are appropriate to, and partially definitive of, that form of activity" are of two sorts. The first is what MacIntyre terms "the excellence of the products" (p. 177). One such "product" is the outcome itself—patients are helped, within the health care environment, to become self-determining. The abilities that enable persons to be as self-determining as possible are enhanced. This standard of excellence in the circumstances surrounding consent recognizes that persons need to be self-determining, both in the sense of possessing authority about their own bodies and in the sense of being the best sources regarding their own interests. But there is a second product whose excellence may be less immediately obvious: the activities that HCPs undertake to enable patient self-determination. Patients can successfully execute decision-making authority and promote their own best interests because clinicians act in ways that not only allow their success but encourage it. The first excellence is the self-determining patient; the second is HCPs' enabling that self-determination.

The practice of free and informed consent recognizes the moral importance of persons' determining their own value structures and applying them in deciding how their lives will go. When clinicians embrace this value as the foundation for consent, and proceed so as to maximize it, they help to achieve that end and testify, on an on-going basis, to its importance.

## The Authority of Practices

This analysis of a practice may not fully indicate its practical import. Practices restrict options. People operating under a practice are not free to step outside the practice to determine how best to proceed— even if the practice obstructs other significant goals or values. As MacIntyre notes (1981, p. 177): "A practice involves . . . obedience to rules as well as the achievement of goods. To enter into a practice is to accept the authority of those standards . . .". Once a practice has been established, its rules are always in force. One cannot, for example, decide that in this case it would be better not to seek a patient's consent. The practice itself forbids choosing to ignore its rules.

As inconvenient as the rules may be, there are good reasons to make them binding. The importance of following practice-generated rules has been discussed by John Rawls (1955, Section III). Rawls notes, correctly, that trying to decide how to handle cases on an individual basis can be confusing, frustrating, and counter-productive. Such an approach often leads to unwanted results. Take keeping promises, for example. Briefly, the idea is this: humans in community take certain goals to be worthwhile, including the pursuit of mutually beneficial goals, helping others in times of need, encouraging sympathy among community members, and so forth. These goals can be attained through promoting feelings of trust among citizens. One mechanism by which trust is developed is the practice of promise-keeping. I get you to help me by promising to help you in return or by promising to pay you, then I keep the promise.

The primary rule on which the practice of promise-keeping depends is the imperative, keep your promises. Its corollary is: do not make promises you do not intend to keep. These rules follow from the very meaning of a promise; it is a serious vow about how the promiser will behave in the future. Promisers may not renege merely because keeping a promise is inconvenient. The rule about keeping one's promises is binding because, were it not, people could make promises to secure benefits for themselves, then renege. Such benefits would be achieved at the expense of others who are duped. If people could decide on each occasion whether or not to keep a promise, social interactions would be seriously impaired. Ultimately, promises would lose their meaning. Saying, "I promise" would mean "maybe I will do what I say, but maybe I won't." People would no longer trust the words or find it reasonable to extend help. In the end, there would be no such thing as promising; the words "I promise" would have no meaning. Then the benefits the practice was designed to promote would not be gained.

In a nutshell, the practice of promising depends on everyone's (or nearly everyone's) following the rule. Widespread, consistent failure to keep promises would make the idea of promise-keeping meaningless, and the benefits of the practice would go unrealized.

Informed consent is analogous to promise keeping. If clinicians must decide in each case whether to seek consent, much confusion would result. Practitioners would have to decide when patients' consents would be sought. They might construct rough guidelines, for their own use, about when seeking consent is appropriate. Different practitioners would develop different criteria, so HCPs would be operating under different systems. In particular cases no one could be certain whether consent should be sought or how to proceed. Bewilderment would be widespread, decision making would be in disarray, and patients' decision-making authority and welfare would not be protected.

A more efficient method for decision making is to establish a practice with formal rules. First, we identify values to be protected—here, patients' autonomous self-determination and well-being. Second, we identify recurring situations (assigning decision-making authority for health care) in which those values play a central role. Third, we agree that these situations will henceforth be rule-governed. Finally, we formulate rules that indicate how to achieve the goals that the practice fosters. In the case of free and informed consent, the rules specify (1) that the patient must be provided with all relevant information; (2) that the patient must be competent; (3) that the consent must be voluntary (i.e., not coerced); and (4) what exceptions can be made.

Regardless of the content of a practice, its procedural requirements are the same:

1. The rules of the practice are logically prior to the particular cases that it addresses.
2. The practice changes the degree of authority each person has regarding unilateral resolution of particular cases.
3. The rules of the practice are not merely guidelines or suggestions for case resolution, but are instructions for those purposes.
4. The rules will more often than not protect the values on which the practice is based (Rawls, 1955, Sec. III).

What does all this mean? The first requirement means that people cannot be involved in the activity without first knowing the rules. The second requirement indicates that those operating within the practice are no longer fully free; they must play by the rules. The third requirement stipulates that the rules define a procedure that *must* be followed; and finally, the fourth requirement (which is not so much a rule as an assurance that there are good reasons for following the rules) claims that adhering to these requirements will help one realize the goals they protect. Note, however, that a practice does not guarantee good outcomes; it merely increases the probabilities that they will occur.

### The Practice of Informed Consent

These concepts apply to the practice of free and informed consent. First, since the rules of the practice are logically prior to particular cases, HCPs in training learn about the necessity of and procedure for ensuring informed consent before they are allowed to manage actual cases. Second, since the practice specifies competent patients as having decision-making authority, practitioners may not fail to seek their consent in particular cases. Third, the rules are not merely guidelines, but specific instructions for obtaining consent. Clinicians must give information to and solicit consent from competent patients. They cannot force patients to accede to their recommendations. The rules dictate behavior. Any clinician who claims that, in this case, it would be better not to seek a competent patient's consent does not understand the practice. Finally, adhering to these rules will more often than not protect patients' autonomous self-determination and promote their well-being. Admittedly anyone involved in clinical medicine can give examples of cases in which adhering to the rules of informed consent led to deleterious consequences, but these are exceptions. In fact, a few words are in order about these exceptions.

The first exception falls under the description of "therapeutic privilege," in which a patient's decisional authority is transferred to another (often a physician) because failing to transfer authority would clearly harm the patient. For example, if a genuine emergency exists and taking time to inform and seek consent from the patient would threaten her life or health, the practice excuses the HCP from the duty to seek consent. The practice presumes that any autonomous patient would consent to the exception rather than risk life or limb. In such cases, the patient's consent is thought to be "implied" rather than given explicitly, overridden, or omitted entirely.

The second exception recognizes that autonomous persons can autonomously choose to waive their decisional authority. Patients who prefer not to hear details of their disorders or treatment plans can defer to the choices of their HCPs. In these cases, professionals do not seek the patient's consent, but administer treatment in accordance with their best professional judgments. These clinicians are advised to check with the patient at regular intervals to assure that the patient has not changed her mind in this regard.

Perhaps the most controversial exception is paternalistic intervention. Paternalism, which usurps a patient's decisional authority "for his own good" and allows another to choose for him so as to promote his own best interests, has two logical forms. First, a clinician judges that giving the patient the information requisite to seeking his consent would so distress the patient that his health and well-being would be severely jeopardized. Such judgments are often made about patients experiencing severe emotional distress (perhaps Mrs. W); the idea is that exposing them to even more unsettling information would "push them over the edge." Second, a clinician judges that a patient's choice, while competently made, is so flagrantly antithetical to his own welfare that the choice must be ignored and the patient's protests or objections overridden. Jehovah's Witnesses who refuse life-saving blood transfusions often have those refusals overridden; the justification is that dying needlessly is never in a person's best interests. The appropriate role for paternalistic interventions in health care continues to be the topic of much debate. Here I merely note that paternalistic interventions are probably required much less frequently than clinicians believe.

## Competence as Part of a Practice

Competence is central to the practice of informed consent. The practice decrees that competent patients are the appropriate decision makers regarding their care and, as such, are the only persons from whom consent should be solicited. There are three reasons for this. First, respecting the capacities of persons to govern their own lives extends only to those who are able to autonomously assemble value structures and plan their lives accordingly. We do not admire, nor find meritorious, the simple capacity to pick A over B, as when a child picks vanilla rather than chocolate ice cream. Only autonomous choice is morally valuable, and autonomous choice can only be made by persons with certain capacities for information management. That is, autonomous choice can only be exercised by competent persons.

Second, some people (1) never have been or (2) are not now, or (3) never (again) will be able to autonomously determine their own interests. Individuals born profoundly and irreversibly retarded, for example, are incapable of such behavior. Consequently, their interests must be determined and protected by others. To offer them an opportunity to participate in the consent process is to expose them to great harms that they have not autonomously chosen. (This is not to say that persons can never choose harm for themselves, but to claim that such harms must be competently and freely chosen by those who will suffer them.) Likewise, it makes no sense to suggest that infants and small children can determine their own best interests. Nor can irretrievably comatose patients state autonomous preferences (even if they once were able to do so). These individuals are unable to understand or even to be aware of a preference, let alone to act on one. They do not, or do not now, have the capacities to be autonomous. Thus, a practice designed to protect autonomy does not apply to them.

Finally, persons who have the valued capacities may lose them temporarily. Persons who are delirious with fever, disoriented from a concussion, or heavily medicated for pain control do not automatically lose their values and goals. They have, however, temporarily lost their capacities to autonomously choose in accordance with them. These individuals are excluded from decision making to prevent their inadvertently acting to thwart their own best interests as they themselves have defined them. These persons are protected by the exceptions specified in the practice of informed consent. Only when persons are capable of acting competently should they be involved in the consent process, because only competent persons can reliably determine and report their preferences.

In summary, a practice is a rule-governed process established to promote certain behaviors and achieve certain outcomes. The practice of informed consent fosters the morally worthy end of autonomous decision making and seeks to allow patients and professionals alike to live self-determined lives. As a practice, informed consent provides opportunities for clinicians to respect autonomous patients by sharing information and promoting their free choices. Competent patients have individual value structures and are capable of conceptualizing their own best interests.

## MORAL IMPLICATIONS OF INFORMED CONSENT

What will it mean to combine the practice of informed consent with the moral requirements to respect autonomy and to act beneficently toward (i.e, satisfy desires of) competent patients? It means, first, that individuals who have particular value structures will have unique reasons for acting in particular ways at particular times. Thus, HCPs and bioethicists are morally obligated to work to understand what patients *truly* desire, and to undertake actions that will promote the satisfaction of autonomous desires that stem from autonomously erected individual value structures.

The principle of respect for autonomy demands, first and foremost, that HCPs identify which patients are competent and, thus, potentially autonomous. To these patients HCPs must not only provide pertinent information, but also avoid both flagrant and subtle coercion regarding particular options. This demand need not (as is all too commonly thought) stop HCPs from offering their recommendations. Nor should it keep professionals from attempting to dissuade a patient from what appears to be a bad choice. HCPs are, after all, experts who presumably have good reasons for preferring certain options. The point is that the principle of respect for autonomy demands that clinicians refrain from forcing patients to choose as they—the clinicians—think best.

In addition, the principle of beneficence obligates HCPs to take positive steps to promote and protect the self-determined well-being of their patients. Professionals can—and are required by this principle to—help patients make decisions. Provision of information obviously plays a key role in this regard, but other, equally important efforts can also be supportive. The first is to furnish patients with an environment that is conducive to decision making. Being available and eager to patiently answer questions about their diagnoses, treatment options, risks and benefits, and so forth creates such an environment. It encourages patients to ask questions and participate in decision-making activities;[15] reassures patients as needed; and recognizes and promptly treats those conditions (e.g., psychopathology, frustration, fear) that impair a patient's decision-making abilities.

To respect autonomous persons is to admit the worth of their value structures and the choices they make in light of them. The practice of informed consent promotes their self-determination (which these value structures and choices express) by supporting and enabling their efforts to make autonomous choices. Patients' welfare is protected when others act to help them bring about autonomous choices.

Health care is one of many decision points in an individual's life, and health care choices are instances of decision making. Illness, especially serious illness, can be a crossroads that requires a revision of lifestyle. Other things being equal, it should be presumed that the person most intimately involved, the patient, has the best understanding of how and to what extent her illness will entail a revision of value structure. Thus, the patient is best positioned to make decisions about what should be done to manage the illness. Illness, after all, does not exist in a vacuum; it exists within people. More particularly, illness exists within people who have value structures on which sickness may be expected to have an impact. (How much impact depends, of course, on the nature of the illness and how disruptive it is to the person's life plan.)

Like all other decisions, health care choices are best made in the presence of as much pertinent information as possible. Patients who can be given all the relevant health care data (diagnosis, possible treatment modalities—including no treatment at all—and risk-benefit ratios of different treatments, variable prognoses, costs in terms of time, effort, discomfort) to be sufficiently informed about the important aspects of their decisions will be best placed to make health care decisions. Of all participants in the decision, patients' access to the full range of values in their lives is the most direct and the least limited. They, and they alone, can best estimate the impact different choices will have on their lives as a whole; which choices will synchronize with their value structures; which values and interests, if any, they are prepared (even if reluctantly) to revise or sacrifice; which options they can comfortably embrace.[16] Put another way, persons' consents and refusals regarding health care are particular instances of the exercise of capacities that make them worthy of respect. That the consents or refusals occur within the health care setting, rather than in some other sphere, makes no morally relevant difference. HCPs hope, of course, that patients will opt for the actions that lead (at least statistically) to the best health outcomes. Nonetheless, given patients' privileged positions regarding evaluations of how their lives should go, clinicians must be prepared to accept patients' decisions—even those that apparently fail to promote patients' well-being. This is not to say that the choices of competent persons can never be overridden. There may be very good, even compelling, reasons for failing to respect particular autonomous choices, but overriding an autonomous choice always demands the strongest justification. Moreover, within the practice of informed consent, appeals to ethical principles or values other than autonomy and beneficence in an effort to override an autonomous decision are illicit. The practice insists that the free and informed choices of competent persons deserve respect. The practice of informed consent was instituted to extend respect to and promote the well-being of autonomous persons in the health care setting. Failure to honor autonomous choices jeopardizes these values. To claim in some case that it would be better not to respect an autonomous choice (but to act in the patient's best interests as interpreted by someone else) is to miss the point of the practice of informed consent and to imperil the moral values, autonomy and beneficence, that it protects and promotes.

## NOTES

1. Much of Kant's discussion is framed in terms of "personhood," where "person" is a technical term, used to designate one who possesses the capacities for rational thought and, hence, for universal moral legislation. Under such an interpretation, persons need not be humans. God and the angels would be Kantian persons, as would intelligent extraterrestrials.

The more interesting question is whether, within a Kantian framework, all humans are necessarily persons. In his discussion of personhood in *Foundations of the Metaphysics of Morals*, Kant seems to use "person" and "human" interchangeably. In the second formulation of the Categorical Imperative, he speaks of respecting "humanity, whether in your own person or in that of another" (*Foundations of the Metaphysics of Morals*, trans. Beck, p. 47=[429]). In this and other such phrasings, the terms appear to be used as synonyms. In a discussion of duty, Kant notes that "[duty] must . . . hold for all rational beings . . . and only for that reason can it be a law for *all human* wills" (*Foundations*, p. 43 =[425], emphasis added). The suggestion here is that duty, as a prescription for "all rational beings" is, *for that reason*, a prescription for *all humans*. Similarly, he notes that ". . . man and . . . every rational being exists as an end in himself and not merely as a means to be arbitrarily used by this or that will" (*Foundations*, p.46=[428]). Again, the implication is that all, as opposed to only rational, humans are worthy of respect.

Nevertheless, confusion arises on this question. In other passages Kant is keen to stress the importance (for morality) not of human beings per se, but of reason. For example, ". . . morality and humanity, *so far as it is capable of morality*, alone have dignity (*Foundations*, p.53=[435], emphasis added). Likewise, he speaks of the "dignity [of every rational being]...over all *merely natural beings* (*Foundations*, p.56=[438] emphasis added). Such passages seem to imply that it is not humans per se that are worthy of respect, but rationality and, hence, only those humans who also possess the capacity for rational thought. If this is his meaning—that is, if Kant genuinely believes that *only* rationality grounds respect, humans who lack the ability to reason (e.g., the severely demented, infants) are not persons and so are not worthy—or at least not inherently worthy—of respect. There may be other good reasons for treating all humans respectfully, but such treatment would then derive from those other reasons rather than from the nature of the humans in question. If, on the contrary, Kant thought all humans, regardless of their particular capacities to reason, deserved respect, then it is unclear why he speaks specifically about that capacity. Given his casual use of the terms, Kant quite likely presumed that all humans were capable of some degree of reason and thus worthy of respect.

The Kantian emphasis on the ability of persons to reason (and especially to reason about morality) has been espoused by many other authors since he wrote in the eighteenth century. Some have fully embraced Kant's grounding of morality in reason. Others have insisted that there is more to morality or personhood than mere rational capacity. I have been tempted to say that reason is a sufficient but not a necessary condition for being worthy of respect. That is, one need not be rational to be worthy of respect, but so long as one is rational, one is automatically deserving of respect (and is, for purposes of the present discussion, a being who is competent and whose decisions ought therefore be respected). I now believe that this assessment is incorrect and that reason is a necessary but not sufficient condition for being respected (both in oneself and with regard to one's decisions). This assessment means that persons who are worthy of respect must possess reason, but they must also possess other capacities as well.

2. For further discussion of the unique nature of personal value structures, see Brody, 1988, Chapter 2.

3. The autonomy of once, but no longer, autonomous persons can be respected by honoring the choices they made when they were competent/autonomous.

4. As common as these sorts of premonitory statements are, they are not necessarily true. Some battered children grow up to be good parents; some embezzlers go free to enjoy their ill-gotten gains; and some patients never learn the truth. The promised ill-effects do not reliably follow. Why not?

There are, of course, many answers one can give about particular cases. The battered child received psychological treatment to overcome the effects of her battering; the embezzler was very good at covering her tracks; the clinician was very convincing or the patient was apathetic. All such answers, however, assume that the promised results would always occur unless they were somehow thwarted. The faith we have in this assumption is misplaced. In truth, we understand very little about how consequences come to pass because we understand very little about what causes things to happen.

This worry is common in both clinical and research settings. Two patients given the same medicine may have different responses. Presumably the drug causes different results, but why? Two different researchers undertake the same protocol, but achieve different outcomes and are at a loss to explain what caused the dissimilar results. We often expect something to happen, only to be surprised when the unexpected occurs. Most clinicians can tell at least one story of a therapeutic "miracle," of a patient who survived against all odds. What causes these survivals?

The problem of causality—that is, the problem of determining what we do and do not cause—was extensively discussed by the Scottish philosopher, David Hume. Hume noted that we assume we cause the effects that follow our interventions. But since different effects can follow, we really have no assurance that they follow because, rather than in spite of, our actions. When particular effects frequently follow particular actions, we infer that the actions cause the effects. But all we can legitimately claim in such cases is what Hume calls "constant conjunction"—that certain states of affairs are, more often than not, conjoined to certain actions. (See Hume, 1966, Section IV, "Sceptical Doubts concerning the Operations of the Understanding.")

Hume's concerns are raised with regard to medical ethics by Eric Mack (1988, pp. 57–74). Mack notes that health professionals are often called on to make judgments about what they should do based on claims about the results they ought to produce. While this is understandable, such judgments are inappropriate without a theory of causality that specifies what, in fact, people can and do cause. Some assurance that a particular action will cause a particular outcome is required. Since a sound theory of causality has yet to be developed, appeals to consequences can only provide imperfect moral warrants for doing particular things.

None of this is meant to dissuade clinicians and bioethicists from appealing to consequences—probably a hopeless task at any rate. However, they should be cautioned that they make such appeals under more uncertainty than they commonly appreciate.

5. Consequentialist moral theories have a long and noble history, largely developed by British moral philosophers. Beginning with David Hume in the eighteenth century, the consequentialist approach to moral

behavior was subsequently refined by such great English scholars as Jeremy Bentham, John Stuart Mill, Henry Sidgwick, and G.E. Moore. Each of these thinkers had a different theory of what made consequences good or bad. Nonetheless, all agreed that morality obligated persons to promote good and prevent bad outcomes. Each captured the intuitively compelling belief that it is better if things go well than ill.

The study of the evolution of Utilitarianism (the most prominent variety of Consequentialism) is a demanding task, in part because of the subtle changes in the theory of the good and in part because writers often use precisely the same terms but mean quite different things. Beginning with Hume, the good was defined as that which has utility, by which Hume meant that which was useful to humans either individually or in society (Hume, 1966, Sections I and V). For Jeremy Bentham, the good was "utility" by which he meant "tends to produce benefit, advantage, pleasure, good, or happiness" (Bentham, 1948, p. 2.). Most commonly Bentham associated utility with pleasure and the absence of pain. Although it is not clear precisely what Bentham meant by "pleasure," he is most commonly taken to mean by that term "pleasant sensations"—the more of them and the greater their intensity and duration, the better. In other words, only the quantity of pleasure mattered. (See also Sidgwick, 1981.)

John Stuart Mill found Bentham's concept of the good too narrow, arguing instead that although utility was the ultimate good and that utility was comprised of pleasure and the absence of pain, pleasure had qualitative as well as quantitative dimensions. That is, the intensely pleasant sensations of, for example, great sex were not necessarily better than the (usually) less intense pleasure of hearing Beethoven's Ninth Symphony, even if the quantity of pleasure attained in the former exceeds that attained in the latter (*Utilitarianism*, especially Chapter 2). In an often quoted passage he noted, "It is better to be a human being dissatisfied than a pig satisfied; better to be Socrates dissatisfied than a fool satisfied" (Ibid., p.14).

In addition to variations on the theme of what is meant by happiness and pleasure, most consequentialist writers incorporate a bevy of different theories of human nature and of rationality that add further dimensions to their analyses. The result is a very intricate system that makes the assessment and prediction of outcomes a very challenging task indeed.

6. For further discussion of the distinction between the obligation to refrain from harming and a positive obligation to help, see Frankena, 1973, p. 47.

7. Hedonism and its defense are extensively developed in the ethical theory known as Utilitarianism. This theory was thoroughly developed by the nineteenth-century philosophers Jeremy Bentham (1948) and John Stuart Mill (1975, and note 5 above). For a twentieth-century defense, see Brandt, 1982.

There are two broad classifications of hedonism: egoistic and universal. Egoistic hedonism states that the good refers only to individuals and their pleasant or painful experiences. Universal hedonism specifies that pleasure and the absence of pain, globally considered, constitute The Good. In the former, it is only *my* pleasure and pain that I am required to consider. In the latter, the pleasure and pain of *everyone*—myself included—must be scrutinized. In this case, it is permissible to subject me to a great deal of pain if in doing so the pleasure of the community at large can be increased. (This notion leads to one of the objections to this theory, since subjecting persons to pain for the benefit of others is always worrisome.)

8. The hedonist must assume either that people really do seek only pleasure and the absence of pain (in spite of their statements to the contrary) or that the other things people seek do not count. The former claim assumes an extremely restricted (not to mention uncomplimentary) analysis of human nature and appears to be empirically false. The latter claim is both empirically and theoretically unsupported.

9. Hedonism is an example of an objective good theory with a very short list. Pleasure is the only item on the list of things that are objectively good. Pain is the only item on the list of things that are objectively bad.

10. Some people do not consider themselves free to compose their own lists of the good because a list is dictated for them by a particular religious doctrine. Since these doctrines vary considerably between sects, none can be considered universally binding; claims to the contrary are matters of faith, not of reason operating impartially or in any universal sense. MacIntyre (1981) and Engelhardt (1986, Chapter 2) discuss the effects of failing to produce a list of universal goods.

11. Note, however, that there are also problems with the desire satisfaction theory. Two, in particular, need to be mentioned. First, most people think that some preferences ought not to be honored. Although different people would make qualitatively different lists, most agree that some preferences are immoral. If so, the morally appropriate response would be to refuse to satisfy them. Illicit preferences might include those that are racist, sexist, speciesist, or "perverted." Jones's desire to enslave people of color, Brown's desire to rape preschool-age children for sexual fulfillment, or Smith's desire to torture kittens are desires that many think it would be immoral to satisfy.

The second problem for the desire satisfaction theory is that some people develop desires in strange or "abnormal" ways. As any mental health professional can testify, desires can be suspect not only in view of their content, but in view of their origin. The man who wants to give all his personal wealth to feed the poor may be considered altruistic and worthy of praise—until it is learned that he thinks he is Jesus Christ, or that as a result of being beaten and denigrated as a child he has come to have an image of himself as being completely unworthy of having any advantage. Many think such abnormal or "abnormally acquired" desires ought to be thwarted, not satisfied. These worries are, sad to say, very real ones in the health care setting. The abused child may, in fact, desire her own death because she has come to see herself as unworthy of clinicians' attentions or of the expenses her treatment would require. Parents may choose to forgo therapy for their sick daughters that they would willing embrace for their sick sons. Families may choose to forgo care for elderly relatives whose lives are burdensome or whose care is expensive.

These are thorny theoretical problems. If the good is satisfaction of desires, then satisfaction of all desires—including these—ought to be sought. On the other hand, some desires do seem to be inappropriate. The problem is how to identify inappropriate (as opposed to idiosyncratic) desires. Unfortunately, the only way to designate desires as truly immoral is through some sort of objective list which, as noted above, has not been forthcoming.

12. Occasionally the question of a patient's immoral or abnormally generated preferences will arise. In such cases, psychological consultations and therapy may alleviate some of the concerns. If therapy fails to resolve concerns about honoring certain desires, the desires should be honored, so long as clinicians are not compromised in doing so. Most such desires will not have sprung, full-blown, from nowhere. If they have, they probably provide further evidence of the need for a psychological evaluation. Thus, they spring from the patient's value structure. If she has determined, for whatever reason, that fulfillment of this desire somehow constitutes the good for her, then the principles of respect for autonomy and beneficence will, other things being equal, require that the requests be fulfilled.

13. The current U.S. Supreme Court presumably supports a desire satisfaction approach. In its June 25, 1990, decision in Cruzan v. Missouri (No. 88–1503), the Court ruled that persons desiring to forgo certain forms of life-sustaining medical care had a liberty right to do so, so long as they explicitly and competently express their wishes.

14. I have profited greatly from discussions with Baruch A. Brody and S. Kay Toombs on this point. See Toombs (1992) on just this point.

15. The need for emphasizing the patient as the decision-making authority cannot be overemphasized. Patients only infrequently see themselves as having decisional control. Even those who think the decision is theirs may have trouble asserting themselves. Lidz et al. (1983, p. 541) remark that only 10 percent of their patients see themselves as the decision makers.

16. An important caveat attends this point. Individuals are not the only persons with a capacity for making the choices that affect them directly, medical or otherwise. Most persons have close relationships with other persons in which their value structures and interests are shared or at least discussed. This sharing can put another person in a position of being able to say, often

with a great deal of accuracy, what their family members and friends would want to have done for them when they are unable to speak for themselves.

This intimate knowledge of others allows the practice of "substituted judgment," both formally and informally, to be adopted as an alternative form of decision making. When a person is unable to speak for herself, medicine (see, e.g., President's Commission, 1982a; Buchanan, 1985; Buchanan and Brock, 1986; Buchanan and Brock, 1989) and the law (e.g., In re Brophy, 1986; and In re Conroy, 1985) have traditionally turned to those close to the patient to determine what she would choose, were she able. Such examples formalize a common and helpful approach to decision making; namely, inquiring "What do you think Mary would want us to do?" when Mary is incapable of providing her own response.

# 3

# Current Confusion Surrounding the Concept of Competence

The lack of an explicit definition of competence is disturbing; however, the absence of a definition does not mean that the subject has not been considered. HCPs appreciate that the practice of free and informed consent requires a competent patient and have produced a rich body of literature devoted to competence. Consequently the absence of a well-articulated definition is surprising. This lack might best be explained by the fact that scholars have often focused on a single capacity when a set of capacities seems more appropriate. Put in philosophical terms, much attention has been devoted to capacities that are necessary, but not sufficient, for competence. Just because a particular capacity is a necessary component of competence to consent does not make it the only capacity that is required. In short, many suggestions have been made, and pockets of consensus do exist about what competence means. This chapter will consider how far existing agreement can take us toward defining competence to consent.

## DEFINITIONS OF COMPETENCE

Though no single definition of competence to consent to health care exists, there is general agreement about competence defined more broadly. Most broadly, "competence" is defined as "the ability to perform a task." But what does this mean?

### A Task-Oriented Definition of Competence

Charles Culver and Bernard Gert (1982) provide a detailed analysis of task-oriented competence. To begin, task-oriented competence means that one cannot decide whether a person is competent to perform a task without first knowing what the task demands (Culver and Gert, 1982, pp. 53–54). To understand competence, one must first understand the nature of a task.

Tasks come in many forms. They can be very simple, such as the task of taking a patient's temperature, or very complex, such as the task of identifying the causes of a patient's fever. Tasks can be very general, such as practicing medicine, or very specific, such as taking a blood pressure. Many complex tasks are collections of simple tasks, and many general tasks are agglomerations of specific tasks. For example, the complex task of identifying the cause of a fever partly depends on many simple tasks—charting temperature curves, collecting blood and sputum samples, and so forth.

All tasks, however, share one characteristic: their successful completion requires that the person undertaking the task know what actions are required to complete the task and have the abilities to perform those actions. Further consideration of this characteristic reveals that successful completion of any task, simple or complex, general or specific, requires (1) a description of actions required, (2) a knowledge of that description by anyone who wants to complete the task, and (3) the ability to perform the necessary actions. This analysis provides a basic definition of task-oriented competence:

> A person is competent to do a task if the person knows what actions are required to complete the task and has the abilities needed to perform those actions.

This definition identifies two components upon which competence depends: knowledge and capacities. In practice, separating the two is difficult because knowledge partly depends on intellectual capacities and intellectual capacities can improve with an increase in knowledge. In theory, however, capacities can be defined as skills or abilities that may be mental as well as physical. Thus, a person has the capacity to perform the task of taking a blood pressure if he possesses the cognitive and physical skills needed to learn and carry out the procedure. Again, in theory, knowledge is the possession of information. Capacities and knowledge are both necessary for competence, because competent performance requires the person to know what actions are required and how they should be performed and be able to perform them. So the competent blood pressure taker must know what to do and how to do it and he must be able to carry out the procedure.

The preceding discussion has provided us with a logic, or structure, according to which we can evaluate competence to perform any task. First, the actions required for the task's completion must be specified. Second, the person must know that the task requires these actions and how to perform them. Third, the capacities—mental and physical—necessary to perform those actions must be identified. Fourth, any person whose competence is under consideration must possess those capacities.

To demonstrate the logic of task-oriented competence, consider the general task of practicing obstetrics. This general task is composed of the more specific tasks of diagnosing and managing obstetrical conditions. These specific tasks can, in turn, be subdivided into more specific tasks. For example, the mid-level task of diagnosing obstetrical conditions includes the particular tasks of identifying conditions that threaten a normal live birth, e.g., placenta previa. But diagnosing placental previa is itself a cluster of more precise tasks. And so on. In short, practicing obstetrics includes a wide variety of particular diagnostic tasks of varying degrees of specificity.

Having delineated this hierarchy of tasks, we are better able to consider competence to perform them. The example of diagnosing placenta previa is useful here. Imagine that we want to know if Jones, an obstetrician, can competently diagnose placenta previa. We can only evaluate this claim if we know what the task, diagnosing placenta previa, requires. The logic of competence reveals that the actions necessary to diagnose this disorder must first be identified. Since we know that diagnosing placenta previa requires (1) knowing that painless third trimester bleeding often signals the presence of placenta previa, (2) ordering an ultrasound examination for placental placement, and (3) performing a careful pelvic examination to confirm the diagnosis immediately prior to delivery (with preparations already having been made for emergency Cesarean section), we have the information necessary to consider Jones's competence. In other words, criteria exist in terms of which to evaluate Jones's, or any other obstetrician's, diagnostic ability. Of course, as the logic indicates, much more information about Jones is needed. The second step is to assess whether Jones knows that diagnosing placenta previa requires these actions and knows how to perform them.

In addition to knowing what tasks are required and what their performance demands, the third aspect of competence is the ability to meet these requirements. Thus, the next component of task-oriented competence is to identify the capacities necessary for the task's completion. Diagnosing placenta previa demands the abilities to understand normal and abnormal anatomy and physiology in general and the female reproductive system and processes in particular, as well as normal and pathological obstetrical conditions; to recognize signals of pathology (e.g., painless third trimester bleeding); to know which techniques are useful in confirming the presence of pathology (e.g., ultrasound, careful pelvic exam); and to appreciate data provided by those techniques (e.g., abnormal placental placement). Lastly, the person whose competence is in question ought to possess the requisite capacities. If competence is specific to particular tasks, and if particular tasks are understood in terms of actions requisite to their completion, and if these actions depend on capacities necessary to behave in the designated fashion, then the competent person must possess those capacities.

Note, also, that the person whose competence is under consideration ought to be able to do the task at hand (Culver and Gert, 1982, p. 54). For example, no one calls an accountant who cannot diagnose placenta previa "incompetent." Because expertise in accounting does not include diagnosing placenta previa, accountants are not expected to have the capacities needed to execute this task. On the other hand, the capacity to diagnose placenta previa is part of the obstetrician's professional responsibility. A residency in obstetrics should provide both the intellectual and manual capacities necessary for this task. Consequently, we expect obstetricians to possess these skills, and those who fail to demonstrate them are rightly considered incompetent.

If we put all this together, we can refine the task-oriented definition of competence:

A person is competent to perform a task, the actions of which are specified, if he knows what actions are required, knows how to perform those actions, possesses the capacities necessary to perform those actions, and, given his position, can reasonably be expected to possess both that knowledge and those capacities.

Thus, Jones is competent to diagnose placenta previa if she knows that placenta previa is a complication of pregnancy, that painless third trimester bleeding may signal that disorder, that sonography and cautious pelvic exams are reliable diagnostic tools for it, and if she can interpret their findings—given her training as an obstetrician, she can reasonably be expected to know these things.

The same logic indicates how to determine Jones's more general competence. If, for example, she is being considered for hospital privileges, she must demonstrate competence to perform a wide array of particular diagnostic and management tasks. On the basis of a constellation of particular competencies, she will be considered more or less competent to diagnose and treat obstetrical conditions and, on the basis of those competencies, she is a more or less generally competent obstetrician.

Not surprisingly, obstetricians demonstrate varying degrees of skill in performing professional tasks. Based upon their capacities to perform particular tasks, each of which requires particular knowledge and capacities, they are more or less competent obstetricians. Practitioners and patients recognize this diversity when they remark, "Jones is great with complicated OB cases, but I wouldn't use her for normal pregnancies." This comment signifies that Jones possesses the specialized knowledge and capacities to diagnose and treat unusual obstetrical conditions successfully, while her knowledge and capacities to manage routine cases are less impressive. Likewise, if a Labor and Delivery nurse comments, that "Smith is good with everyday deliveries, but don't let him near a complication," she is indicating that Smith demonstrates competence in one area, but lacks it in another.

### A Preliminary Definition of Competence to Consent to Health Care

The logic of task-oriented conceptions of competence can be applied to consent. The specific task of giving consent is an example of the more general task of making a decision, or selecting one option from a mutually exclusive set.[1] Virginia Abernethy has addressed competence to consent as competence to make decisions. She defines a generally competent decision maker as "informable and cognitively capable of making ordinary decisions on matters unrelated to the crisis at hand" (Abernethy, 1984, p. 57). Her claim is that anyone who possesses these qualities in everyday life is competent to give or withhold consent in a medical setting. She asserts that persons who successfully complete most of the decision-making tasks they face in everyday life can successfully complete the task of making a health care decision. This claim is compatible with the general presumption of competence discussed in Chapter One, and it correlates nicely with the triggers of suspicion of incompetence noted there. But does it apply to the more particular competence of health care decision making? Combining Abernethy's account of general decision making with the idea of task-oriented competence provides a very general preliminary definition of competence to consent:

> Persons are competent for the task of giving a free and informed consent if they are generally informable and cognitively capable of making decisions.

The logic of competence indicates how to develop this definition: The acts required for decision making and the knowledge and capacities on which those actions depend must be identified.

Decision making is, by nature, goal-oriented. The purpose of making decisions, or choices, is to promote wanted and avoid unwanted states of affairs or outcomes. This task includes five actions. First, a person must perceive a current state of affairs, X, as undesirable. Second, the person must identify a preferred state of affairs, Y. Third, the person must recognize actions that would likely change X to Y. Fourth, the person must evaluate possible actions, a process that requires determining, for each action, (a) the likelihood that Y will occur, (b) burdens that must be borne, and (c) risks entailed. After a careful consideration of these factors, the person must, fifth, rationally select the preferred action.

Consider, for example, a patient with angina. First he perceives a recurring chest pain as undesirable. Second, he identifies being free from pain as preferable. Third, he recognizes the options that could rid him of pain: sedentary lifestyle, cardiac medications, coronary artery by-pass graft. Fourth, he evaluates these options, considering the likelihood that each will leave him pain-free, the burdens he faces with each (e.g., inability to pursue enjoyable activities vs. having to remember to take medication several times daily vs. postoperative pain), and the risks of each (e.g., early death vs. medication side effects vs. anesthesia death). After carefully considering these facts, he chooses the option he prefers.

Note how these actions correlate with Abernethy's definition. She suggests that decision making has three broad aspects: informability, cognitive capability, and deciding per se. Each of the actions involved in decision making requires that the person be capable of receiving relevant information ("informability"), of rationally considering that information ("cognitive capability"), and of using it to choose ("deciding"). In addition, Abernethy's definition, combined with the nature of the task of decision making, captures the essential elements of human nature and behavior that are presupposed by decision theory in general: (1) that persons have (or can obtain) information, (2) that they prefer some states to others, and (3) that they are capable of rational choice. We will begin our consideration of these concepts with some brief remarks about rationality and its role in decision making.

A rational choice is generally understood as a choice that maximizes one's own welfare (or the welfare of those one cares about) and is consistent with one's other choices (e.g., one does not simultaneously choose to live a long life and choose to forgo life-saving surgery).[2] In fact, choices in which a person sacrifices her own well-being without good reasons are considered irrational (Culver and Gert, 1982, pp. 26–7). Understood this way, "rational" describes actions, not persons, while "competent" describes persons, not actions; "rational" and "competent" are not synonyms. Competent persons can, of course, make rational choices, because competent persons can evaluate states of affairs, relate present and preferred states to their interests, evaluate options that may improve their states of affairs, and insure that their choices are not self-defeating (in conflict with one another). But an incompetent person can also make a rational choice, that is, one that promotes her welfare and does not directly conflict with other choices. Quite likely when we describe persons as rational we mean that they are cognitively capable of making rational choices.

With these ideas in mind, we can refine our preliminary definition of competence to consent:

> A person is competent for the task of giving a free and informed consent if (1) he is generally informable and cognitively capable of performing the actions involved in making a decision, (2) he knows that decision making requires these tasks, (3) he knows how to perform these tasks, and (4) given his situation, we can reasonably expect him to be able to make decisions.

Further elaboration is needed, however, because decision makers must not only know what actions are required and how to execute them; they must also possess the capacities needed for execution. A complete definition requires that we identify the characteristics that competent persons must possess.

Capacities that define "competence" have been much discussed. Virtually all writers who have addressed the nature of competence have referred to different capacities.[3] Those most commonly considered fit nicely into Abernethy's structure, so we will introduce and consider them in that light. Their role in a decision-making structure will be expanded and justified in Chapters Four and Five.

Informability, the first capacity required for competence, correlates with the first trigger of suspicion—the patient who cannot acquire the facts necessary to make a decision. To be informable is to be capable of acquiring relevant information. Informable persons can receive facts about their situations.[4] They must at the least be alert; they cannot be comatose or obtunded. They must also be able to recognize relevant information as information, not as meaningless or unimportant stimuli. This capacity includes the ability to recognize information about the environment itself—the person must know that she is in a situation in which a choice must be made. The capacity also includes an ability to recognize the nature and importance of the facts being presented.[5] Patients must recognize that they are sick, what treatments are (or are not) available, and so forth. Lastly, informability includes the capacity to retrieve, or remember, information for use in the on-going process of decision making.[6] Information cannot go in one ear and out the other.

To be informable, then, one must be conscious, aware of the environment, educated (or educable), and aware that incoming data are not random stimuli that one is free to ignore. An informable person cannot be out of contact with reality for physiological (e.g., coma) or psychological (e.g., autism) reasons. One cannot suffer from delusions that radically impair one's perception of the world (e.g., believe that clinicians are medieval inquisitors whose purpose is to extract professions of faith). Nor can one be unable to learn (e.g., profoundly intellectually developmentally disabled). To be informable is to be able to *receive, recognize the relevance of,* and *remember* facts.

Being informable is quite distinct from being informed. The former is a capability; the latter is a state of affairs. Informed consent requires that patients be informed about their diagnoses, prognoses, and treatments. Such information allows patients to understand, choose, and cooperate with therapeutic courses.[7] Patients cannot be informed unless they are informable. They are informable only if they are able to receive information.

The distinction between being informable and being informed is important for practical reasons. There are many reasons why informable patients are uninformed. Some explicitly request that their HCPs not give them information about diagnosis, prognosis, or treatment. For whatever reasons, they prefer to leave decision making to their HCPs with the instruction to them to "do what you think is best." The informable patient who chooses to be uninformed has transferred decision-making authority and may reclaim it at any time.

Other patients refuse information for religious reasons. For example, Jehovah's Witnesses may not want to hear about therapeutic options that require the use of blood or blood products because given their religious beliefs, these treatments are genuinely not options for them. Though informable, they choose not to be informed about certain alternatives.

The second capacity required for competence is cognitive capability.[8] It correlates with the second trigger of suspicion—the inability to appreciate relevant facts or apply them to oneself. Like informability, this criterion is made up of several distinct capacities. One must be able to discern if and how information relates to oneself, and to reason about how various choices may alter one's status and plans.[9] The Olympic ice skater must consider the varying impact of repeated joint injections with steroids and local anesthetics vs. meniscectomy on her future career. In addition, persons must be able to examine how different choices produce different outcomes, and to assess which, based upon their own values and lifestyles, is preferable. One must also be able to understand that different options have different prognoses, and be able to include these prognoses in decision-making calculations.[10] Again, the skater may have to determine whether she wants maximal mobility and minimal pain for a few years or for a lifetime.

Since most problems admit different solutions, persons should be able to rank possible choices according to their preferences and the likelihood of outcomes.[11] Patients need to be able to order their prospects from "most desired" to "least desired." Ideally, patients will be able to employ the therapeutic option they most desire; however this is not always possible. The Olympian may have to forgo steroid injections because the Olympic Committee forbids them. Likewise, a patient with end-stage cardiac disease may most prefer to have a transplant, but if no heart is available, he must be able to specify his second choice (and, if that is impossible, his third choice, and so on). In sum, cognitively capable persons can see relationships between information and themselves, can weigh risks, burdens, and benefits that attend different options, and can place options in a hierarchy. Cognitively capable persons can *relate to themselves, reason about*, and *rank* options.

Since the third trigger of suspicion was an inability to come to a decision, the third capacity required for competence is that persons must actually be able to decide. All the foregoing abilities are irrelevant if the process does not culminate in an actual choice. Thus, after informable patients cognitively consider their options, they must be able to choose their preferred approach.[12] The patient who is intractably undecided cannot move to resolve his health care problems.

Moreover, persons must be able not only to select an option, but to commit themselves to their decisions. They need not be enthusiastic about their choices, but they must be committed to them. To continue our example, the patient with end-stage cardiac disease may not be eager to undergo a cardiac transplant. Such an option is risky, frightening, painful, and expensive—good reasons to be less than zealous about undertaking the procedure. Nonetheless, the patient must be able to at least resign himself to its being the least of the possible evils.[13] If he is not at least convinced of that, he will lack the motivation to proceed with the therapy. Thus, competent patients must be able to *resolve* their situations and (at least) *resign themselves* to their choices.

Thus, our preliminary definition of competence includes eight distinct but functionally inseparable capacities. These are the capacities to receive, recognize, and remember relevant information; to relate to oneself, reason about, and rank alternatives; to resolve situations; and to resign oneself to those resolutions. In health care settings it may also require a ninth capacity: to recount one's decision-making process to others. More will be said about this requirement later. Here we need only note that HCPs, family, and friends who participate in patients' decisions will be more comfortable if patients can give some justifications for their choices—especially those that are risky or idiosyncratic.

Proof that this preliminary definition of competence is correct requires the detailed discussion and justification of all these capacities in later chapters. The remainder of this chapter examines the problems with the concept of competence as it is currently understood.

## CURRENT PROBLEMS WITH THE CONCEPT OF COMPETENCE

In spite of the fact that competence has never been explicitly defined, tests for competence do exist. This odd state of affairs is the first predicament we will address.

## The Need to Distinguish the Definition from the Tests

Since persons are competent to do a task, T, if and only if they possess the necessary capacities, we cannot know they are competent to do T without first knowing what capacities T requires. From this it follows that we cannot test their competence. Unless we know what capacities T requires, we do not know what to test for.[14]

Recall Jones. The claim that she is a competent obstetrician because (among other things) she has the capacity to diagnose and treat placenta previa is meaningless unless it has been determined that the capacity to diagnose and treat placenta previa is part of competent obstetric practice. Unless this capacity is required of competent obstetricians, Jones's ability to do it says nothing about her professional competence. Similarly, if someone were to claim that Jones is an incompetent obstetrician because she cannot grow grapes, we should have to know that grape-growing abilities have nothing to do with obstetrics to refute the charge of incompetence. But without a definition of obstetrical competence even this obvious claim cannot be made. Only when it is known what "obstetrical competence" means can we undertake to test Jones's competence. In sum, we cannot test Jones's competence as an obstetrician without first knowing what capacities are required of any competent obstetrician. Only after such guidelines have been established do we know what to test for.

Likewise, we cannot say that a person is competent to give informed consent unless we know what capacities are required for the task. We cannot dependably test for competence to consent unless we know what to test for. So the first project in the conceptual analysis of competence to consent is to decide what we should be testing for. That is, we must determine whether the capacities included in our preliminary definition of competence to consent are the proper capacities. Until that task is completed, we cannot devise a test for competence.

A question naturally arises: Why is the distinction between a definition and a test important? Quite simply, definitions and tests serve different functions. A definition serves a theoretical function—it tells us what we mean by competence. The capacities that define competence specify the criteria for being a competent person. To be competent is to have the particular capacities. (Jones is a competent obstetrician because she has the necessary capacities, including the capacity to diagnose and treat placenta previa.) Tests serve a practical function—they are tools that identify the presence or absence of capacities, and determine whether particular persons have the appropriate abilities. (Jones correctly answers questions about or takes appropriate measures for the management of placenta previa.) Tests identify actual competent and incompetent consenters.

Previous work on competence to consent has often confused these two projects. In fact, the cart—testing—has generally preceded the horse—definition. To date there has been much discussion about testing for competence, but little effort to define it clearly. Moreover, there is no guarantee that success in one project will assure success in the other. We may be able to identify the capacities a person needs to be competent, yet be unable to test for them. For example, most HCPs believe that some capacity to weigh risks and burdens against benefits is required for competent decision making, though we have no functional test for this capacity. Conversely, we may be able to test for particular capacities, but lack confidence that those capacities constitute competence (e.g., we can measure intelligence, but we cannot say that intelligence guarantees competence).[15] In short, for the concept of competence to be useful, it must be defined. Until a definition is secured, attempts to construct a test for competence are premature, a fact that may account for the historical difficulty of settling on any particular test.[16]

The missing definition is of practical importance, because lacking an established definition of, and dependable tests for, competence, it is impossible to determine which patients are appropriate decision makers. Thus, clinicians cannot be certain their patients' consents for diagnostic and therapeutic procedures are valid. Without a valid consent, practitioners cannot be morally or legally authorized to provide or withhold care and proceed, when they do, without appropriate authority. Moreover, this practical problem can become a legal problem because HCPs are liable if they expose patients to risks to which they have not competently consented. Consider the competent patient who understands he is at risk for an allergic reaction to IVP dye, yet consents to the X-ray. If he has an anaphylactic response, it is just very bad luck. The radiologist is neither morally nor legally responsible for this harm (assuming he has not been negligent), because the patient competently chose to accept the risk. But if the patient was not competent, the radiologist is responsible because he was the only competent decision maker.

What we have said so far is this: A patient can only give valid consent if he is competent to consent. We can only know if a patient is competent if we know what "competent to consent"means. But since there is no widely accepted definition of "competence to consent," we are uncertain about its meaning. Further, since we are uncertain about the meaning of "competence to consent," we cannot devise a reliable test for it. Therefore, we currently have no reliable test for competence to consent and therefore we do not know which patients are competent to consent.[17] Therefore we do not know which consents are competently given and, therefore, valid.

### Alleged Tests for Competence to Consent

The failure to specify the capacities that define competence has not, oddly enough, impeded competence testing. A wide array of tools are currently used to assess competence (e.g., the Mental Status Exam (Strub and Black, 1987), the Mini-Mental Status Exam (Folstein et al. 1975), the Neurobehavioral Cognitive Status Examination (Kiernan et al. 1987), the Short Portable Mental Status Questionnaire (Pfeiffer, 1975), the Cognitive Capacity Screening Examination (Jacobs et al. 1977)).[18] Of course each test evaluates something, but since competence has not been defined, there is no guarantee that these tests measure competence. Moreover, even in this practical arena one finds confusion between defining competence and testing for it. As evidence for this claim, consider the highly regarded work of the Pittsburgh Group (Roth et al., 1977).[19] Their examples will demonstrate the lack of precision in this area.

The Pittsburgh Group is plagued by the general confusion that surrounds the notion of competence. Without explicitly defining competence, they suggest five tests for its presence: "(1) evidencing a choice, (2) "reasonable" outcome of choice, (3) choice based on "rational" reasons, (4) ability to understand, and (5) actual understanding" (Roth et al. 1977, p. 280). How useful are these tests?

A test is a measurement tool; it determines the presence or extent of something. For example, a test for glycosuria determines the presence of sugar in the urine (- or +), as well as its extent (0 - 4+). Similarly, a test for competence should determine the presence or absence of competence in a consenter, as well as its extent (from fully competent to fully incompetent). Each of the "tests" proposed by the Pittsburgh Group fails to do one or both of these things.

Consider, the first test—"evidencing a choice." Under this criterion: "The competent patient is one who evidences a preference for or against treatment. This test focuses . . . on the presence or absence of a decision. Only the patient who does not evidence a preference either verbally or through his or her behavior is considered incompetent" (Roth et al. 1977, p. 280).

This test does measure the presence of something—a choice—and choice is an important factor in decision making. The problem is that the Pittsburgh Group gives no justification that the mere presence of a choice is either a necessary or a sufficient condition of competence to consent. No one would claim that a two-year-old who vehemently chooses not to have a penicillin shot for pneumonia is competent, though she surely "evidences a preference for or against treatment." Likewise, Mrs. W and Ms. Y evidenced choices, but in neither case did their HCPs believe their indications of a preference settled the matter. Thus, even if choice is a necessary aspect of competent consent, there is reason to suspect that it is not sufficient, that additional capacities are required.

Next consider whether "reasonable outcome of choice" tests for the presence or extent of competence. Here the focus is on results, and the patient who chooses to promote a state of affairs that is contrary to the choice of a "reasonable" person will be found incompetent (Roth et al. 1977, p. 281). But this cannot be right. What HCPs want to know is whether competence is present in patients whose choices are unexpected. When Mrs. W refuses a C-section, her HCPs want to know if she is competent to do so. Saying that the majority of rational persons would choose otherwise does not answer the question. Her choice may be reasonable (if, for example, she is a Christian Scientist), even though most would choose differently. More important, even if others find her choice unreasonable, if she is competent she holds decision-making authority, and that authority protects her freedom to choose "unreasonably."

The same can be said of the "choice based on 'rational' reasons." Here attention is directed toward the explanation given for one's choices, but what makes a reason rational, and why? Many otherwise competent people choose—at least according to others—on the basis of nonrational reasons. Perhaps the best example here is love. Most of us have at least one friend who married exactly the wrong person (unreasonable outcome) because he was in love (nonrational reason). We are apt to describe such decisions as unreasonable or even perhaps as irrational, but we rarely question the person's competence. Perhaps people can make rational choices to behave nonrationally; or perhaps acting in concert with a strong emotion, itself nonrational, is rational. But the more worrisome problem continues to be knowing what counts as a rational reason. When Ms. Y said, "Do whatever you want because I don't care what you do," was her choice based on rational reasons? Would her choice be reasonable? In any case, would she be competent? *Should* her HCPs follow her instructions? The point is that neither "reasonable outcome of choice" nor "choice based on 'rational' reasons" indicates that the patient is competent.

Next, take "actual understanding." On the one hand, actual understanding does indicate the presence of something—understanding. Again, the relationship of understanding to competence to consent needs to be shown. Actual understanding may help to define competence. That is, maybe competent decision makers must actually understand something about the decisions they are making. But even if "actual understanding" is a necessary aspect of competence, it may not be sufficient; other capacities may be needed. In short, what this "test" contributes to assessing a patient's competence to consent is not clear.

Finally consider "ability to understand": "[A]t a minimum the patient must manifest sufficient ability to understand information about treatment. . . . What matters in this test is that the patient is able to comprehend the elements that are presumed . . . to be a part of treatment decision making" (Roth et al. 1977, p. 281). The key phrase here is "able to comprehend"; it designates a capacity for which a test is needed. "Ability to understand" is not a test but a criterion for competence.[20]

Let's put this objection another way: When is a person, P, competent to consent? One answer is when P has the "ability to understand risks, benefits, and alternatives to treatment" (Roth et al. 1977, p. 281). That is, P possesses a particular capacity—the capacity to understand relevant information. But there is still the further question: How do we know P has the relevant capacity? Answer: P is tested to determine its extent. The Pittsburgh Group in fact makes this distinction (though apparently without realizing its conceptual import), saying: "The patient's capacity for understanding may be tested by asking the patient a series of questions concerning risks, benefits, and alternatives to treatment" (Roth et al. 1977, p. 281). In other words, the *definition* of competence to consent includes a *capacity* for understanding, while the *test* for that capacity is a set of questions that determines the presence or extent of that capacity. So, for example, Ms. Y might be competent to choose between radiation alone and radiation with chemotherapy if she understands the risks and benefits of both. We might test her understanding by asking her questions about these alternatives (What are the side effects of each? What are the different chances of success? How would each alter her schedule for work or recreation?).

In the end it is hard to assess the The Pittsburgh Group's "tests." The greatest strength of their work is that it identifies important aspects of competent decision making, and "passing" any of these tests may serve as a mark in favor of competence. As our provisional definition indicates, patients ought to be able to make (or evidence) a choice. Moreover, cognitively capable patients ought to be able to consider a problem rationally and choose in ways that are likely to promote their own welfare ("reasonable outcome" and "rational reasons"). Similarly, the importance of informability gives credence to The Pittsburgh Group's concerns with understanding, whether potential or actual, and their emphasis on abilities to receive and recognize relevant information, relate information to oneself, and reason about options.

In short, while the Pittsburgh Group's "tests" are not tests in the usual sense, they do indicate capacities that belong in the definition of competence. The point is that without first defining competence, reliable tests for it are difficult to construct. One first needs to determine what "competence to consent" really means. This definition requires a conceptual analysis, a process to which we now turn.[21]

## Basic Issues Regarding the Concept of Competence

### General and Specific Competence

Virginia Abernethy has argued that competence is a general notion, that "the presumption of competence should be overcome only when significant dysfunction in an *array* of cognitive and interpersonal domains can be demonstrated" (Abernethy, 1984, p. 57, emphasis added).[22] This means that persons would be competent for all tasks whenever they could successfully complete most tasks that they routinely encounter. Then persons who could perform most normal activities of daily living (e.g., hold jobs, balance checkbooks, raise children) would be considered—in virtue of those abilities—competent to consent to health care. On a general notion of competence, actual competence to do most things means competence to do all things.

Most scholars have rejected a general notion of competence, arguing instead that the definition of competence (i.e., the requisite capacities) should vary according to context.[23] As context-dependent, competence must be determined for specific tasks. Under a specific notion of competence, a person would be competent for a particular task if she possesses the capacities requisite to its performance. The fact that a person competently completes most activities of daily living would not extend to competence to consent (or, for that matter, to competence to complete any individual task). With context-dependent (specific) competence, it would be necessary to possess the capacities required for particular tasks.

Schematizing the possibilities for competence is helpful, since doing so helps exhibit the differences between them. Schema for general competence (GC) and specific competence (SC) are as follows:

> **GC:**    A person (P) is competent (C) for *any* task (T) if a Standard (S) is met (or met to Degree D).
>
> **SC:**    P is C for *this* T if S is met (or met to Degree D) for *this* T.

Clarity regarding the implications of this distinction is important. If competence is a general notion, then competent persons are competent to manage all situations that arise. Generally competent persons are competent to make stock market investments, plant a garden, execute a will, sell a house, consent to health care, and anything else they want to do. They have decision-making authority for their lives in general and their health care in particular.

Alternatively, if competence is a specific notion, persons are competent for particular projects only if they possess the capacities demanded by those projects. If making stock market investments requires different capacities than making decisions about health care, persons may be competent—in virtue of possessing some capacities but not others—to buy stocks but not to consent to health care. They may be competent to do some things but not others. Here it makes no sense to speak of competent or incompetent *persons* (except those who are incompetent for all tasks, as, for example, the permanently comatose). Instead, individuals are competent or incompetent for particular tasks at particular times. One can simultaneously be a competent stock broker and an incompetent gardener.

The point is that general competence is competence to do whatever one undertakes. On a general analysis there are only competent and incompetent persons who sometimes perform well and sometimes perform poorly. On a specific analysis persons are competent for some tasks but not for others, depending on what capacities they possess.[24]

The distinction has important ramifications for health care providers and bioethicists. If competence is general in nature, the patient who can satisfactorily complete most of his normal activities is because of that fact competent to consent. So Mrs. W and Ms. Y are competent to consent. Although the notion that the ability to grow tomatoes, repair small engines, or write scientific treatises can be transferred, without loss, to the ability to make health care decisions seems counter-intuitive, such assumptions are common and not wholly unwarranted. The presumption that persons are competent unless there is compelling evidence to the contrary makes both moral and practical sense. Patients are assumed to be competent, and the burden of proof is on those who assert otherwise.

Still, the implications of general competence may not be fully appreciated. To be clear: general competence asserts that persons are competent to consent if they are generally able to make decisions. The person who can make the decisions necessary to produce good tomatoes, well-running engines, or scientifically respectable papers can be considered a generally competent decision maker. Such persons are the appropriate persons from whom to solicit consent for treatment, and their decisions to give or withhold consent must be respected, as must be their assessments of their own best interests.[25] Moreover, this respect must be granted regardless of any evidence of particular decision-making incapacity. Generally competent decision makers who appear to understand none of the risks or benefits that attend a specific decision will still be the persons from whom consent must be sought and whose decisions settle the issue. Because they are generally able to make sound choices, the principle of respect for autonomy, rather than the principle of beneficence will govern their care. Under this approach Mrs. W is competent to refuse the C-Section and Ms. Y can turn over decisional authority to her physician.

On the other hand, persons who are unable to manage the details of everyday life will—because of that fact—be deemed generally incompetent. If they cannot hold down a job, run a household, tend a garden, and balance the checkbook, they will not be considered competent for any other activity. So no matter how capable they appear to be to make decisions about health care, they will not be considered appropriate decision makers. Instead, surrogate decision makers must be appointed. The principle of beneficence, rather than of respect for autonomy, will govern their care (unless they have previously left very precise instructions about any health care they may need).

If competence is context-dependent, the implications differ dramatically. With a specific notion of competence, patients' capacities in other spheres are irrelevant (though, of course, they give rise to expectations about how persons will perform any particular task). The person who is incompetent to sell stocks may still be competent to consent. The person who adequately manages his everyday affairs may still lack the ability to make competent health care decisions. Whenever consent is required, it must be determined whether the patient is the appropriate decision maker *here and now*. Under this approach, Mrs. W. and Ms. Y may or may not be competent to consent.

Consequently, questions of general vs. specific competence are important to health care professionals and bioethicists for two reasons. First, consent needs to be solicited from the appropriate party. Since informed consent must be given by a competent person, clinicians must determine competence so as to know whom to inform and from whom they can accept a consent. Second, when a patient appears incapable of making a decision (as may be the case with generally competent but specifically incompetent persons), one may rightly worry that he is, in fact, if not by definition, incompetent to relate his current situation to his value structure. If so, doing what the patient asks may actually thwart his best interests and harm rather than help him. Put another way, the question is whether to shift the ethical principle governing the patient's care from autonomy to *general* beneficence. These concerns, then, require a decision regarding whether informed consent assumes general or specific competence.

Further issues to address include (1) whether competence is a matter of a threshold or of degree (i.e., what constitutes the standard); (2) whether competence will vary according to what is at stake (i.e., what, if any, role consequences play in the analysis of competence); and (3) the respective roles of cognition and affect (i.e., what sorts of capacities will be included in the definition of competence). We will consider these questions in turn. In these discussions I will speak neutrally of competence without specifying whether it is general or specific.

### Threshold and Degree Competence

Is competence all or nothing, or does it come in degrees? If there is a threshold for competence, a boundary separates competent from incompetent persons. Those on one side are completely competent to consent, while those on the other are completely incompetent. That is, persons on the competent side of the boundary are generally competent. People on the incompetent side of the line are generally incompetent. On a threshold conception of competence to consent, any person who sufficiently possesses the necessary capacities is competent to make all decisions. Anyone lacking the necessary capacities would have any and all decisions made for her by someone else.[26] The implications of threshold competence are precisely those previously discussed above under general competence.

Competence may not, however, conform to a threshold notion. Instead it may depend on the *extent* to which persons possess particular capacities. If capacities are present in greater or lesser amounts, competence is a question of degree. On a degree conception, persons may be more or less in possession of the necessary capacities, and thus more or less competent.[27] The more competent a person is, the stronger his claim to decision-making authority and the more likely it is that he can reliably determine and report his own best interests. Then, we would have a greater obligation to recognize his decision-making authority and to respect both his assessments of his own interests and his notion of how to promote them. The less competent the person, the less others are bound to solicit or respect his decisions. Others would also be less obligated to respect any choices he expresses. This is not an unfamiliar approach. In reality, persons may be more or less involved in decision making, depending on their interest, ability, or opportunity. Moreover, patients' decisions may be more or less respected, depending on their decisional facility and their intensity and persistence with regard to particular choices. Clinicians may be more inclined to respect a strongly felt choice, even if the patient's decision-making capacities appear reduced. Respect may also vary according to perceptions as to whether a patient's choice is likely to further her own best interests.[28]

Consider the schema for threshold competence (TC) and degree competence (DC):

**TC:** P is C if S is met.

**DC:** P is C to degree D if S is met to Degree D.

As an example of the difference between the threshold and degree conceptions, consider the "ability to understand" criterion in the case of Ms. Y, the woman for whom post-lumpectomy adjunct therapy has been recommended. On a threshold notion of competence, she is probably competent to decide about therapy if she at least can recognize that she is ill; that particular treatments have been recommended; that she is in a health care setting where such treatment can be provided; that if she undertakes those treatments, the probability of recurrence is reduced; and that this is a new approach by her physician. (I say "probably competent" because a definition of competence has not yet been defended. Thus to claim certainty for such assessments would be presumptuous.) If she can appreciate these facts, she can be said to have the ability to understand the situation and, on that basis, to be competent to make decisions about her treatment. Her decision-making authority, as well as her statements about the nature of and best means for promoting her own best interests, would be recognized. The principle of respect for autonomy would govern her care.

Under a degree notion, one must consider not only whether Ms. Y possesses an ability to understand, but also the extent to which that capacity is functioning. She may be able to understand not only that she is ill, but also what her prognosis is with and without treatment; not simply that chemotherapy and radiation have been recommended, but what alternative therapies exist, and what her prognosis would be with each; not only that she is in a hospital, but in a hospital that has demonstrated its ability for treating persons in her condition; and not only that this approach will probably reduce her long-term morbidity and mortality, but also the risks with each alternative and the chances that these risks will occur in her case. On a degree theory of competence a distinction can be made between persons who understand more and those who understand less. We can distinguish the patient who understands the situation incompletely from the one who understands it thoroughly. This distinguishes DC from TC, where the only distinction to be made is between people who do and do not understand "enough." (Practically speaking, DC will ultimately look much like TC. Clinicians must eventually decide if a patient is competent "enough," and that decision becomes a cut-off point. We can consider the similarities and differences in more detail later.)

This dichotomy, like that of general vs. specific competence, has important implications for clinicians and bioethicists. First, DC and TC differ in the extent to which others—HCPs, family, friends—are permitted to "officially" participate in a patient's decision-making activities. The patient who meets or exceeds a threshold will be expected to make decisions about her care. Her competence establishes her decision-making authority and her ability to reliably assess what will promote her interests, and ensures that the principle of respect for autonomy governs her care. The professional should focus on the provision of information.

On a degree conception, competence determinations and decision-making authority will be less precisely specified. Without a line of demarcation that clearly specifies competence, there is less precision in the determination and, derivatively, greater room for the participation of others. If the patient is more or less competent, then the level of his competence falls upon a competence continuum. Less competent patients have less decision-making authority than do more competent patients. The principle of respect for autonomy applies less and the principle of beneficence applies more in the less competent person. With the less competent patient, there will be a greater opportunity for the (beneficent) participation by others. This opportunity will diminish as the degree of competence increases and the principle of respect for autonomy gathers or regains strength.

Second, this distinction has crucial consequences concerning our respect for particular choices. The threshold-competent person's decisions must be accepted as the final word. What he elects must be honored. The degree-competent persons exhibit a range of competence. Persons who understand things more thoroughly are more competent than those who understand to a lesser degree. Thus, they have greater decision-making authority than those whose understanding is reduced. Those whose competence is diminished have weaker claims to decision-making authority and to others' respect of their choices. (Again, DC cannot escape a pragmatic identity with TC. Clinicians eventually must decide whether to obey or override a patient's choice.)

If decision-making authority is less firmly established (as a result of decreased competence), other morally relevant appeals may participate in the decision-making process. For example, when a patient has reduced competence, his choices are less binding on others, and it may be morally legitimate to override decisions that others view as unwise. Assume Ms. Y, the woman for whom postlumpectomy adjunct therapy has been recommended, is competent on a threshold determination. If she chooses to forgo both therapies, this choice, with its important consequences, must stand. If DC prevails there may be room for negotiation. Diminished decision-making capacity commensurately reduces decisional authority and expands the legitimacy of input from other agents and other morally relevant appeals. Just as competence is on a continuum, so is the movement between the principles of respect for autonomy and beneficence. The more competent the patient, the greater the reliance upon autonomy; the less competent the patient, the greater the reliance on general beneficence.

When the consequences of decisions are serious and the patient has diminished decision-making capacity, the argument favors increasing other people's participation in the decision-making process. In fact, other participants frequently appeal to the projected outcomes of health care decisions. When persons choose to forgo benefits or suffer heavy burdens, others are increasingly concerned that they may not have done so competently. In turn, this concern often motivates consideration of the perceived consequences of the choice and gives rise to suggestions that consequences should always play a role in assessing competence. For example, when a person has a reduced capacity to understand the facts, and the consequences of the decision are serious, an appeal to those consequences and to the person's diminished capacity might argue against the person's decision-making authority.

### Consequence-Dependent and
### Consequence-Independent Competence

The third conceptual possibility is that competence determinations could be consequence-dependent. If so, definitions of competence will change with the seriousness of situations.[29] If competence is tied to consequences, persons may be competent to consent to a therapy of minor import but not one that is critical to their well-being. Put another way, the definition of (requirements for) competence will change depending on the consequences of the decision. When choices have sufficiently important results, a high level of ability—manifested by particularly stringent criteria—is demanded for competence to make decisions. Only the most capable persons will be granted decision-making authority for choices with potentially devastating outcomes. Only the most able persons will be viewed as reliable reporters of their own best interests when repercussions are momentous.

Profound effects are common in health care settings. Choices that determine morbidity and mortality are an everyday occurrence. For example, patients can refuse life-saving therapy or request that they not be resuscitated in case of cardiopulmonary arrest. Since the outcome of these decisions—death—is serious and irrevocable, clinicians want to be quite certain that persons issuing them are competent. They want strong assurances that patients who choose death are appropriate decision makers, and that death really is in the person's best interests.

Conversely, when choices have minimal import, decision-making competence is less crucial. Virtually everyone can be competent to resolve little problems. We would be hard-pressed to overrule a patient's decision to take her sleeping pill at 10:00 P.M., rather than at 9:30 P.M. With less at stake, it is more difficult to insist that the patient's decision is harmful or that autonomy should give way to general beneficence.

The dynamic nature of importance is recognized in the claim that competence is consequence-dependent. Under this approach, Ms. Y may not be competent to refuse all adjunctive therapy, though she may be competent to refuse a daily multivitamin. Again differences may be clarified by the schema. Consequence-independent competence (CIC) and consequence-dependent competence (CDC) may be schematized as follows:

CIC: P is C for any T if nonvarying S is met (or met to D).
CDC: P is C for this T if S, which varies in terms of this T's consequences, is met for this T.

CIC is phrased in "general" terminology because general competence necessarily precludes an appeal to consequences. Conversely, CDC's need for assessing outcomes of particular decisions requires the "specific" wording.

### Considerations of the Three Options

Each of these six options has its advocates. Consider CIC and CDC.[30] On the one hand, James Drane (1984, 1985) claims that capacity to consent should vary according to the medically significant consequences the situation holds for the patient. He argues that less competence is necessary to refuse a major harm or accept a major benefit than is needed to refuse a major benefit or accept a major harm. On the other hand, Stephen Wear (1991) reminds us that people often choose to behave in ways that can lead to noxious outcomes (e.g., they take up sky-diving, or buy fast cars instead of life insurance). Unless we are prepared to routinely forbid all risky decisions, there are no in-principle reasons to do so in health care settings. Just because potential catastrophe attends certain health choices is no reason to require that standards of competence be more stringent than those demanded in other settings.

Next, consider TC and DC. Faden and Beauchamp argue that a threshold conception of competence will facilitate competence determinations. Decision-making authority is more easily ascribed, and issues of competence are more reliably settled. Meanwhile, proponents of a degree conception (e.g., Baruch Brody) insist that this approach captures the reality to which common sense attests: people really are more or less able to manage situations; they are more or less reliable reporters of their own best interests, and their decisions should sometimes command more, sometimes less respect.

Abernethy (1984) recommends that we understand competence as a general capacity, that we recognize the full decision-making authority of the normally competent; and that their choices be respected, regardless of circumstances. Most writers, however, agree with Culver and Gert (1982) that specificity is preferable and that competence needs to be repeatedly evaluated as conditions change. A person's decision-making authority and respect for her choices depend on particular situations.

A conceptual analysis of competence will need to address all three dichotomies. As important as each is in contributing to our understanding of the concept, none addresses all the issues contained within it. Rather each theory, in virtue of its failure to attend to more than one aspect, is conceptually incomplete. The narrowness of focus makes each pair inadequate as is illustrated by the following questions that led to these dichotomies: (1) Is this person competent for all tasks or merely for this task? (GC vs. SC); (2) Is this person fully, partly, or not competent to make a decision? (TC vs. DC); and (3) Should the potential outcome of this decision affect the designation of this person as competent? (CIC vs. CDC). To answer one or two of these questions is to answer incompletely. We need answers to all of them to decide if persons are competent.

Assume for the moment that a conceptual analysis shows that SC is preferable to GC. Then clinicians and bioethicists must only determine if Ms. Y is competent to decide here and now about these therapeutic options. However, knowing that competence is context-dependent says nothing about whether determinations of competence will proceed according to a threshold or degrees. We must still determine if Ms. Y is fully competent (TC) or more or less competent (DC). If the latter, her decision-making authority is not precisely specified; she may be competent for some tasks, but not for others. Other people may also play a greater role in the decision-making process. Ms. Y's ability to relate her situation to her value structure may wax and wane, as may her ability to determine what will promote her own interests. As a result, the extent to which her decisions must be respected may vary.

Finally, deciding between TC and DC does not determine the role to be played by consequences. Consequences could be ignored and a single threshold set. Or if competence varies with consequences, a series of thresholds may be established: $T_1$ for catastrophic consequences, $T_2$ for major consequences, $T_3$ for moderate consequences, and so forth. Alternatively, with DC, patients would have to be more competent for decisions with serious consequences, less competent for decisions with less serious consequences, and so forth. Clinicians and bioethicists must assess the relationship of competence to decision-making authority, to patients' abilities to specify their best interests and how to promote them, and to the extent to which their decisions are immune from interference.

Clearly, competence is not merely a matter of (1) general vs. specific, (2) threshold vs. degree, or (3) significance of consequences, medical or other. Instead, competence incorporates all these notions. As Table 1 shows, there are various combinations of these aspects.

Correlation of Table 1 with the previous schema reveals what these possible combinations will mean:

*OPTIONS*   *COMBINATIONS*

1)   P is C for all T if nonvarying S is met.

2)   P is C to D for all T if nonvarying S is met to D.

3)   P is C for this T if varying S is met for this T.

4)   P is C for this T if nonvarying S is met for this T.

5)   P is C to D for this T if varying S is met to D for this T.

6)   P is C to D for this T if nonvarying S is met to D for this T.

Table 1. Combinations of the Aspects of Competence*

| Options | GC vs. SC | TC vs. DC | CDC vs. CIC |
|---------|-----------|-----------|-------------|
| 1 | General | Threshold | Not consequence-dependent |
| 2 | General | Degree | Not consequence-dependent |
| 3 | Specific | Threshold | Consequence-dependent |
| 4 | Specific | Threshold | Not consequence-dependent |
| 5 | Specific | Degree | Consequence-dependent |
| 6 | Specific | Degree | Not consequence-dependent |

* One might expect eight combinations of the aspects of competence—four general, four specific. However, since GC by definition precludes appeals to consequences, only six combinations are possible.

The question of GC vs. SC is the question of the context in which competence determinations will be made: Is P always or only sometimes competent? The question of TC vs. DC is the question of the nature of the standard for competence: What qualities are necessary for P to be competent, to what extent must P possess them, and will that extent fluctuate? The question of CIC vs. CDC is the question of whether of not the standard will change according to projected outcomes: Will the standards be fixed, or vary directly with the possibility for disaster? A conceptual analysis that fails to answer each of these questions is incomplete and, as such, not helpful to clinicians and bioethicists who must identify the appropriate decision-making authority and the principles that govern medical decision making. Discussions to date have focused on single components of the concept; hence their inadequacy.

### Cognition and Affect

In addition to these distinctions, we must also consider what sorts of capacities ought to be included in the domain of competence. Clearly, competence to consent requires mental (as opposed to merely physical) capacities, but what mental capacities are relevant?

Mental function includes at least three functionally distinct but interactive mental systems: intellect, emotionality, and control. The intellect is the information handling system and includes thought processing, perception, orientation, memory, judgment, and intelligence. Emotionality includes feelings and motivations. Control refers to the expression of behavior. These components are closely intertwined, and there has been much discussion about how disorders of emotionality and control may interfere with the function of the intellect.[31] The effect of strong emotions (e.g., fear and hatred) on one's choices is also well known. However, no commensurate attention has been given to whether and how these systems can promote or enhance intellectual function. As a result, the consensus is that competence to consent lies exclusively within the domain of the intellect.[32]

This exaggerated emphasis on the intellect will be considered in a later section. Here I will only suggest that it seems inadequate. Emotion or control (hereafter, the affective components) are crucial in both the assessment and the conceptual analysis of competence. Dysfunctions such as severe depression or irrepressible rage, which commonly impair decision-making ability, illustrate the negative link between affect and competence; however, positive links exist between them as well. Love, for example, can motivate persons to perform actions that are "rationally required" but personally distasteful (e.g., giving up smoking to please a partner).

The more crucial question is whether only the cognitive or intellectual components should count. Most persons include affective components in making important decisions; they attend not only to reason but also to feelings.[33] Decision-making data usually include not merely facts, but how one *feels* about those facts; not merely the variety of possible outcomes, but which of those one would most prefer. One's preferences commonly count as reasons for choices, and these preferences do not come from reason alone.

Return to Ms. Y: In her decision regarding adjunctive treatment she may include cognitive aspects (e.g., burden-benefit estimates and different prognoses with different treatment regimes), but also affective factors (e.g., she hates the idea of noxious side effects or, alternatively, she loves the idea of a team of people devoting so much time and energy to her). In fact, most HCPs would think it odd to hear patients declare that feelings have nothing whatsoever to do with their major health care decisions. The patient who has a well-documented horror of surgery yet announces that she has no preference for vasodilators and beta-blockers over coronary artery by-pass grafting would surely bear further investigation. At the very least we would want to ascertain why her strong dislike of surgery has not caused her to reject an open-chest procedure.

Affective components usefully participate in decision making in two well-established ways and, perhaps, also in a third. First, as noted above, affect and cognition are practically inseparable. Strong feelings can impede or enhance cognitive facility, and cognition can provoke or extinguish strong feelings. Second, persons include affective data in their decision-making processes. People generally consider which outcomes—as well as the means to their realization—would make them feel best (or least bad). Moreover, affective responses can support decisions. A feeling of assurance following a tough choice reinforces one's belief that the choice was correct and gives one the resolve to carry through. Alternatively, affect can correct the decision-making process. A feeling of dismay following a hard choice leads one to reconsider and sometimes to rescind a decision. These processes are familiar occurrences.

But affect may participate in decision making in a third and, for many people, very unsettling fashion: It can fully determine one's choice. There are times when rational decision making is apparently a fiction, when decisions are based on "gut-level feelings." In such cases, feelings are divorced from reality—at least for the activity in question. Sometimes persons "just know" what to do.[34] They know how they will proceed, not because they have rationally deliberated about their opportunities but because they have strong feelings that put the matter outside the realm of rational reflection. Whether people rely on feelings to reinforce, correct, or generate decisions, they would be hard-pressed to defend their decisions in a world that demands unadulterated rationality as the basis for choices.[35]

The respective roles of cognition and affect are meaningful for clinicians and bioethicists. Affectively directed decision making occurs frequently in the medical setting where circumstances are often laden with emotional content. This need not preclude capable decision making. As Drane remarks:

> . . . ability to understand is not the same as being capable of conceptual or verbal understanding. . . . Real understanding . . . may be more a matter of emotions. Following an explanation, the patient may grasp what is best for her with strong feelings and convictions, and yet be hard pressed to articulate or conceptualize her understanding or conviction (1985, p. 20).

Thus, clinicians and ethicists need to understand how emotions impede, facilitate, supplement, or supplant cognitive choices. They must also determine if cognition impedes, facilitates, supplements, or supplants affectively directed decisions. They need to know the nature and the extent to which affect and cognition contribute to decision-making competence. Is white-hot hatred of surgery a competent basis for refusing a hysterectomy for a Class I cervical cancer *in situ*? Or must that emotion be supported by an intellectual analysis of the risks and benefits of forgoing surgery? Do strong emotions impair, obliterate, enhance, or insure one's capacity for competent choice? Do they mandate a move from respect for autonomy to beneficence? The answers to these questions are important; they help determine where decision-making authority lies and the extent to which one is obligated to respect another's strongly felt, but "irrational," decision.

At first glance the distinction may seem to be cognition vs. affect. However informed consent, by definition, requires information exchange and management. Information management requires cognition. Thus, the distinction is actually between cognition alone and the conjunction of cognition and affect.

To date, the role of affect has been largely unexamined. Efforts to attain patients' consents focus on the transfer and manipulation of information. Feelings are generally considered only as impediments to cognition. But this exclusion is inappropriate given the intimate relation between the cognitive and affective aspects of the mind and the role of affect in decision making. Recall that emotionality and control interact with intellect, that persons include affective data in their decision-making calculations, and that some people make some decisions on the basis of affect alone. Consequently, an adequate conceptual analysis of competence must include an analysis of affect. Such an analysis may reveal that affect is irrelevant to competence. If so, its exclusion from decision-making competence will have been justified. However, this exclusion is premature and will remain so until we have an analysis of competence to consent that addresses the relationship of cognition and affect in competent decision making.

### Summary

If each of these distinctions contributes to the definition of competence, that concept will be much more complex than is generally recognized. What constitutes competence to consent will depend on which particular capacities are essential and on which set of distinctions truly defines competence. Returning once more to Ms. Y's "ability to understand" will help illustrate this point. We assume she was independent prior to her illness and that her independence is limited now only because of that illness. Then on GC she will be competent to consent since she understands more than she fails to understand (because she has been and continues to be self-determining in most spheres of her life). On SC she will be competent to consent in this situation only if she understands the nature of this situation. On TC she will be competent to consent to this and all other interventions if her capacity to understand reaches the threshold (however that is defined). On DC she is more or less competent to consent relative to the greater or lesser extent of her understanding. In addition we need to determine if competence requires that both her affective and cognitive abilities be intact or if only cognitive abilities are required. On CIC she is competent to consent to any decision if her capacity to understand meets the relevant standard. On CDC she must be more competent to understand if the consequences of her decision are serious rather than trivial.

## SUMMARY

In this chapter we have seen that the concept of competence to consent has not been fully developed or described, and that it is, in fact, a much richer, more elaborate concept than has generally been appreciated.

A conceptual analysis of competence must reflect all necessary conditions for competence to consent. It must specify (1) the context (GC or SC) within which determinations of competence will take place; (2) the standard—i.e., the extent (TC or DC)—to which the requisite capacities must be present; (3) the role of consequences (CIC or CDC); and (4) the capacities—cognitive and affective—that individually or collectively define competence. Ultimately, competence must be defined by specifying its context, standard, appropriate capacities, and the role of consequences. Until these analyses are complete, neither clinicians nor bioethicists can know when decision-making authority is being properly assigned, which patients can accurately relate their own value structures to health care, and which moral principles govern individual therapeutic choices. To date none of these has been firmly established.

In spite of the challenging uncertainties about the nature of competence, its definition is crucial if HCPs and bioethicists are to understand which patients possess decision-making authority. Admittedly, since patients are presumed to be competent to consent, questions of competence may arise infrequently. Nonetheless, when the question is raised, it must be answered. To ignore it is to place the patient at risk for significant harm. Competent patients whose decision-making authority is usurped suffer the loss of self-determination. Incompetent patients who are granted decision-making authority may not have their interests protected. Only if competence is defined can we determine which moral principle—respect for autonomy or beneficence—governs a patient's care.

## NOTES

1. For analyses of consent as decision making, see Abernethy, 1984; Appelbaum and Roth, 1981; Buchanan, 1985; Buchanan and Brock, 1989; Culver and Gert, 1982; Capron, 1974; Faden and Beauchamp, 1986; Green, 1941; Katz, 1984; King and Cross, 1989; Lidz et al., 1983; Lynn, 1988; Miller, 1981; President's Commission, 1982b; and Wikler, 1979.

2. For further discussions of decision theory see Edwards, 1954; Pollay, 1970; Tversky and Kahneman, 1981.

3. For suggestions of capacities that comprise competence, see Abernethy, 1984, 1991; Appelbaum and Grisso, 1988; Appelbaum et al., 1987; Appelbaum and Roth, 1981, 1983, 1984; Baumgarten, 1980; Beauchamp, 1991; Beauchamp and McCullough, 1984; Brody, 1988; Buchanan, 1985; Buchanan and Brock, 1986; Capron, 1974; Carnerie, 1987; Drane, 1984, 1985; Dworkin, 1982; Eth, 1985; Faden and Beauchamp, 1986; Gaylin, 1982; Leikin, 1982; Lesser, 1983; Lidz et al., 1983, 1984; Lidz and Meisel, 1982; McCartney, 1986; Meisel et al., 1977; Morreim, 1991; Meisel and Roth, 1981; Pellegrino, 1991; Perl, 1991; Robertson, 1991; Rosoff and Gottlieb, 1987; Roth et al., 1977, 1982a, 1982b; Tancredi, 1982; Wear, 1991; Weinstock et al., 1984; and Wikler, 1979.

4. Discussion of the necessity of being able to receive information may be found in Appelbaum and Grisso, 1988; Appelbaum et al., 1987; Beauchamp, 1991; Beauchamp and McCullough, 1984; Buchanan, 1985; Carnerie, 1987; Kiernan et al., 1987; King and Cross, 1989; Meisel and Roth, 1981; President's Commission, 1982b; and Roth et al., 1982a.

5. Discussion of the importance of the ability to recognize decision-making situations and to understand the meaning of information about those situations may be found in Appelbaum et al., 1987; King and Cross, 1989; Pellegrino, 1991; and Roth et al.,1982a.

6. Discussion of or support for the abilities to remember and retrieve information may be found in Anthony et al., 1982; Appelbaum and Grisso, 1988; Buchanan, 1985; Buchanan and Brock, 1986, 1989; Carnerie, 1987; Dodd and Mood, 1987; Folstein et al., 1975; Green, 1941; Kiernan et al., 1987; Meisel and Roth, 1981; Miller and Germain, 1988; Pellegrino, 1991; President's Commission, 1982b; Tancredi, 1982; and Wear, 1993.

7. For further discussion about the role of information in health care decisions see Alfidi, 1971; Appelbaum and Roth, 1981, 1983; Baumgarten, 1980; Buchanan and Brock, 1986, 1989; Carnerie, 1987; Dodd and Mood, 1981; Faden et al., 1981; Katz, 1984; Lankton et al., 1977; Lidz et al., 1983; Meisel et al., 1977; President's Commission, 1982b; Rennie, 1980; and Stanley et al., 1984.

8. Many consider informability to be a component of "cognitively capable." (For a representative sample of this position, see Nelson et al., 1986, or Kiernan et al., 1987.) Here I split the concept into separate constructs, since one can be informable without being otherwise cognitively capable. Persons can receive and retain data without being able to analyze it.

9. Discussions of and support for the criterion of being able to consider whether information relates to oneself, and to consider various choices with regard to how they might alter one's present or future status and plans can be found in Appelbaum and Grisso, 1988; Appelbaum et al., 1987; Beauchamp, 1991; Beauchamp and McCullough, 1984; Bloom and Faulkner, 1987; Buchanan, 1985; Buchanan and Brock, 1986, 1989; Carnerie, 1987; Green, 1941; Hahn,1982; Lesser, 1983; Meisel and Roth, 1981; Miller and Germain, 1988; Pellegrino, 1991; Pincoffs, 1991; President's Commission, 1982b; Roth et al., 1982a, 1977; Sherlock, 1983; and Weinstock et al., 1984.

10. Discussions of and support for the criteria of being able to examine how different responses may lead to different outcomes; being able to assess which, based on one's values, would be preferable; being able to understand that different probabilities of success attend each of the different options; and being able to include those probabilities in one's decision-making calculus may be found in Appelbaum and Grisso, 1988; Appelbaum et al., 1987; Beauchamp, 1991; Beauchamp and McCullough, 1984; Bloom and Faulkner, 1987; Buchanan, 1985; Buchanan and Brock, 1986, 1989; Carnerie, 1987; Green, 1941; Kiernan et al., 1987; Leikin, 1982; Meisel and Roth, 1981; Miller and Germain, 1988; Pellegrino, 1991; Pincoffs, 1991; President's Commission, 1982b; Roth et al., 1982a, 1977; Sherlock, 1983; Tancredi, 1982; Thompson, 1982; Weinstock et al., 1984; and Wikler, 1979.

11. Discussion of the criterion of being able to rank possible choices may be found in Appelbaum et al., 1977; Buchanan, 1985; Buchanan and Brock, 1986, 1989; Gert and Clouser, 1986; and Sherlock, 1983.

12. Discussion of or support for the criterion of being able to actually make a choice among options may be found in Appelbaum and Grisso, 1988; Appelbaum et al., 1987; Beauchamp, 1991; Beauchamp and McCullough, 1984; Buchanan and Brock, 1986, 1989; Carnerie, 1987; Lidz et al., 1984; Meisel et al., 1977; Miller and Germain, 1988; Pellegrino, 1991; Pincoffs, 1991; President's Commission, 1982b; Roth et al., 1982a, 1977; Sherlock, 1983; Taylor, 1983; and Wikler, 1979. A particularly sophisticated account of the role of volition and noncoercion in choice is found in Schaffner, 1991.

One case in which these characteristics can be distinct is that of pathological indecision. (For concerns about pathological indecision, as well as "normal" ambivalence, see Appelbaum and Grisso, 1988; Drane, 1984; Morreim, 1991; President's Commission, 1982a; and Rosoff and Gottlieb, 1987.) Pathologically indecisive persons can be informable and cognitively capable of weighing various options, seeing relationships between those options and their own expressed values, appreciating how different choices would achieve different outcomes, assigning probabilities to projected outcomes, or some combination of these activities. What they cannot do is settle on an action. (A word of caution is in order here. One needs to take care not to confuse the person who is especially careful in making decisions and may take an inordinate amount of time in choosing among options with the person who is genuinely cognitively incapable.)

**13.** Discussion of or support for the criterion of being able to psychologically commit to one's choice may be found in Appelbaum et al., 1987; Beauchamp, 1991; Beauchamp and McCullough, 1984; Buchanan, 1985; Buchanan and Brock, 1986, 1989; Drane, 1984, 1985; Green, 1941; Lesser, 1983; Miller and Germain, 1988; Pellegrino, 1991; Pincoffs, 1991; President's Commission, 1982b; and Sen, 1977.

**14.** Perhaps we can know post facto that P is competent to do T by checking to see if T got done (by P or at P's behest). This approach might be acceptable in some contexts. For example, P can be retrospectively recognized as a competent cook if the meal is tasty. However, in other contexts competence will need to be determined before allowing a person to undertake an activity. For example, most of us would want some evidence that P is a competent surgeon before we consent to her operating. Or, determining competence in advance might be a necessary part of assigning a task. No matter how competent Smith is as a pediatric cardiologist, if he is not a competent orthopedic surgeon, we would not assign him the task of setting Brown's fractured femur. At least sometimes we need to know who is competent to do T *before* T is undertaken.

Competence is important for consent because it is necessary for assigning decision-making authority. Incompetent people are not asked to give consent. Only competent decision makers get to make decisions. Consequently, prospective determinations of competence are required to identify appropriate decision makers. They are necessary to determine persons from whom, in virtue of their competence, consent can be solicited.

**15.** In philosophical terms, defining competence is an ontological project. Ontological investigations determine the nature of reality—in this case, the nature of competence. Testing for competence is an epistemological issue. Epistemological ventures determine how we know what we know—in this case, how we know that someone is competent.

**16.** Regarding the difficulties in constructing tests for competence, see Anthony et al., 1982; Appelbaum and Grisso, 1988; Appelbaum et al. 1987; Beauchamp, 1991; Buchanan and Brock, 1986; Burch and Andrews, 1987; Carnerie, 1987; Erikson and Scott, 1977; Eth, 1985; Folstein et al., 1975; Green, 1941; Jacobs et al., 1977; Keller and Manschreck, 1979; Kendell, 1968; McCartney and Palmateer, 1985; Meisel et al., 1977; Morreim, 1991; National Conference of Commissioners on Uniform State Laws, 1982; Nelson et al., 1986; Robertson, 1991; Roth et al., 1977, 1982a; Roth, 1979; Schwamm et al., 1987; Smith, 1967; Stone, 1976; Tancredi, 1982, 1987; Tversky and Kahneman, 1974; and Weinstock et al., 1984.

In fact, Roth et al. claim that such efforts are futile when they assert: "The search for a single test of competence is a search for a Holy Grail" (1977, p. 283). Their pessimism stems from the belief that different tests will be required for different sorts of consents (e.g., tougher tests for situations that have a great deal at stake). Other scholars express pessimism that a single test will ever be forthcoming because tests are dependent on values or culturally determined interests and goals. Because different people and different societies have different values, the tests will vary accordingly (Abernethy, 1991; Wikler, 1979).

**17.** Actually, there may currently be a reliable test for competence; but since we have not defined competence, this reliability would be accidental.

**18.** For discussions and critiques of the various forms of mental status examinations used for competence testing, see, Nelson et al., 1986; Roe, 1982; Roth et al., 1977; Schwamm et al., 1987; Taylor et al., 1980; Burch and Andrews, 1987; Jacobs et al., 1977;Strub and Black, 1985; Anthony et al., 1982; Tancredi, 1982; and the psychiatric literature generally.

**19.** For further examples of competence "tests," the reader is referred to Abernethy, 1984, 1991; Beauchamp, 1991; Black and Strub, 1986; Drane, 1984; Folstein et al., 1975; Ginsberg, 1985; Jacobs et al., 1977; Kiernan et al., 1987; Keller and Manschreck, 1979; Lezak, 1983; MacKinnon and Yudofsky, 1986; Reitan and Wolfson, 1985; Roe, 1982; Schwamm et al., 1987; and Tancredi, 1987.

**20.** E. Haavi Morreim raises the same objection (1991, pp. 121–122, note 3). My analysis of this conceptual problem was reached prior to my discovery of her analysis.

**21.** Robert Arnold, M.D., has proposed in discussion that the Pittsburgh Group's "tests" may actually *be* quite useful as tests, and we will understand that when we have a definition of competence. While this is an interesting suggestion, subsequent discussion will show that it is wrong. Most of these "tests" appeal to outcomes rather than process, an appeal that is incompatible with respect for autonomous choice. I would, however, like to thank Dr. Arnold for his many helpful suggestions on an early version of this chapter.

**22.** To my knowledge the only other advocate of a "pure" general notion of competence is Stephen Wear (1991). Morreim (1991) seems to lean toward general competence when she argues that the burden of proof of incompetence falls on those who would, in the face of a patient's general competence, charge that he is incompetent for medical decision making.

23. Additional discussions of a context-dependent, or specific, notion of competence may be found in Appelbaum and Grisso, 1988; Appelbaum et al., 1987; Appelbaum and Roth, 1981; Beauchamp, 1991; Bloom and Faulkner, 1987; Beauchamp and McCullough, 1984; Brody, 1988; Buchanan, 1985; Buchanan and Brock, 1986; Culver and Gert, 1982; Drane, 1984, 1985; Eth, 1985; Green, 1941; Pellegrino, 1991; The President's Commission, 1982a; Robertson, 1991; Roth et al., 1977, 1982a, 1982b; Stone, 1976; and Wikler, 1979.

24. Faden and Beauchamp (1986, Chapter 8) also draw a distinction between competent persons and competent actions, arguing that general competence can function in a "gate-keeping" role. That is, consent should be sought from generally competent persons (i.e., those with general decision-making ability). Generally incompetent persons are usually those for whom others must assume the decision-making role. When persons are generally incompetent, others must be approached to obtain consent for their health care procedures. Nonetheless, the generally competent person may be specifically incompetent for a particular choice, while the generally incompetent person may competently give a specific consent.

25. For discussions of the relationship between competence and decision-making authority, see Appelbaum et al., 1987; Baumgarten, 1980; Beauchamp, 1991; Beauchamp and McCullough, 1984; Buchanan, 1985; Buchanan and Brock, 1986; Lesser, 1983; Lynn, 1988; Morreim, 1991; Pellegrino, 1991; Pincoffs, 1991; Robertson, 1991; and Roth, 1979. For support of the claim that competence not only confers decision-making authority, but also requires that such authority be respected, see Morreim, 1991; Pellegrino, 1991; and Beauchamp and McCullough, 1984.

26. Discussions of threshold competence are in Abernethy, 1984; Appelbaum et al., 1987; Beauchamp, 1991; Beauchamp and McCullough, 1984; Buchanan, 1985; Buchanan and Brock, 1986; Faden and Beauchamp, 1986; Green, 1941; Pellegrino, 1991; Robertson, 1991; Weinstock et al., 1984; and Wikler, 1979.

27. For discussions of degrees of competence see Abernethy, 1984; Appelbaum and Grisso, 1988; Appelbaum et al., 1987; Appelbaum and Roth, 1981; Baron and Hershey, 1988; Beauchamp, 1991; Beauchamp and McCullough, 1984; Brody, 1988; Buchanan, 1985; Buchanan and Brock, 1986; Green, 1941; Morreim, 1991; Pellegrino, 1991; and Stone, 1976.

28. For further discussion see Beauchamp, 1991; Brody, 1988; Buchanan, 1985; Wear, 1991; Faden and Beauchamp, 1986; Morreim, 1991; Pincoffs, 1991; President's Commission, 1982a; Robertson, 1991.

29. For excellent general discussions of the nature of both CIC and CDC, as well as of some of their diverse implications for health care, see Buchanan

and Brock (1986) and Brody (1988). Advocates of consequence-dependent competence include Appelbaum and Roth, 1983; Beauchamp and McCullough, 1984; Buchanan and Brock, 1986; Buchanan, 1985; Drane, 1984, 1985; Gaylin, 1982; Green, 1941; Owens et al., 1987; Pavlo et al., 1987; President's Commission, 1982b; Roth et al., 1977; Weinstock et al., 1984; and Wikler, 1979.

30. The considerably shorter list of advocates for competence as consequence-*independent* includes, to my knowledge, only Eth (1985), Robertson (1991), and Pellegrino (1991). Of course Abernethy (1984, 1991) and Wear (1991) (and possibly, Morreim [1991]), as advocates of general competence, are also committed to this notion because, by definition, generally competent persons cannot be constrained by appeals to consequences. So long as persons are generally competent, they are competent to make all decisions, regardless of the fact that some choices place them at significant risk for poor outcomes.

31. For discussions of how disordered emotionality can impair the function of the intellect, see Appelbaum and Roth, 1981; Brand and Jolles, 1987; Buchanan and Brock, 1986; Callahan, 1988; Capron, 1984; Carnerie, 1987; Drane, 1984; Folstein et al., 1975; Roth et al., 1982a, 1982b; and Wear, 1991. Nonetheless, mental illness does not necessarily impair a person's decision-making ability. For example, paranoid schizophrenics need not be incapable of making competent decisions in realms that are unaffected by particular delusions or other aberrant thought processes. For extended discussions, see Abernethy, 1984, 1991; Appelbaum and Grisso, 1988; Beauchamp, 1991; Bloom and Faulkner, 1987; Meisel et al., 1977; Robertson, 1991; Roth et al., 1982a, 1982b; and Stone, 1976.

32. Jacobs et al., 1977, and Tancredi, 1982, discuss exclusively intellectual competence.

33. For more on the role of affect in decision making, see Abernethy, 1991; Appelbaum and Roth, 1981; Baumgarten, 1980; Callahan, 1988; Carnerie, 1987; Drane, 1984, 1985; Faden et al., 1981; Fennell et al., 1987; Ingelfinger, 1982; Leeb, Bowers, and Lynch, 1976; Lesser, 1983; Perl, 1991; Tancredi, 1982, 1987.

34. Drane, 1985, and Fennell et al., 1987, discuss such instantaneous decision making.

35. The critic will claim that such purely affective decisions are infrequent or somehow odd. Nonetheless, many persons have found themselves eschewing rationality during decision making. Do such persons rationally eschew rationality? That is, do they say to themselves something like the following: "I know I am not rationally evaluating all the data as I should do or as I would usually do; however, I feel so strongly about this case that I wish to forgo rational deliberation in favor of acting in accordance with my feelings. Given their strength, that is the only rational thing to do."

Or is the process rather more like this: "When I am presented with a situation that immediately invokes a strong affective response, I quickly act in light of that response and without reasoning at all about how I will act. Later when I reflect upon my actions, I might come to believe either that reason would have supported or refuted the decision; but reason's counsel in no way motivated my act. Given the strength of my feelings, reason had nothing to say about the matter."

Can affective choices be completely independent of cognition? Presumably not, at least insofar as strong feelings about something require knowledge of the nature of that object or state of affairs. Such knowledge would seem to require some understanding of the details, implications, or impact on one's life; and this would seem to require certain cognitive (i.e., datagathering) capacities.

A related question is whether some things can only be affectively known. Are certain kinds of knowledge completely inaccessible to rational processes? That is, will reason interfere with or absolutely prevent the acquisition of certain kinds of knowledge? One good candidate for pure affective knowledge is romantic love. Presumably one cannot be in love without affectively experiencing it. The question is, can one be in love while intellectualizing it? The claims are often made that rationally dissecting love is a sure way to destroy it (love is blind); that relying on reason would guarantee that love would never, could never, be known. For our purposes, this would mean that certain kinds of knowledge can only be known through the affective system.

# 4

# Defining the Structure of
# Competence to Consent

We now turn to elaborating the structure of competence introduced in Chapter Three. We recall that the commonly considered options for organizing competence included: general (GC) vs. specific (SC) competence, threshold (TC) vs. degree (DC) competence, and consequence-dependent (CDC) vs. consequence-independent (CIC) competence. In addition, the previously unconsidered issue of cognitive vs. affective capabilities was introduced. This chapter examines these options in greater detail, looking at the justifications for, implications of, and criticisms surrounding each option. In its entirety, the chapter will identify and justify the structure of competence to give a free and informed consent in health care settings. (Not surprisingly, the structure might differ in other settings.)

## DECISION-MAKING SUCCESS AND FAILURE

We assume that competent decision makers make "good" decisions. But what are the characteristics of a "good" decision? Must good decisions promote the decision maker's well-being? Are decisions that fail to promote a person's interests evidence of incompetence.[1] Everyone occasionally makes decisions that fail to promote—or that even work against—his interests. These "mistakes" occur because decision making is an imprecise (i.e., nondeductive) activity. In making decisions, people get the facts, consider them, and compute the probabilities of each option's promoting their well-being. They then choose the alternative that insofar as they can determine will best achieve their purposes. Such choices do not guarantee that the desired outcome will occur. In spite of one's best efforts, bad outcomes may result. If all that is required is a good outcome, lucky people will be considered good decision makers and the unlucky, even though conscientious, will be designated as decision-making failures.

Since even the most adept decision making cannot guarantee uni-
formly good outcomes, competent decision making refers not to
results, but to a process. In fact, the four general criteria do just this.
Informability, cognitive and affective capability, and the abilities to
make and explain a decision enhance—but do not guarantee—a person's chances of achieving desirable outcomes. Because chance can
wreak havoc on schemes and dreams, we must appeal to a process
that persons undertake to structure their lives rather than to results.[2]
A good decision is one that has the greatest probability of satisfactorily resolving choice-requiring situations while simultaneously protecting other values or interests the decision maker has. For example,
a person may choose the least probable outcome if it is the one she
most fervently hopes to achieve, or a less preferable outcome that is
more affordable or that better preserves other values she holds. Consequently, good decision makers are able to choose courses of action
that seem most likely to achieve their greatest goals (or more of
them), promote their strongest interests, and conform most closely to
their value structures considered in their entirety. Such a process
requires that persons be able to determine what their alternatives are
and to estimate what chance each has to secure the desired result.

This analysis of competence does not require that all choices actually maximize or even merely promote one's well-being. What it does
require is that decisions be made according to a procedure for acquiring information and exercising cognitive and affective capacities so as
to have the best foreseeable opportunity of realizing one's goals.

## GENERAL VS. SPECIFIC COMPETENCE

### Understanding the Concepts

There is nothing mysterious about the distinction between general
and specific competence. It is an example of the common discrimina-
tion between the general and the particular. Most broadly, one can be
a generally competent person, capable of managing most situations
that arise in the course of life. One may be competent, for example, to
perform a job, manage a home, feed and clothe oneself, enjoy hobbies.
This description fits most people with whom we live and work and,
for that matter, most of the people we know. They do some things better than others, and they get most things done adequately. Persons
who are generally competent "at life" are not able to do everything.
General competence implies that most of the time one can adequately

do most of the things one needs to do in everyday life. As Abernethy (1984, p. 57) puts it, general competence implies appropriate functioning "in an array of cognitive and interpersonal domains."[3] The generally competent person is able to satisfactorily complete most of the tasks he faces (including perhaps, but not necessarily, making most of the decisions he faces).[4]

There is a second, narrower, sense of competence—a general competence to perform most tasks within a particular sphere of activity. One may be a generally competent nurse in this sense. A generally competent nurse may still perform some actions better than others. She may be quite good at some tasks (e.g., inserting intravenous catheters), but quite poor at others (e.g., inserting urinary catheters), while being adequate for most nursing duties. To be a generally competent nurse is not to be a perfect nurse, but to be capable, more often than not, of adequately completing the tasks most nurses face. Similarly, to be a generally competent decision maker is to be capable of adequately managing most decision-making situations. One might be capable of deciding which career to pursue, whether to marry, and so forth, though incapable of deciding whether to buy stock in IBM. Generally competent persons usually exhibit competence in several more precisely circumscribed spheres.

Lastly there is a strictly limited, or specific, sense of competence that applies only to particular tasks. For example, a nurse may be specifically competent to insert a particular intravenous catheter without being capable of inserting other intravenous catheters, performing other nursing tasks (e.g., inserting a urinary catheter), or managing other aspects of life (e.g., being competent to make financial investments). A specifically competent person is able to do one thing, but not necessarily anything else. A specifically competent decision maker can make one decision without necessarily being competent to make other decisions, or to do anything else. Thus, one can be specifically competent to make a particular health care decision without being competent to make different decisions, health care or other, or without being more generally competent. Again, generally competent persons exhibit numerous more particular and specific competencies. In health care the general/specific distinction is acknowledged in the old saying that generalists know less and less about more and more until finally they know nothing about everything; while specialists know more and more about less and less until eventually they know everything about nothing. Thus, one could be a competent family practitioner, but not a competent cardiologist, or vice versa.

The question is this: Which sense of competence should be required for a patient to give her or his informed consent? There are theoretical and practical answers to this question, and both are important. Theoretically, we can easily dispense with the broadest sense of competence. What is wanted within the practice of consent are patients who can give particular consents. Since consent is a form of decision making, patients must be able to make (at least some) decisions, but the ability to perform most activities of daily living is not the competence we are seeking. Competence to consent depends on the abilities identified earlier—informability, cognitive and now, possibly, affective capacity, and the abilities to reach (and resign oneself to) a decision and recount the process. From the theoretical perspective, other abilities simply do not apply within this context.

There is, however, an important practical relationship between general competence and competence to consent: patients' abilities to do other things are valuable indicators of what to expect from them in decision-making situations. Most generally competent persons are also competent decision makers, and most generally competent decision makers are competent to make particular health care decisions. As a result, HCPs assume that patients who adequately manage the other aspects of their lives are competent to make health care decisions unless there is evidence to the contrary. The moral importance of freedom and autonomy generate a reluctance to intrude into the decisions of others. Consequently, as long as nothing triggers suspicions about patients' decision-making abilities, HCPs quite properly give advice but do not usurp their patients' decision-making authority.

Clearly, however, a general inability to manage the activities of daily living calls for a careful evaluation of a patient's decision-making abilities. In addition, patients who suffer conditions (e.g., hypoxemia, uncontrollable fear) or demonstrate behaviors associated with decision-making inability (e.g., intractable indecisiveness) prompt concern about their decision-making capacity. As a result, HCPs want to examine these patients' decision-making capacity more closely.

What, then, of general decision-making competence? General decision-making competence is a general ability to make decisions in choice-requiring situations. On our preliminary definition, generally capable decision makers are generally informable, cognitively and affectively capable, able to make and resign themselves to their decisions, and able to recount the decision-making process.[5] So long as these four broad criteria are generally met, a person is considered a generally competent decision maker even when she is unable to make some decisions. On this conception, the patient who is having problems making a particular decision but who has been able to make past decisions successfully, or the patient who is presently able to make other decisions, will still be considered a competent decision maker.

Let us consider general decision-making competence in terms of our preliminary definition. Generally competent decisionmakers usually demonstrate informability, cognitive and (possibly) affective capacity, and abilities to choose and recount the decision-making process. First, being generally informable is being able to receive information from one's surroundings and recognize it as information relevant to the problem at hand. Generally informable persons also have the capacity to remember facts pertaining to present decisions. Second, cognitive and affective capability is a general ability to consider and appreciate—cognitively and affectively—relevant information. Persons can consider if or how information relates to themselves, their value structures, and their interests. They are able to consider how choices might affect their present or future well-being. They usually understand the probabilities of different eventualities, are routinely able to examine how different choices would lead to different outcomes, and can decide which, based on their sets of values, would be preferable. Having completed these considerations, generally competent decision makers can make a decision, act on the basis of it, and explain themselves when questioned. That is, generally competent decision makers are sufficiently informable, cognitively and affectively capable, and able to make and justify decisions within the framework of their lives. If these four broad criteria are generally met, a person is considered generally capable of making decisions.

We now understand that general competence (GC) refers to general decision-making competence. We can schematize this decision-making competence as follows:

A person (P) is competent (C) for *any* task (T) if a standard (S) is met (or met to D).

Using this procedural approach, where T is "making a decision," the context for competence becomes "generally." If the standard (S) is described as:

can acquire information about options, cognitively and affectively consider their probabilities of achieving chosen aims, choose on the basis of those considerations, and recount the decision making process,

then GC translates to:

P is C to make any decision if P generally can (or can to Degree D) acquire information about options, cognitively and affectively consider their probabilities of achieving chosen aims, choose on the basis of those considerations, and recount the decision-making process.

Lastly, what of specific competence? We recall that persons are specifically competent if they have the ability to perform a particular task. For the purpose of free and informed consent, persons are specifically competent if they can give or refuse to give consent to a particular treatment where that includes reference to a particular condition, a particular practitioner, a particular place, and a particular time or span of time.[6]

Although the four general abilities still apply, they have different qualifications. One still must be informable, that is, capable of receiving and remembering information and of recognizing its relevance to oneself, but specific competence requires that the patient be able to be informed about the particular project, to receive and remember some particular information, to understand particular data, and to recognize it as information that is pertinent to the present situation and must be used here and now to make a particular decision about a particular problem. That one is generally informable, was informable at some time in the past, or will (again) be informable some time in the future is irrelevant, except as a predictor of how one will perform here and now.[7] That one is able to do something else (say, ride a bicycle) is also unimportant. The capacities to do a particular task—to make this decision—determine competence to give a specific consent.

As with general competence, cognitive and affective capability implies a capacity to manipulate information. Here persons must be able to consider whether or how this information relates to themselves, their value structures, and their interests. Persons must be able to consider how this choice relates to and may alter their present or future status. They must be able to understand the probabilities of the different options, and incorporate them into this decision. They must be able to examine how different responses to this information would lead to different outcomes, and to decide which outcomes, based on their values, would be preferable. Again, usual, previous, or anticipated possession of these abilities is suggestive only; one must possess them for this consent. Persons must be able to make, resign themselves to, and justify this choice.

Thus, specific competence presupposes that persons are sufficiently informable, cognitively and affectively capable, and able to make and explain decisions within a very particular framework. What they are able to do in normal circumstances matters not at all (although, as noted above, a person's history will provide a useful guideline as to what we can expect). Specific competence demands that a person's competence be assessed for a very particular set of conditions: the one at hand. Even if the four broad criteria are generally met, a person should not be considered competent unless she is capable of managing this particular situation. (But recall that in the absence of evidence to the contrary, competence for particular decisions is assumed when patients are generally competent.)

On a specific notion of competence, the task (T) is making *this* decision. The standard (S) does not change, but the context becomes "for this decision."

Then SC, or,

P is C for *this* T if S is met (or met to D)

translates to:

P is C to make this decision if for this decision P can (or can to a specified degree) acquire information about options, cognitively and affectively consider their probabilities of achieving chosen aims, choose on the basis of those considerations, and recount the decision-making process.

### Implications

The general and specific analyses of competence are more alike than different. On both accounts persons must be informable, cognitively and affectively capable, and able to make and explain (some) decisions. Their differences do not lie in what must be done or in what abilities one must have; rather, they lie in the circumstances under which tasks must be executed. As a result, the analyses can affect different patient populations differently.

Within the context of consent, the task immediately at hand is to determine whether the patient is competent to consent to treatment. Whether by GC or SC, the patient's decision-making ability must be assessed. On a general conception, the patient's broad decision-making capacities must be evaluated; on a specific conception, only the patient's ability to make a particular decision needs to be examined. With GC, the distraught or merely recalcitrant person who fails to resolve a particular health care decision but who continues to make other sorts of decisions remains competent because her decision-making capacities are generally intact. With SC, this person would be incompetent because she must be able to apply her decision-making abilities to the consent at hand. Concerns about general vs. specific competence arise in two groups of patients: those whose decision-making abilities are usually above reproach (whether this refers to a past ability to make decisions or to a current ability to make most other decisions), but who are now unable to give a particular consent; and those who appear able to make the decision at hand, but have difficulty with most others.

The crucial difference between general and specific competence is the extent to which the relevant capacities apply to a particular decision. Certain capacities enable persons to undertake a process by which decisions are made that, other things being equal, will likely lead to their well-being. These capacities may attend decisions generally or particular decisions. If they attend decision making generally, the person is a generally competent decision maker. If they attend the making of a particular decision, the person is specifically competent. Most patients are both generally competent and competent to make a specific decision about consent for treatment. Others are capable of making most decisions, but incapable of making a specific health care decision. Yet other persons are generally incompetent while being specifically competent for a certain health care decision. Finally, some persons are both generally and specifically incompetent (e.g., a comatose person). To illustrate the differences between GC and SC, let us consider two cases.

*CASE I:* Mr. A is a 42-year-old unmarried male who lives with his brother and sister-in-law. He is poorly educated, but able to understand most information that is presented to him in layman's terms.

He works as an assistant to his brother, a brick mason. By his account he makes a "decent living" and enjoys his job. He has been hospitalized several times over the past six months with stiff neck, headaches, and disturbances of balance. Repeated lumbar punctures have revealed persistent meningeal inflammation, but all procedures to date have been unable to isolate the causative organism. A diagnosis of chronic meningitis has been made. Because several courses of broad spectrum antibiotics have failed to cure the disease, a cisternal tap has been recommended with the hope of being able to isolate the causative organism.

Mr. A understands what his illness is, why treatment has failed, and what his HCPs now want to do. He states that he is eager to be healed and to return to his former productive life. He has signed the consent form, but on two different occasions, upon being taken to radiology for the procedure, became quite agitated and adamantly insisted that he had changed his mind about having the procedure done. He admitted after the fact that he was worried about revoking his consent and that he knew his "only chance" for the cure he desires was to have the test. Nonetheless, he stated that he "just couldn't go through with it," a reluctance he himself was at a loss to explain. A work-up by psychiatry ultimately revealed that Mr. A suffered from intermittent auditory hallucinations that told him "the doctors are trying to kill you." Even though the "voices" were not active during the attempted cisternal taps, Mr. A was responding subconsciously to their warning.

*CASE II:* Mrs. B is a 73-year-old nursing home resident. She has always been an ardent supporter of family planning issues, donating time and money to Planned Parenthood and other organizations that address reproductive concerns. Several years ago her activities intensified. On three occasions she submitted application forms to agencies soliciting women to be surrogate mothers. She began roaming the streets day and night, "counselling" homeless people about family planning issues. On two occasions, her purse was stolen; once she was mugged. Her son's attempts to dissuade her from her late-night wanderings were unsuccessful. She insisted that his concerns for her safety were unwarranted. Ultimately, she refused to allow her son in her home and began carrying a loaded gun to ward him off. At this time her son, concerned for her safety, successfully petitioned to be made her legal guardian, and admitted her to a nursing home.

Mrs. B is excitable and "nervous," and requires assistance in most activities of daily living. Her son makes all her financial and legal decisions. When diagnosed with a carcinoma of the cervix for which a hysterectomy has been recommended, Mrs. B originally indignantly refused the operation because the surgery would "make it impossible for me to help all those sad women who can't have children on their own." However, after conferring repeatedly with her physician, primary care nurse, and her son, she is able to understand that she is sick, that her life will be threatened if she does not have the surgery, and that if she is dead she can help no one. If she has the surgery, she can continue to "advocate" for family planning issues within the facility. She agrees to have the surgery.

Is Mr. A or Mrs. B competent to consent to or refuse treatment? Mr. A's case gives one pause because he admits the importance of the same facts as do his HCPs. Moreover, he seems to want the same outcome they do—his recovery. Thus his repeated last-minute revocations of consent are bewildering and lead his HCPs to suspect that he might not be competent. Mr. A exemplifies the first category—those who are generally able to make decisions, but incapable of making a particular choice. He lacks the capacities to resign himself to his choice, and to recount the process that leads him to repeatedly change his mind. (Note, also, that not only can he not explain his indecision to his HCPs; he cannot explain it to himself either.) His hallucinations preclude his carrying out a program that he believes to be to his advantage, a belief with which his HCPs concur. Since he was previously able to make decisions and can still make other decisions, he is a generally competent decision maker. Thus, on GC he is competent; on SC he is incompetent.

Mrs. B, one the other hand, has long been unable to manage any of the important decisions in her life. She is generally incompetent to consent or refuse because she lacks the capacities necessary for self-sufficient decision making in her life as a whole. She is unable to reason about information (e.g., that she is too old to serve as a surrogate mother), or relate information to herself (e.g., she fails to appreciate that her late-night outings endanger her well-being and even her abilities to usefully pursue her goal of supporting reproductive programs). Still, persistent attempts at explanation and reassurance have enabled her to understand the nature of the situation in which she now finds herself: what is wrong with her, what the recommended treatment entails, the pros and cons of proceeding with treatment, and the effect of the surgery on her life. In virtue of that understanding, she seems competent to make the concrete decision she now faces. As such, she represents the second class of patients—those who are generally incompetent while being specifically competent.

The upshot of these remarks is that on a general conception Mr. A is competent and Mrs. B is not, while on a specific conception Mrs. B is competent and Mr. A is not. If a general conception of competence is adopted, persons who can manage their lives successfully will be considered competent to manage whatever health care situations they face.[8] Patients who cannot make most other decisions will be presumed incompetent to make medical decisions as well. Conversely, on a specific conception persons who manage their lives successfully will not necessarily be competent to manage their health care situations (although they may be), while persons who cannot manage their daily affairs may nonetheless be competent to manage their health care situations (although they need not be). The problem lies in deciding which approach is properly ascribed to competence to consent.

### Justification

The question naturally arises: Why have conflicting conceptions emerged? What is the moral justification for each? The most fundamental moral justification for a general conception of competence is the principle of respect for autonomy. The argument goes like this: (1) Autonomous persons are special sorts of creatures, worthy of respect because they possess certain abilities. (2) One of these abilities is the capacity to order their lives according to self-defined values, goals, beliefs and interests. (3) Since autonomous persons best understand their own values and goals, they have legitimate decision-making authority regarding their own lives.[9] This decision-making authority holds even when others disapprove of their goals or their means for achieving them, so long as their decisions continue to be autonomous.[10] We respect their autonomy by not interfering with autonomous persons' pursuit of their goals.

General competence can also be justified by appealing to the principle of beneficence. The principle states that we are morally obliged to promote good consequences for others. Two additional premises are needed: (1) Autonomous persons know best what consequences are most desirable from their own points of view; and (2) If they have adequate information about therapeutic alternatives and their probable results, they can choose the intervention that will most likely produce the outcomes they prefer. The conclusion of this argument is that regardless of which intervention or outcome seems most desirable to others, a person's autonomous choice is most likely to promote her best interests. Thus anyone interested in maximizing good outcomes will support persons who choose autonomously.

When everyone agrees with a patient's choice, there is no problem. Occasionally, however, HCPs worry that a patient has chosen poorly. If the choice is "bad" because the person is choosing in light of uncommon, unshared values, the situation can be resolved by respect for autonomy. Autonomous choices should be respected even when others disvalue the goals they promote, because respecting autonomy protects the freedom to march to the beat of a different drummer. This liberty is highly valued. Persons are free (if not encouraged) to undertake risky behaviors (e.g., mountain climbing, motorcycle racing) even though such behavior may lead to "poor" outcomes (e.g., injury, death). Indeed, agents themselves may disvalue these consequences. Nonetheless, the value that accrues to one's life, all things considered, often includes chancy endeavors. Part of freedom is the freedom to fail.[11]

Justification for a specific conception of competence also appeals to the principle of respect for autonomy. Recall that one way of respecting autonomy is to foster the conditions under which persons can exercise it. Here the argument is: Autonomous decisions ought be honored; however, sometimes generally autonomous persons, because of a temporary loss of or reduction in their capacities, make specific inautonomous choices that thwart their own espoused value structures; in such cases, the principle of respect for autonomy demands that we act to preserve, enhance, or restore the capacities of these individuals, even if this means temporarily usurping their decision-making authority. So, in the case of Mr. A (whose "voices" prompted his repeated repeal of consent for a cisternal tap), the claim can be made that his own strong preference for treatment is best served (and his autonomy best respected) by performing the cisternal tap, even in the face of his adamant objection at the time the procedure is actually attempted.[12]

Since usurping a patient's decision-making authority may seem an odd way to preserve autonomy, let us consider this claim in greater detail. We recall from Chapter Two that there are two occasions for self-determination. The first is a general opportunity to define (or defend) the values, goals, and interests by which autonomous persons structure their lives. The second occasion is the recurring opportunity for people to apply their values. Generally competent decision makers generally do well in particular decision-making episodes. Suspicion is triggered, however, when a generally competent decision maker's choices are at odds with his own values. This is the case with Mr. A. He repeatedly insists that he is eager to resume his previous healthy life; he understands that the procedure is the first step toward that goal; he consents to the procedure. But he is unable to follow through. When he revokes his consent, he is acting against his previously stated and long-held goals and values. He is acting to destroy, rather than protect, his interests. In this case, his specific incompetence threatens his general competence and—more important—his return to health which, by his own admission, he desires. In such cases, we respect a patient's autonomy by promoting the conditions under which he can continue to exercise it. We promote his well-being by overriding his (incompetent) choice. Put another way, we acknowledge his specific incompetence as a reason for transferring decision-making authority to others so that his general competence can be restored.

Although appeals to autonomy and beneficence support both general and specific conceptions of competence, an argument can be made that competence, at least as it applies within the practice of free and informed consent, refers to a person's capacity to make a specific decision rather than to his general decision-making capacities. That argument is this: When HCPs seek a person's consent, they are seeking his permission to intervene in his life in a very particular way and for a very particular purpose. They may be concerned with how this will affect his life as a whole. Indeed, therapy is often contemplated because they are greatly concerned to restore him, as fully as possible, to that life. Nonetheless, HCPs seek a patient's informed consent for specific interventions. If the patient lacks the capacities necessary for evaluating that problem or its postulated solutions—that is, if he is incompetent, then allowing him to choose puts him in harm's way. First, if he is incompetent he is incapable of autonomous choice. If his choice is not autonomous, there is no good reason to think it will promote or protect his own values. If the patient's autonomy is not protected he is, for that reason, subject to harm. This is why the practice of informed consent, which was established to protect autonomy and promote beneficence, demands a competent consenter at the outset. This is why the practice demands that the person be competent to give this consent. The moral principles of respect for autonomy and beneficence require specific competence.

No problem arises if the patient is both generally and specifically competent. If she is generally competent but incompetent for this decision, clinicians will want to diagnose and eliminate the source of her present inability (e.g., transient memory deficit, the options are equally favorable or distasteful, and so forth). If possible, HCPs should postpone decisions until competence is restored. If this is impractical, transferring decision-making capacity to someone who is familiar with the patient's value structure is the best way to respect and promote both her values and her future capacity for autonomy.[13]

### Summary

Because autonomy and beneficence are better protected when specific competence is adopted, the moral principles of respect for autonomy and beneficence justify SC over GC. Moreover, the practice of free and informed consent requires a specific, rather than a general, context for competence. We move next to defining the best standard of competence to consent.

## THRESHOLD VS. DEGREE COMPETENCE

We have resolved that competence is better understood as a specific rather than general notion, but the analysis of the concept remains incomplete. We still need to know what the standard (S) for competent decision making should be. This is the issue of threshold vs. degree, or of how much ability is required. Just as the GC vs. SC dichotomy raises the question of the appropriate context for decision making, the TC vs. DC dichotomy considers the extent of the capacities under discussion.

### Understanding the Concepts

The distinction between threshold and degree is analogous to the distinction between "all-or-none" and "more-or-less." The degree (more-or-less) approach assumes that competence (actually, the capacities that constitute competence) lies on a continuum. The end points of this continuum are "fully competent" and "fully incompetent." Between these ends lie many points that correspond to extents to which the capacities are present.

The threshold (all-or-none) approach designates a single point of demarcation that transects the competence continuum. Persons whose capacities fail to reach this point are incompetent. Persons whose capacities reach or exceed the point are competent. The cutoff point allows, at least in theory, clear designations about which persons are and which are not competent. The schema show that on a degree conception (DC):

P is C to Degree D for this T if S is met to Degree D;

while according to TC, the threshold conception:

P is C for this T if S is met.

In medicine the degree/threshold distinction is illustrated by severity of illness indices and the management of seriously ill patients. Patients can be classified as more or less sick on the basis of the scores they receive on such systems as APACHE II (Knaus et al. 1985), TISS (Cullen et al. 1974; Keene and Cullen, 1983) or APS (LeGall et al. 1984; Lemeshow et al. 1985, 1987). For example, patients with APACHE (Acute Physiological and Chronic Health Evaluator) scores in excess of 40 are considered to be very sick, while those whose scores are 5 or below suffer minimal physiological derangement. Individual patients' scores fall on a continuum between zero (no pathology) and 128 (major, widespread pathology). The patient who scores "one" (i.e., who is virtually normal) is clearly less sick than is the person who scores "51" (i.e., is critically ill). Likewise for patients with scores of "7" vs. "40," "10" vs. "30," "20" vs. "21," and so on.

For institutional populations, where some patients are more and some are less sick, one can set a threshold that will determine treatment loci and modalities. For example, if a hospital sets an APACHE score of 22 as an admission threshold to the Intensive Care Unit (ICU), patients with scores of 22 or higher are "sick enough" to require intensive care; that is, they meet that institution's threshold for admission to ICU. Likewise a patient whose APACHE score exceeds 40 may be defined, again according to a hospital's threshold, as too sick to recover. Because the threshold indicates an inability to benefit from ICU care, these patients may be barred from ICU even if they or their families request such care. The treatment location of patients who are more and less sick depends on whether they reach certain thresholds.

Is the standard for competence to consent a threshold or a degree notion? Do the capacities that constitute competence fall on either side of a threshold, or are they organized to form degrees of competence?

As with general and specific competence to consent, thresholds and degrees are related to informability, cognitive and affective capability, and the abilities to choose and recount the decision-making process. The concern now is with the extent to which a patient must demonstrate these abilities. How informable—how capable of receiving, recognizing as relevant, and remembering data—must a patient be to be considered competent? To what extent must persons possess cognitive and affective capability (manifested as some ability to reason about information, relate it to their value structures, and rank options)? How able must one be to resolve a situation and to recount the decision-making process? Thus, on a threshold conception, the standard (S) becomes:

possesses to extent E the capacities for decision making.

Then TC, or,

P is C for this T if S is met,

translates to:

P is C for this T if P possesses to E the capacities for decision making (i.e., can to E acquire information about options, cognitively and affectively consider their probabilities of achieving chosen aims, choose on the basis of those considerations, and recount the decision making process).

Conversely, on a degree notion of competence persons are rarely (if ever) said to be fully competent or fully incompetent. When they display a particular extent of capacity, they are competent (or incompetent) to that degree. Thus if they are informable and in possession of cognitive and affective capacity and decision-making ability to degree D, they are competent to degree D.[14] Here capacities are located on the continuum. If one can be accurately informed about six of ten particular facts, one is capable to degree six. (The value "6" is illustrative only. It does not represent any actual measurement procedure.)

Thus on a degree conception of competence S becomes:

possesses to degree $D_n$ the requisite capacities for decision making,

and DC, or,

P is C to D for this T if S is met to D,

translates to:

P is C to $D_n$ for this T if P possesses to $D_n$ the requisite capacities for decision making (i.e., can to $D_n$ acquire information about options, cognitively and affectively consider their probabilities of achieving chosen aims, choose on the basis of those considerations, and recount the decision-making process).[15]

## Implications

The conceptions of threshold and degree competence are more alike than different. On both accounts persons are evaluated according to the same criteria: informability, cognitive and affective capability, and the abilities to make and resign oneself to decisions and to recount the process. Here the differences lie not in what capacities are present, but in the extent to which those capacities must be present for a person to be competent. For both TC and DC the patient's decision-making ability must be assessed. Additionally, both approaches will locate the extent of a patient's capacity on a continuum, and both require a reliable method for quantifying capacities.

From here on the implications diverge. On a threshold conception the requisite extent of competence (i.e., the threshold) must be explicit. There must be some determination of the extent of capacity necessary for a person to be competent. Whatever extent is chosen will require some justification as to why everyone below that point will be, at least within the practice of free and informed consent, an incompetent decision maker, while everyone above it will be a competent decision maker. Once the threshold has been established, all those falling on or above it will be competent to consent. Those failing to attain the level are incompetent to consent.

Since the context of competence is specific situations, competence must be determined for particular situations. This will make setting thresholds difficult, as well as enormously time-consuming. Surely a patient will need to understand that he is sick, what is wrong with him, the nature of the recommended treatment, and what chance it has for success. But to what extent? Any designated level of capacity is, from a substantive perspective, arbitrary. As Faden and Beauchamp (1986, pp. 289–290) note, cutoff points are often established as a matter of expedience. In the form of laws (e.g., no one below the age of majority is legally competent) or policies (e.g., no one with an APACHE greater than 22 may be admitted to ICU), they enable certain evaluation of a person's status and give precise guidance. With regard to informed consent, a threshold would establish cutoff points that may be used to distinguish patients who hold decision-making authority from those who do not. The danger, both in clinical and legal settings, is that cut-off points may be designated solely in virtue of bureaucratic convenience rather than because they indicate competence in any objective sense.[16] Thus while pragmatic concerns may support a point of demarcation, one is hard-pressed to justify, from a *moral* point of view, disenfranchising persons for failing to meet a standard whose main virtue is convenience.

Such worries help to make a degree conception of competence theoretically more attractive. In addition, individuals usually do possess capacities to greater or lesser degrees. Some patients can receive and remember few facts; others, many. Some understand their diagnoses anatomically, physiologically, and biochemically; others understand only that they are "sick." Where one patient will appreciate only that the doctor recommends surgery, another will precisely understand the actual details of the surgical procedure. Where one patient knows only that treatment will "probably" make her better, another will appreciate the probability for complete vs. partial cure, with and without complications. The latter patients in each case are surely more competent to consent than the former. To the extent that greater competence is present, the patient will have a greater claim to decision-making authority. To illustrate the difference between TC and DC, let us consider two more cases:

*CASE III:* Mr. C, a 47-year-old street person, is brought to the emergency room by police officers who discovered him, collapsed and confused, in an alley. He is a poorly nourished, dirty, dehydrated man who is oriented to person only. There is no evidence of substance abuse. He has a 6 X 10 cm. coccygeal ulceration extending into the gluteal crease. The ulcer is draining a purulent material. Blood cultures reveal a gram negative septicemia. After three weeks of hospitalization, adequate nutrition and hydration, antibiotics, and debridement of the ulcer, Mr. C is alert and oriented to time, place, and person. He is comfortable and requesting to be released. His ulcer is healing nicely, though T.I.D. sitz baths and antibiotic ointment applications are still required. Upon questioning, Mr. C states, "I got sick because I was on the street." Mr. C's HCPs wish to transfer him to a skilled nursing facility (SNF) until his ulcer has completely healed. Mr. C vigorously resists this suggestion. He reports that he is miserable in the hospital (though, unless the subject is raised, he appears content).

When questioned as to how he plans to care for himself after discharge from the hospital, he replies he will "soak in water and put medicine on my sore." He is unable to remember the specific details of his wound care. Still, when supervised, he is able to complete the procedure satisfactorily. When asked where he plans to carry out these measures, he says only "I have friends to help." He is, however, unwilling to provide their names. Thus they cannot be reached to determine their availability to assist with his postdischarge care, or to take him home from the hospital. He knows he has to "take care of my sore or it will get bad again" and that if that happens "I have to come back to the hospital." He also agrees that his recovery is better assured by transfer to the SNF. Still, he wants to be discharged. When asked why he wants to leave the hospital and what he plans to do after discharge, he replies, "Anything I want to."

*CASE IV:* Mr. D is a 32-year-old homosexual male with AIDS. He is in the emergency room with respiratory distress, diagnosed as having Pneumocystis pneumonia. His failing health forced him to resign his job as a registered pharmacist six months ago. The loss of his job resulted in the loss of his insurance. He has exhausted his savings and is unable to pay his rent or purchase food, medicine, and any further medical care. He has two close friends who have welcomed him into their home and arranged their work schedules so that one of them is always available to tend to his needs.

Mr. D understands that he has a terminal illness, that with medical care his life can be extended for some brief but unspecified period of time, that he has at least a 50/50 chance of recovering from this bout with pneumonia, but that without treatment this pneumonia will probably result in his death. He requests that his friends (who are present and whose names, address, and phone number Mr. D gives for the record as persons to be notified in case of emergency) be allowed to take him back to their home and keep him as comfortable as possible. His friends indicate they are willing to do this. He wants to spend his "remaining time saying good-bye to friends and family," and tells his HCPs that he has "gotten all my affairs in order." He requests that he be given a prescription for injectable Morphine Sulfate to minimize his respiratory distress.

Mr. C demonstrates minimal informability and decisional capacity. He knows what is wrong with him: he has a sore. He knows the recommended treatment: bathing and medication. He knows his prognosis: if he fails to care for it, he will get worse. Nonetheless his HCPs are genuinely concerned that his minimal capacities are insufficient to deem him competent. They fear that his limited access (or, as is more likely, no access) to facilities for personal hygiene virtually guarantee that his wound will become infected and he will again require hospitalization for sepsis (if he does not die before he can receive care). More to the point, they fear that his low level of understanding has lead to his failure to appreciate these risks and their implications for his welfare. They are reluctant to honor his request.

In contrast, Mr. D's HCPs are inclined to honor his requests. He fully understands his diagnosis, his treatment options, and his prognoses with and without therapy. He understands his entire situation as Mr. C does not. He has planned for his (admittedly brief) future in ways that Mr. C has not. Mr. D clearly has a greater (qualitative and quantitative) understanding of the facts of his illness. Moreover, he has a greater capacity for autonomy (e.g., abilities to set and pursue goals and to choose in light of his values) in view of which we deem his decision worthy of respect. In sum, Mr. D seems more competent than Mr. C, and his choice more deserving of respect.

Are both patients competent on a threshold conception? Without a designated threshold this question cannot be answered with certainty, but some speculations might be made. If one rules out appeals to "more or less" (which is, after all, what setting a threshold does), one must seek some sort of minimal set of criteria by which persons will be designated as competent decision makers. A "minimal" set is needed for the following reasons: The goal is to identify appropriate patients to whom to extend (as well as to exclude from) decision-making authority. We are seeking a cut-off point below which persons are deemed unable to make health care decisions. The cut-off presumably should denote the least restrictive set of criteria persons can possess and still actually promote and protect their own values. Given that the basic principles that underlie the entire exercise are respect for autonomy and beneficence, one is rightly concerned not to usurp decision-making authority in persons who are capable of autonomously defining, revising, promoting, and protecting their own best interests. Therefore, the threshold should be set in the least restrictive way to protect these values.

Using a minimal sense of informability, Mr. C seems competent. He knows what is wrong with him (a "sore") and what the treatment is ("soak in water and put the medicine on"). He has displayed at least rudimentary cognitive capability in that he knows his prognosis differs with and without treatment (recovery vs. rehospitalization). He knows that his street life contributed to his illness and that he may have to come back to the hospital if his symptoms recur. One might also argue that he is cognitively capable insofar as he recognizes that he has to convince his HCPs that a relapse is unlikely. This may be why he insists that his (nameless, faceless) friends can give him the help he needs. He has made a choice—for discharge—and has persisted in it.

Given the paucity of detail that Mr. C remembers, as well as his minimal appreciation of his situation, his HCPs are concerned about his competence to make this decision. Nonetheless, he does fulfill a minimal set of criteria for a threshold conception of competence. If this conception is adopted, HCPs will have no recourse but to honor this clearly and repeatedly stated decision. Having attained the threshold, Mr. C is the appropriate decision maker about his care. Moreover, unless there is evidence that Mr. C's discharge offends his value structure or fails to promote his (admittedly unusual) interests, there is no further reason to keep him institutionalized.

If respect of patients' choices is accorded or denied on the basis of respect for autonomy, then respect for the one should vary directly with respect for the other. That is, more autonomy commands more respect; less autonomy commands less respect. This is why Mr. C's case is somewhat unsettling: he seems to have qualitatively and quantitatively fewer of the qualities that contribute to autonomy. His established value structure seems rudimentary at best; his known interests are limited to getting out of the hospital and doing "anything I want to." At best he has a limited frame of reference for making the decision he faces. He seems only minimally informable and somewhat deficient in the cognitive capacities required to assess risk-benefit ratios or to evaluate the different outcomes that different interventions would promote. In short, his decision seems somewhat but not very autonomous. But this sort of ambiguity is irrelevant on a threshold conception of competence. On a threshold analysis, Mr. C is either competent or incompetent. If he is competent, his ignorance of the finer details of his disability and care is irrelevant—in spite of the worries they raise in his caregivers. Conversely, if he is incompetent, what understanding he does posses regarding his disability and its impact on his life style is irrelevant.

Because competence is considered in specific situations, HCPs need to determine if patients are competent to give particular consents. If the standard for competence is a threshold, a threshold must be established for each and every situation in which consent is sought. While this may be theoretically possible, it is a practical nightmare. The most obvious implication is that HCPs must devote enormous amounts of time to defining all relevant details of each situation, relating those details to the criteria of competence, and establishing a threshold for competence for this situation. It seems safe to assume that they would have time for little else—neither diagnosis nor treatment—a state of affairs that clearly does not promote patient welfare. The nature of thresholds is simply not compatible with the specific context of competence.

On the other hand, a degree conception captures the variable nature of health care decisions, as well as life's complexities. A degree notion of competence acknowledges that the abilities to undertake this process vary between individuals and, as a result, so does respect for their particular health care choices. Some decisions have more variables, or greater predictive uncertainty, or greater impact on one's values and future length and quality of life. These complex issues demand a higher level of ability than those that are simple. As a result, a single patient who demonstrates a particular degree of competence may be competent enough for some choices, but not for others. From the practical point of view, it is generally easier to determine if a particular patient knows too little, enough, or more than enough to make a particular choice than to determine if the patient meets a pre-set threshold. Moreover, HCPs do not need to undertake the onerous task of setting infinite thresholds. The downside is that, without a well-defined measure of "enough," there is less intersubjective certainty about judgments of competence.

Lastly, a threshold version does not accord well with autonomy or beneficence. These values are best protected by a process that allows persons to select goals and values that are important to them, and to use these values to make choices. Because autonomously chosen values define what will promote a patient's best interests, enabling autonomous choices based on these values preserves autonomy and promotes beneficence. Cutoff points that arbitrarily obstruct this process fail to promote or protect these values. To usurp the decision-making authority of a patient who is engaged in, if not perfectly adept at, decision making endangers his well-being rather than protecting it. Thus, the principles of autonomy and beneficence support a degree notion of competence.

### Justification

The findings of the previous section may give small comfort to advocates of either notion. TC can, in theory, precisely specify who is competent to consent; but in practice TC is nearly impossible. DC is possible in practice, but does not absolutely define who is competent to consent. Perhaps further appeal to autonomy and beneficence will lend support to one conception. Recall that autonomous persons are generally worthy of respect because they can plan their lives according to value structures they determine for themselves. Once in place, these value structures indicate what will serve the person's best interests. That is, they tell HCPs how to be beneficent toward their patients. One way to respect autonomy and promote beneficence is to refrain from interfering with autonomous choices. This approach extends to patients in consent-requiring situations. HCPs who want to promote their patients' welfare should respect patients' autonomous decisions. The first step toward this end requires some means of ascertaining which patients are competent. There are two options. We can designate a level of decision-making capacities. Those whose abilities exceed the level are competent; those whose abilities fail to reach the point are incompetent. Or we can consider patients as more or less competent to assume decision-making authority, in accordance with their greater or lesser abilities.

The justification for a threshold conception then runs as follows: Competent persons have certain capacities. They possess them to certain extents. Competent decision makers display decision-making capacities to at least extent E. Accordingly, to respect competent persons (i.e., those with E decision-making ability) and to protect incompetent patients (i.e., those whose decision-making ability falls below E), E is set as the threshold for competence. Patients whose capacities fall at or above E are competent decision makers. Patients whose capacities fall below E are not competent decision makers.

Designating a threshold has two advantages. First, it settles, at least for health care decision making, which patients are and which are not competent. Second, it is easier to assess patients using a single value, according to which they either pass or fail, than to assign them along a continuum and then decide, on the basis of a potentially infinite number of values, whether they are competent.

On the other hand, a degree conception of competence also has its attractions. People really do fall many different places along a continuum of capacities. DC recognizes that decisions come in all degrees of complexity. A patient at a single point in time may be competent enough to make a simple decision, yet not competent enough to make a complex one. This finding correlates nicely with the belief that we must respect autonomous decisions, though not arbitrary choices. By honoring only autonomous (competent) choices, DC both respects autonomy and promotes beneficence. The impaired, but not completely incapable, patient retains decisional authority for simple choices; however, when choices are so complex as to exceed her impaired abilities, decisional authority is transferred. This approach best protects and promotes the patient's goals, values, and interests (including the interest in retaining decision-making authority in one's own life).

Further, the logistical advantages that a threshold conception would confer do not alter the fact that any threshold is artificial. That the question of competence is settled by fiat is, and ought to be, disturbing if we have reason to suspect that the fiat does not accord with the facts of the matter. And the fact of the matter is that people are more or less competent to manage particular situations which are themselves more or less complex. Likewise, the ease of assessing patients according to a single value is, and ought to be, distressing if there is reason to believe that a single value fails to reflect the complexity of the evaluation being performed. The fact that autonomous choices deserve respect requires recognition. The better way to admit such respect will be through a degree notion of competence, in part because this approach respects persons' decision-making authority, even when they have limited decision-making skills—so long as the situation requires no greater facility. In addition, because autonomous persons determine what acts and outcomes promote their own well-being and presumably choose in light of those interests, this approach is also beneficent.

### Summary

While both TC and DC appeal to the principles of respect for autonomy and beneficence as justification, DC better protects those moral values. In addition, thresholds are both artificial and practically impossible to implement. DC, in virtue of less precision, is easier to implement and has the additional advantage of according better with common sense. And while DC is not necessarily more reliable than TC, neither is it less so. Lastly, while DC more fully protects decisional authority, it admits expanded external decision-making participation—traditionally important in health care settings—as competence decreases.

## CONSEQUENCE-DEPENDENT VS. CONSEQUENCE-INDEPENDENT COMPETENCE

Whether competence is general or specific, threshold or degree, its complete analysis must indicate the extent to which consequences affect competence determinations. This is because one reason commonly given for transferring a patient's decision-making authority to someone else is that allowing patients to make their own decisions will have bad consequences.

### Understanding the Concepts

With consequence-independent competence (CIC), consequences have no place in defining or assessing competence. With consequence-dependent competence (CDC), appeals to projected outcomes are relevant to competence definitions and assessments. As Drane puts it, ". . . as the consequences flowing from patient decisions become more serious, competence standards for valid consent or refusal of consent become more stringent" (1985, p. 18). As the consequences of choices become more sobering, as more can be gained or lost, the definition of competence—either the number or the extent of necessary capacities— should change.

The first possibility, consequence-independent competence, merely specifies that consequences are irrelevant. Competence to consent will be a matter of general vs. specific and threshold vs. degree determinations. Once those analyses are completed, all that needs to be said will have been said.

The alternative is consequence-dependent competence, in which competence again lies on a continuum, whose end points are "minimal chance of catastrophe" and "maximal chance of catastrophe." Between these extremes lie many points by which competence may be designated according to greater or lesser chances for catastrophic outcomes. Persons can be more or less competent, but instead of varying only with a person's capacities to manage the situation, competence also varies with the nature of the projected outcomes of particular choices. That is, P may be C for T because T will (probably) have minimal negative consequences for P. At the same time P may be incompetent for $T_1$ if the projected consequences for P of $T_1$ are disastrous.

On the basis of CDC, the anticipated impact of choices determines the requirements for competence. This is not the same thing as competent-for-simple—incompetent-for-complex decisions. A choice can be simple, yet have immense consequences. If one has no health insurance and little money, the choice between medical and surgical treatment of angina is simple: take medicines. The consequences, however, of this "simple" choice (e.g., fear of sudden death, medication side effects, exertional angina) are substantial. In any case, a consequence-dependent conception of competence requires a series of thresholds along a continuum: where the consequences of choices are insignificant, the level of competence required is minimal; where the consequences are significant, the level of competence required is maximal. The number or extent of required capacities (i.e., the standard [S]) will vary directly with the seriousness of the projected consequences. When the consequences are severe, the standard will be higher than when the consequences are minor. We recall that a consequence-dependent conception (CDC) states:

P is C for this T if S, which varies in terms of *this* T's consequences, is met;

while according to consequence-independent competence (CIC):

> P is C for this T if S, which does not vary in terms of conse-
> quences, is met.

What does it mean to be competent to consent on consequence-
dependent and consequence-independent notions? Regarding CIC
this question is quickly dispatched: it means whatever it means on
whichever other notions are chosen, and nothing more. Thus, S
becomes whatever specific and degree notions determine.

With CDC, however, the decision maker's capacities and the magnitude of consequences for differing situations must be specified. A
person is competent if she possesses the particular set or extent of
capacities that correspond to the magnitude of the potential consequences of the options about which she must decide. Because capacities and outcomes are ranked along a continuum, a CDC conception
of standard S becomes:

> possesses the requisite capacities for decision making in a situa-
> tion of Magnitude M.

Then CDC, or:

> P is C for this T if S, which varies in terms of *this* T's conse-
> quences, is met

becomes:

> P is C to $D_n$ for this T if P possesses to $D_n$ the requisite M-level
> capacities for decision making in a situation of Magnitude M, and
> this situation's magnitude is M.

### Implications

CIC and CDC, unlike the previously considered conceptions, are
more different than alike. There are no implications that attach to CIC
uniquely, only those that attach to SC or DC. For CDC, persons will
still be evaluated according to the criteria of informability, cognitive
and affective capability, and the abilities to make decisions and
recount the process. For CDC, however, options with projected maxi-

mal or minimal negative effects will require maximal or minimal capacities. CDC requires that the varying magnitude of potential effects of postulated actions be identified; that both levels of capacities and magnitudes of effects be located on a continuum; and that some way of quantifying consequences be determined so as to place them on a continuum. In sum, CDC requires a method for scoring capacities, a method for assigning the scores on a "capacity continuum," methods for scoring the magnitude of consequences and placing the scores on an "effects continuum," and a method for correlating the two continua.

If we fulfill all these methodological requirements, we will have no further problem identifying patients whose consents or refusals ought be respected. Persons who have the capacities necessary for particular tasks of particular magnitudes are competent to make decisions regarding those tasks. They are not, by extension or without further evaluation, competent to make other decisions. A great deal of time—of HCPs and patients alike—will be devoted to grading situations and to competence testing. Each new task demands a new scoring procedure relevant to that task. Thus, CDC is problematic in the way TC was problematic: the amount of time and energy necessary for its implementation makes it practically impossible.

There is one further implication of a CDC conception. Because HCPs are the best source of expected outcomes from health care interventions (or refusal thereof), they will quite likely have significant input into whatever criteria and testing methods ultimately prevail. As the bias of HCPs is usually for rather than against treatment, we risk adopting an ascending scale of criteria that will effectively preclude patient self-determination for any serious or major therapeutic intervention. This threat may, in fact, be inherent in this approach. Eth, for example, has argued that a consequence-based, sliding scale notion presumes incompetence, in that patients must prove that they are able to handle risky decisions. Criteria can be demanded in so great a number and to so great an extent that very few, if any, persons would be judged competent for momentous choices. Such a system effectively undercuts both the rationale (protecting and promoting autonomy and beneficence) and the procedure for free and informed consent. After all, the practice was established as a way of enhancing and protecting, not annihilating, patient self-determination. Should consequences become a part of a definition of competence, it will be important to take precautions against unbridled enthusiasm for treatment and, derivatively, against patients' autonomous choices. A single case should illustrate the difference in the two approaches.

> *CASE V:* Ms. E is a 58-year-old insulin-dependent diabetic who has developed end-stage renal disease. She has been on hemodialysis for three years, during which she has continued to work as a marriage and family counselor. In her spare time she is a volunteer counselor for several youth clubs. Unfortunately, she has begun to have complications associated with dialysis. While awaiting kidney transplantation, Ms. E gives her situation a great deal of thought and decides against further treatment. Her reasons include having lived a full life, her preference that the kidney go to a younger person who has "more time," and increasing psychological intolerance of the restrictive lifestyle her disease has imposed upon her. She notes that, as rewarding as her life has been, she is ready for it to be over. She plans to discontinue dialysis. She understands this will result in her death and that the dying process will be, at least for some time, uncomfortable. Nonetheless she has thoroughly considered her options and chooses to terminate treatment.

On a CIC conception, Ms. E demonstrates a high degree of competence to make this decision. She understands her illness, the various possible treatments, the prognoses with each, and what her future holds psychosocially as well as physiologically. She has made a choice based on those facts, her personal value structure, and her conception of her own best interests.

On a CDC conception the magnitude of the consequences that will likely follow from her decision are sufficiently great that her competence to make this decision must be questioned. CDC proponents might want to argue that she is competent to make this choice if she chooses to undergo therapy because then her death would (probably) not occur so soon; i.e., the nature of the consequences would change. But is this an acceptable way to circumscribe patients' options? CDC will effectively close off many options—for example, choices to forgo life-sustaining treatment or to undergo risky procedures where positive outcomes are less likely than negative ones—to virtually all seriously ill patients.[17] CDC would quite likely impede patients' participation in experimental therapies as well, especially if the patient himself would not directly benefit.

To argue that more extensive capacities are required in serious circumstances circumscribes patients' options. Many persons in such circumstances will suffer some impairment of informability and cognitive and affective capacities, although Leeb et al. (1976) found that "nervous" patients actually remember more than their more relaxed counterparts. If this reduction is significant, it should be reflected in a reduced degree of competence. Thus, to require a varying standard is another way to impose a threshold (actually a number of thresholds) which, for the reasons noted, is unacceptable. What CDC entails is that whenever the case is serious, the ante is upped, and patients are more frequently excluded from the decision-making process.

## Justification

Consider again how such conflicting conceptions might be justified. The justification for CIC will be the same as that for the preceding options. But for CDC the primary moral justification is, obviously, an unqualified appeal to *general* beneficence. The natural concern for human well-being suggests that major decisions should be approached by people whose "eyes are wide open" and who fully appreciate the ramifications of their choices. When outcomes seem especially threatening, consequentialists act so as to encourage "better" results. One method alleged to achieve better outcomes in terms of the Big Three is the adoption of an increasingly stringent definition of competence.

As plausible as this approach may seem, it has great potential for harming, rather than helping, patients. First, consequence-based competence encourages actions that fail to respect autonomy. As noted in Chapter Two, respect for autonomous choice recognizes persons' capacities to plan their own lives in accordance with self-determined value structures. Nothing indicates that these value structures must include any particular values, goals, or interests, nor that any particular outcomes must be included (e.g., life, health, and pleasure) or excluded (e.g., death, disability, suffering).

There are, in fact, a number of reasons why unqualified appeals to consequences should be forestalled. First, people can agree on the facts of a matter, yet recommend diametrically opposing actions because they (1) evaluate the facts differently, (2) rank outcomes differently, (3) reason with varying degrees of facility, or (4) focus their reasoning on different facts. For example, some cultures do not contain, conceptually or pragmatically, risk/benefit analyses (Hahn, 1982). Moreover, different people operate under different value structures and conceptions of best interests. But respect must be tendered to all autonomous choices, even those based on values, goals, and means that fall outside the mainstream.[18] To insist on a more rigorous definition for competence, whether in number or extent of capacities, because citizens generally or professionals particularly consider certain choices unacceptable flies in the face of autonomy and beneficence. "Wrong" choices may give HCPs good grounds for more rigorous attempts to inform patients to insure full understanding. They may require intensive efforts to understand why the patient chooses as she does. But any move to inherently restrict the range of choices fails to respect autonomous choices or to promote beneficence because it fails to take seriously the unique value structures that inform those choices. As noted in the preceding section, there may be legitimate reasons for overriding a "less" competent person's choice.[19] These reasons would quite likely include appeals to consequences. But such appeals are not the same thing as incompetence and should not be confused with it. Calling persons incompetent is not synonymous with saying they have made foolish, risky, or even overtly dangerous choices. If they are competent and their choices are autonomous, they must be allowed to do foolish or dangerous things.

Second, even when appeals to general beneficence are appropriate, we need to recall that beneficence itself mandates fulfilling (or at least not thwarting) autonomous choices of the decision maker. In other words, HCPs must satisfy the patient's autonomous desires, not their own. If there were certain objective values (e.g., life, health), HCPs would be obliged to promote those. But as we have seen, no list of universally objective goods is available.

Part of the temptation to assume that life and health are universally and objectively good no doubt originates in the professional's commitment. HCPs are dedicated to promoting their patients' welfare, and this usually means acting to save patients' lives and return them to healthy (or less unhealthy) states. Clinicians are committed to "doing something" for their patients, and generally have very specific ideas of about how to help patients—by treating them. In this day and age many things can be done to patients.[20] These interventions have varying probabilities of success. They also have varying costs—physical, emotional, and financial. How one assesses benefits and burdens varies between individuals and depends heavily upon personal value structures. Because the value structures that inform decision making are unique, it is not surprising that different people, presented with the same facts, make different decisions.

Nor is it surprising that the value structures of most HCPs include a commitment to providing the best care possible to their patients. Problems arise when the clinician's appraisal of what is best is at odds with the patient's appraisal. With the HCPs' bias toward treatment, the patient who labors under an ascending scale of competence runs a significant risk of being treated when, given her personal value system, treatment is *genuinely* not in her best interests.[21] Moreover patients and HCPs may disagree about the "facts" of the matter (e.g., how distressing a correctable condition is) or about what treatment would be most compatible with the patient's expressed values. Each might try to persuade the other to her point of view, but agreement is not always possible. HCPs who are unaware of or cannot accept a patient's value structure, or who disagree with patients about the facts, may be able to mount some other justification for treating a patient against her will. But the justification for overriding an autonomous choice should not be a spurious label of incompetence.

## A Limited Role for Consequential Concerns

HCPs' own predictions of consequences and evaluations of probable outcomes commonly dictate the number and extent of capacities they require of their patients in particular decision-making situations. While this is often understandable, it is inappropriate.[22] Any effort to analyze competence in terms of consequences is misdirected, because competence depends on a set of capacities that persons possess, not on the choices they make by using those capacities. Put another way, competence is about a process, not about results (although the former presumably contributes to the latter). Since competence has to do with how rather than what people choose, competence must be defined and assessed without recourse to outcomes. Decision making must be evaluated as a process that patients undertake precisely to overcome the capriciousness of the world. To evaluate decisions only in terms of their outcomes is to expose the unlucky to inappropriate charges of incompetence. Insofar as patients can execute the appropriate process, they should retain decision-making authority. That the process on occasion *inadvertently* leads to poor outcomes cannot impugn decision-making competence. If it could, none of us would be competent, for we all occasionally rue particular decisions that resulted in unanticipated and undesired results. By this same argument, decisions by patients to undertake risky options (where the chances for catastrophe are high) or to undertake options that virtually guarantee what others consider undesirable outcomes cannot be overridden by appealing to consequences as evaluated by others. The patient's ability to undertake the process determines competence to consent.

Confusion about the relationship of competence to consequences may arise because so many of the issues competent patients consider have to do with consequences. Presumably they seek health care in order to promote good rather than bad outcomes. Much of the information about diagnoses, treatment, and prognoses is phrased in terms of outcomes. The entire professional-patient encounter seems fraught with consequential concerns. Some concerns bear further consideration.

First, consequences often trigger concerns about a patient's competence. The patient who either ignores projected outcomes altogether, or who chooses the treatment with the worst projected effects raises suspicions about her competence. Since HCPs are concerned to benefit patients, choices that appear to harm rather than help generate suspicion that the patient's decision-making capacity may be impaired. If there are good reasons for the choice, the competent patient will give them and the professional's concerns may be assuaged.[23] If not, the patient's capacity to make the choice should be determined.

In a similar vein, HCPs often cite the problem of false negatives or false positives as a reason for including consequences in competence determinations. Virtually all studies to which patients may be subjected have some margin of error. Thus, a patient who is actually infected with, for example, the HIV virus can test negative for it (a false negative). Likewise, a patient who has not been infected can test positive (a false positive). HCPs worry that, since their diagnoses and prognoses are less precise because of such unavoidable errors, the probability of negative consequences may be even greater. As a result, they are even less eager to accept patients' already risky choices.

While false positives and negatives pose a genuine risk to patients, there is no reason to believe they differ from other risks. Thus, the possibility of false positives or negatives can be managed like any other—by informing patients of their likelihood and their consequences.[24]

Finally, in health care settings there is general agreement that while choices belong to autonomous patients, other moral factors have import as well. Consider patients with irreversible illnesses who early in the course of their diseases forgo treatment. Even when all those involved (HCPs, family, friends) agree that the patient's choice is an autonomous one that will benefit him, there can be disagreement about whether to accede to his wishes. Such patients are often subjected to appeals to reconsider, lest some new treatment become available in the near future. No one disagrees with the patient's decision-making authority, or even with his decision-making abilities. Rather, the disagreement is with other morally relevant factors in the situation. Family and friends may insist that the consequences to them have moral weight. They may exhort the patient to "try everything" so that their relationship does not end sooner than is absolutely necessary. They may appeal to virtue, entreating the patient to be courageous in the face of adversity, or to be compassionate toward others, including his clinicians, recognizing how hard it is for them to "give him up" prematurely. There may be good reasons to urge competent patients to include the consequences for others in their decision-making calculations. Their failure to do so, however, need not indicate incompetence.

### A Warning

Note that clinicians who carefully avoid defining competence in terms of consequences can be tempted by these other appeals into smuggling consequences into competence assessments. They may insist on a greater degree of competence in circumstances where outcomes are especially worrisome. That is, when consequences are projected to be disastrous, HCPs may demand a greater degree of competence before recognizing a patient's decisional authority. Then, although the definition of competence would not include appeals to consequences, its assessment would.

When decisions are weighty and time for consideration is short, HCPs are understandably tempted to elevate the criteria to insure that only those persons who are maximally competent meet them. This might reduce the number of untoward medical outcomes. The advocate of such an approach will claim that he or she is not defining competence in consequential terms. This claim, while strictly true, ignores the fact that consequences are being introduced at a different point in the decision-making calculus. This approach is a more subtle way of making competence to consent turn on consequences. What it amounts to is this: if the outcome looks bleak, patients have to be *really* competent to retain decision-making authority; if the outcome looks innocuous, patients can retain decision-making authority with quantitatively and qualitatively fewer capacities.

Such maneuvers are false labels of incompetence. If there is genuinely a need to introduce consequences into medical decision making, why not honestly admit that competing values are at work? Respect for autonomous choices is one value. Promoting good outcomes in terms of the patient's own value structure is another. Promoting good medical outcomes is yet another. Other moral appeals (e.g., virtue, rights, equity) may also be introduced. Under such an approach there may be powerful moral reasons to override autonomous choices, but the patient's competence would no longer be spuriously impugned. This admission seems preferable to calling competent patients incompetent—especially since the general consequences of being labelled incompetent can themselves be immensely harmful. If this pluralistic moral approach were adopted, we would expect competent persons to have their choices circumscribed by competing moral claims rather than illicit designations of incompetence. As an example, a patient's competent choice to receive a second liver transplant following rejection of the first might be overridden by claiming that equity requires providing all claimants with a first liver before providing any with a second. Of course, such an approach would mandate statutory changes (e.g., in grounds for malpractice). The point is that the subterfuge of incompetence would no longer be necessary as the only mechanism by which to nullify individual choices.

### Summary

Consequence-dependent competence fails to protect patient autonomy and beneficence in consent situations. As such, CDC fails to protect or promote the values for which informed consent was instituted. While HCPs may understandably wish to override choices that place patients at greater risk of death and disability than other options, they must understand that they may be protecting their own professional and personal values rather than those of their patients. Consequence-independent competence is the appropriate approach within the practice of free and informed consent.

## COGNITIVE VS. COGNITIVE-AFFECTIVE COMPETENCE

### Understanding the Concepts

Cognition broadly understood includes both the information handling system of the brain and cognitive capacities per se. Thus, cognitive competence applies to the capacities of attention and perception, language usage (fluency, articulation, and comprehension), memory, and cognition itself (intelligence, calculation, insight and judgment, manipulation of data, and abstract thinking). Affect broadly understood includes the emotional and motivational systems.[25] Affective competence applies to feelings, motivations, and behavioral control. These abilities to internalize and respond to one's circumstances determine how persons feel, and when, to what extent, and how they act upon their feelings. Dually (i.e., cognitively and affectively) competent persons are able to acquire information from the world, respond emotionally and behaviorally to that information, and use it to increase their knowledge and control of their environments.

Cognitive and affective competence both play crucial roles in day-to-day health care activities. Sick people almost always experience changes in both systems, as illness can reduce or heighten both cognitive and affective abilities. Cognitive and affective capacities contribute to all previous partial definitions because they are part of any standard (S) by which competence is judged. For clarification we can think of the standard of dual—i.e., cognitive and affective—competence as follows:

P possesses to $D_n$ the requisite cognitive and affective capacities for decision making (i.e., can to $D_n$ acquire information about options, cognitively and affectively consider their probabilities of achieving chosen aims, choose on the basis of those considerations, and recount the decision-making process).

### Justification

Cognitive and affective competence are mutualistic rather than mutually exclusive. Healthy persons function effectively in both spheres, exercising both cognitive and affective abilities with facility.

There are three separate arguments why an analysis of competence must attend to both the cognitive and affective systems. The first is that the two systems are so functionally intertwined that whatever affects one variously affects the other.[26] Any situation that provokes a strong emotional response stimulates, in virtue of that response, changes in cognitive processing as well.[27] HCPs often assert that excessive emotionality provokes choices that fail to promote a patient's best interests. A less common, but equally noteworthy, claim is that excessive rationality also has a negative impact. If only reason's input is recognized, the emotions can wreak havoc with the body in subversive ways, both physiologically (e.g., ulcers) and psychologically (e.g., depression).

Second, human information systems include more than the ability to calculate. They also depend on the capacity to recognize and take note of important data, some of which are feelings. Emotional responses signal that situations or events are important. Emotions convey vital information about how a person feels. Part of the reason individuals embrace different goals is that they feel differently about them. Two persons presented with the same choice can admit the same facts but choose different options because their feelings about the facts or the options differ. Even people who share goals may, because of different feelings, adopt different means to them. When emotions are ignored or suppressed, the information they carry is not incorporated into the decision-making process. Decisions are then made without complete information. Because thinking and feeling are both important sources of information, anyone interested in insuring autonomous choice and the welfare of persons is advised to consider both systems in assessing decision making.[28]

A third reason for including both affective and cognitive systems in a conceptual analysis of competence is that each contributes to the values that the practice of informed consent was designed to protect—patient autonomy and welfare. That affective impairment can preclude autonomy is commonly known. What is less commonly appreciated—as will be discussed at length in the following section—is that affective well-being also plays an important role in decision making.

Currently, HCPs consider persons competent if their cognitive abilities are functioning properly, relative to a standard (S). To be cognitively effective is to be competent. But why should we believe that competence is only about cognition? [29] If people actually made decisions based only on rational data analysis, competence might be defined exclusively in terms of cognitive ability. In fact, people make decisions based on feelings as well as reason. How they feel about particular options and projected outcomes is, for most decision makers, an important factor to be considered. Most cardiologists would not deem a patient unreasonable if, other things being equal, he chooses medical management rather than a coronary artery bypass graft to control his angina because he fears surgery. For the patient who would rather avoid surgery, the CABG's 90 percent chance of controlling angina may not be enough better than the 80 percent chance the medications have of relieving his pain. To account for such factors, competence must incorporate affect.

Of course choices based on feelings become worrisome if feelings overpower reason. HCPs worry that a person may be willing to sacrifice life or health solely on the basis of a powerful emotional response. The woman who genuinely understands the risks, but still adamantly refuses a hysterectomy for an (easily cured) cancer *in situ* of the cervix because she has a white-hot hatred of surgeons, rightly raises worries about her competence. Nonetheless, HCPs' worries about patients' decisions are not pathognomonic for incompetence.

For most people emotions play a role in decision making. The question is, should they? The argument that affect helps define competence to consent is complex and turns in part on the roles of cognition and affect in decision making. The argument can be made in practical terms: one can argue that affective capacities play a role because affective and cognitive capacities are functionally intertwined; feelings are part of the data that the cognitive system assesses; and the practice of informed consent was designed to promote and protect autonomy (which can be focused by affective competence and impaired by affective incompetence) and beneficence. In addition, the practical argument is buttressed by another argument, one that depends on an understanding of the nature of persons to whose welfare HCPs are professionally committed. Traditionally this argument has been framed in terms of the sorts of beings that are worthy of respect (where "respect" not only obligates us to protect autonomous *choices*, but also autonomous *persons*, in part by promoting conditions under which they can flourish—i.e., "respect" requires respect for autonomy and well-being).

The history of philosophy considers two major schools of thought regarding the nature of persons worthy of respect. The first school respects only beings capable of rational thought. The second acknowledges the importance of rationality, but insists that persons to whom respect is due have other, equally important attributes. Both traditions will be considered.

### Persons as Merely Rational

The persons-as-merely-rational concept claims that persons are worthy of respect because they have the capacity for rational thought. This capacity—and this capacity alone—entitles persons to special treatment. Although the first known proponents of this concept were the ancient Greeks,[30] we will consider the account presented by Kant, in his discussions of the "autonomous agent."

In the *Critique of Pure Reason*, Kant considers what makes persons worthy of respect. He acknowledges that persons, by nature, possess both sensory and cognitive capacities. Moreover, sense and reason contribute to human experience, but reason alone gives us truth (*Critique of Pure Reason*, p. 121 =[A86=B118], trans. Smith). Senses, on the other hand, give rise to perceptions that are prone to error and, as such, are not to be trusted. Errors arise because (1) sense organs can malfunction (e.g., near-sightedness, deafness); (2) sense perceptions can be erroneous (e.g., a mirage); and (3) sense perceptions can be contaminated by wishes or needs (e.g., John, who loves Jane, "sees" love in her unfocused stare in his direction).

Being sensual creatures, humans naturally pay attention to data acquired through sensory apparatus. But, given the unreliability of the senses, humans engage reason to assess sense data, retaining only the perceptions determined to be true and discarding the remainder. More crucially, Kant believed reason to be capable of pure, unfettered analysis whereby humans can completely ignore their particular circumstances and feelings and consider the world from a universal perspective. By using reason, individuals can surmount their particular circumstances and adopt an impartial point of view.[31] For Kant this "pure" (i.e., universal) activity of reason qualifies persons for respect (*Critique of Practical Reason*, [61]=p. 63, trans. Beck). Unlike information acquired through sense perception, information gained through the pure use of reason is wholly reliable and leads to genuine knowledge whose truth can be recognized by all rational beings.

According to Kant, reason's power lies in its ability to distance persons from their particular situations. Protected from the pull of feelings and desires, reason can impartially prescribe goals and values that all reasonable beings will acknowledge. Put another way, Kant held that particular rational beings are capable of determining what is right and good for all rational beings, because all rational beings can identify universal values that serve as exceptionless guides to (rules for) behavior. Anyone capable of doing this is capable of moral agency and, as such, is intrinsically valuable and inherently worthy of respect. Persons also happen to possess feelings, but these are irrelevant to their value. Only reason—the source of truth—qualifies beings for respect.[32]

The tradition of persons-as-merely-rational is not commonly advocated among twentieth-century philosophers. For the most part, current scholars prefer an expanded definition of persons that includes other faculties. However, physician-philosopher, H. T. Engelhardt, Jr., has developed such an account.[33] In his definitive work, *The Foundations of Bioethics*, Engelhardt argues that there could be no morality at all without rational beings because rational beings make morality possible.[34] They alone are interested in the moral projects of defining good and bad, in assigning moral responsibility, and in determining worthiness of praise and blame (Engelhardt, 1986, p. 107). Morality also requires persons who are "rational, free to choose, and in possession of a moral sense" (p. 105). They must be rational because reason enables them to construct rules capable of impartially guiding the behavior of beings who want to be moral, and to understand that persons have options and that different options lead to different states of affairs. They must be free to choose so as to be capable of being held responsible for outcomes. They must possess a moral sense in order to recognize that some acts are good while others are bad, and that those who commit good acts are praiseworthy while those who commit bad acts are blameworthy. Engelhardt argues that persons can do these things only in virtue of reason; thus, only in virtue of reason is morality possible. Persons, as "containers" of reason, are worthy of respect.

According to both Kant and Engelhardt, only rational beings are capable of autonomy, and autonomy alone enables persons to identify not only existing values, goals, and rules of behavior, but also those that ought to exist. Thus, rational beings alone are worthy of respect because they and they alone can (and want to) define moral values and moral behavior.[35] That Kant and Engelhardt differ in their definitions of moral values and moral behavior is an interesting issue that cannot be developed here. We should, however, note that Kant considers reason synonymous with what I am calling cognitive competence. Reason alone enables universal (i.e., non-subjective) definitions of values and actions, thus reason alone enables autonomy and morality. For our purposes, reason should be understood as assuming a procedural rather than substantive role. As such, reason is necessary, but not sufficient, for competent decision making. Reason will be practically useful for choosing the means to, or identifying incompatibility between, particular values, goals, beliefs, or desires. Of any anticipated undertaking, rational persons can consider the present situation, the desired situation, the odds that treatment will change a present to a desired state of affairs, and the risks involved. Reason empowers persons to evaluate whether a given action is "worth it." But "worth it" in terms of what? In terms of an individual—that is, subjective—value structure that is only partly the product of reason. This process will be developed below. Here reason's insufficiency in defining competence raises the conception of persons as rational—and more.

### Persons as Rational and More

Rationality surely contributes to worthiness of respect; but does reason alone command respect? History provides us with alternative accounts which claim that respect is based on more than a capacity for reason. These accounts insist that qualities beyond rationality contribute to worthiness of respect.

One of the more compelling accounts of persons-as-rational-and-more comes from John Stuart Mill. The son of political reformer James Mill, and the intellectual heir of the great nineteenth-century political philosopher, Jeremy Bentham, Mill was schooled from the crib in the activities of reason. By his twenty-first birthday he had become a scholar, philosopher, logician, reformer, writer, and linguist. Yet, as he notes in his *Autobiography* (1924), intellectual capacity alone did not make a full life; feelings were necessary as well. Moreover, intellectual endeavors carried to extreme may thwart the development of a full life. Mill's record of this discovery is worth quoting at length:

For now I saw . . . what I had always before received with incredulity—that the habit of analysis has a tendency to wear away the feelings: as indeed it has, when no other mental habit is cultivated, and the analysing [sic] spirit remains without its natural complements and correctives. . . . All those to whom I look up, were of opinion that the pleasure of sympathy with human beings, and the feeling which made the good of others, and especially of mankind on a large scale, the object of existence, were the greatest and surest sources of happiness. Of the truth of this I was convinced, but to know that a feeling would make me happy if I had it, did not give me the feeling. My education, I thought, had failed to create these feelings in sufficient strength to resist the dissolving influence of analysis, while the whole course of my intellectual cultivation had made precocious and premature analysis the inveterate habit of my mind. I was thus . . . left stranded at the commencement of my voyage, with a well-equipped ship and a rudder, but no sail; without any real desire for the ends which I had been so carefully fitted out to work for: no delight in virtue, or the general good, but also just as little in anything else. The fountains of vanity and ambition seemed to have dried up within me, as completely as those of benevolence.

. . . neither selfish nor unselfish pleasures were pleasures to me. And there seemed no power in nature sufficient to begin the formation of my character anew, and create in a mind now irretrievably analytic, fresh associations of pleasure with any of the objects of human desire (pp. 97–8).

Mill adds that he "never turned recreant to intellectual culture," but that "The maintenance of a due balance among the faculties, now seemed to me of primary importance" (p. 101).

Mill's point is that life's goals are, in an important way, both the products and producers of feelings. They not only motivate, but also accompany the pursuit and attainment of goals. Goals, considered in their entirety, both produce and are underpinned and partially defined by feelings. Without feelings, goals and efforts are hollow and incomplete. Thus, on Mill's account, persons are worthy of respect in virtue of reason and feelings. Each is important to the well-being of the whole person, and should be cultivated, acknowledged, and respected.

The persons-as-rational-and-more account includes qualities in addition to rationality when considering worthiness for respect because persons are more than just their capacity for rational thought. Humans are to be prized not merely because they can reason, but because they can participate in certain sorts of affective encounters as well. In virtue of their feelings, they can develop personal bonds and be active members of moral and social communities. Nineteenth and twentieth century philosophers have by and large adopted this approach which depends in part on a different (non-Kantian) conceptual understanding of morality.

Consider the relationship of respect and morality developed by L.W. Sumner (1981, pp. 142–46). Morality requires us to promote the well-being of others. To promote someone's well-being is to see that things go better for him rather than worse. But things can only go better or worse if there are states of affairs he would prefer or not. In other words, things go better or worse in virtue of experiences that produce suffering or enjoyment; or things go better for people when they experience pleasure than when they experience pain. Now since pleasure and pain are feelings, morality is about promoting and preventing certain feelings in others. Therefore, morality is about beings with feelings.

Note that on Sumner's account reason is irrelevant to the value of one's existence though it can be instrumental in promoting that value. In fact, he says that were persons to have only reason, it would be utterly impossible to promote their well-being because they would have no interests. If there is only reason, there are no better or worse states of affairs because there is nothing to be desired or avoided, nothing to be enjoyed or suffered. We would be like rational androids or computers. As a result, there is no possibility for promoting well-being except in beings who have something in addition to reason—feelings.

Another contemporary theory that depends on a conception of persons-as-rational-and-more is put forth by Baruch A. Brody (1988). Brody writes:

> We think of persons as having the potential to perform a wide variety of actions whose performance we value greatly. These include the potential to make rational (and especially principled) choices, the potential to engage in a variety of interpersonal relations, the potential to appreciate beauty, and the potential to desire to know the truth. We therefore value the person who has those potentials (p. 33).

Brody's point is that persons possess important characteristics beyond rationality. The capacities to participate in psychosocial, aesthetic, religious, and scholarly communities are also valued. Part of this value lies in persons' ability to interact with others and with their environments in ways that are mutually satisfying; that is, in ways that they enjoy. When persons demonstrate any of these valuable characteristics, we ought to support (or at least not interfere with) such behavior. Reason is not the only source of value.

Brody's and Sumner's positions, then, are much like Mill's: Persons to whom respect is owed possess a composite nature that includes abilities to participate cognitively and affectively in their world. Those who possess all such characteristics are to be valued. Those in whom any of these traits are reduced or absent have less value; those who completely lack them have no value at all.

### Respect for Persons and Competence to Consent

What has all this to do with competence to consent? We established in Chapter Two that HCPs have obligations to respect their patients' autonomous choices and to promote their patients' welfare. Moreover, we noted that having one's autonomous decisions respected is one way to fulfill both of these obligations. In the persons-as-rational tradition persons who are (merely) rational will have their merely rational decisions, medical or other, respected. The presence, absence, or functional level of affective capacities is irrelevant. On the other hand, the persons-as-rational-and-more account attributes value not merely to the capacity to reason, but also to the capacity to function well affectively. Such persons will use affective capacities in making decisions. The question is which conception of persons is preferable?

Given the goals of health care in general and of the practice of informed consent in particular, there are good reasons for adopting the persons-as-rational-and-more account. HCPs are committed to promoting their patients' well-being. If that well-being derives even in part from affective capacities, then HCPs are committed to promoting healthy affective functioning. Most people, patients and HCPs included, agree that life is better than (unwanted) death, health is better than disease, and pleasure is better than (unwanted) pain. As a result, the professional commitment to promoting patients' well-being usually means that HCPs should do whatever is necessary to minimize the patient's pain, promote or restore the patient's health, or save the patient's life. Usually, but not always. At least sometimes HCPs and patients disagree about what best promotes a patient's interests. They may disagree about whether or how to minimize pain, about whether or how to promote or restore health, and even about whether or not to save the patient's life. Now, it is commonly true that patients *feel* more strongly about certain outcomes than about others, and that they choose, at least in part, in accordance with those feelings. Different feelings on the part of different participants can lead to disputes about what to do. Different feelings can also explain why the practice of informed consent was established. In cases of disagreement, this practice recognizes competent patients as the final authority regarding their own best interests. Their own best interests are partially derived from feelings they have about how their lives will go, all things considered. As a result, the practice obligates HCPs to promote their patients' welfare by supporting the autonomous choices patients make in light of their own value structures.

An understanding of the health profession's goals, coupled with an understanding of the relationship between feelings and well-being, must lead to a recognition that the persons-as-rational-and-more is the appropriate account. The issue then becomes not how to ignore affect, but how best to understand its role in decision making and how best to include feelings in the decision-making process. The question is how to understand affective competence. To answer this question, we must consider how cognition and affect contribute to decision making. The working hypothesis will be that both contribute information important to the choice at hand. Since the contributions of cognition are better understood and more widely accepted, we will look at cognitive competence first.

### Competence and Cognition

We may begin by asking about the function of reason. Presumably in cases of consent, cognitive competence will indicate whether or not there are "good reasons" for picking one option over another. Cognitive capacities enable patients to analyze information. Precisely what information particular patients consider depends on the situation; but all patients must have certain pieces of information if their consents are to be truly informed. They must know their diagnoses, treatment options, and the risks, burdens, benefits, and probable outcome of each option. They must also know the recommendation of the clinician in charge of their care, and that they (the patients) are the decision makers for their own cases. Cognition's first function is to receive information. Once this information has been received, reason has something to reason about.[36]

Next, persons use their cognitive capacities to assess information. Relevant information must be recognized as relevant information.

Extraneous facts must be ignored while salient data are retained and stored for on-going analysis (remembered). The decision at hand and the information relevant to its resolution must be related to oneself; patients must see its importance to their own lives and values. Next, the patient must reason about the problem at hand. While there may be some dispute as to just how reason works, in the context of consent, reason enables patients to recognize that their situations require intervention, and that different choices may lead to different outcomes, some of which are more compatible with their value structures than others. To complete this assessment, patients must have some understanding of probabilities, namely, that certain options are more or less likely to succeed and, hence, more or less likely to promote their goals and values. They must know that there are no guarantees—that as likely as it is that things will go well (or poorly), no outcome is ever assured but only more or less probable. In addition, there ought to be some appreciation of the difference in risks and benefits that attend particular options, so that patients understand that not all options are equally safe. In sum, to reason about possibilities is to understand them in terms of their likelihood of promoting one's own goals and values, as well as the burdens of doing so.

Next, patients must be able to rank the options in order of preference, in the event that the first option is foreclosed (e.g., one prefers a kidney transplant to dialysis, but no kidney is available). Having completed a cognitive analysis, patients must be able to resolve the situation—to actually choose. Then, having formulated a plan of action (even if the plan is to do nothing), patients must resign themselves to that plan. Resignation enables patients to proceed as indicated. Lastly, patients are able to recount this process to others who may have questions about how they came to a particular decision.[37] This entire process, then, is what is meant by "having good reasons" for a decision. The "good reasons" are those which, established by the preceding process, specify the choice that will most likely promote one's values. This process is what cognitive competence contributes to decision making.

### Competence and Affect

What does affective competence contribute? Presumably, since the goal is to make choices that promote one's well-being, affect also contributes information that is important for selecting the right alternative. But what information does affect provide?

In his volume on human creativity, *The Mind's Best Work* (1981, pp. 114–121), D. N. Perkins discusses the role of feelings as a source of knowledge.[38] While much of what he says is specific to the role of feelings within the creative process, his structure is so useful for understanding the role of emotions in decision making that in what follows I have adopted both his approach and his terminology. The content is altered to reflect the nature of decision making.

On Perkins' account, there are three routes by which affect contributes to knowledge: "felt emotions," or what one feels in particular situations (1981, p. 116); "cognitive emotions," or feelings that are intrinsically part of the process of inquiry (1981, p. 118); and "expressions," or displays of felt emotions that can be perceived by others (1981, p. 119). Each carries specific sorts of information.

Within the context of informed consent we must ask, first, what felt emotions can tell us. Most basically, they contribute to an understanding of the overall nature of one's current situation. We feel anger upon realizing that others have acted against our well-being. We feel happy when others promote our welfare. We feel secure when we know we are not threatened, frightened when we think we are. How one feels conveys important information about the nature of one's situation. Were the situation different, one's feelings would differ as well. Moreover, feelings direct behavior because they not only communicate facts, but motivate us to certain sorts of action.[39] Anger, for instance, moves one to promote or reestablish her own well-being (or, perhaps, to seek revenge). Fear motivates one to strengthen a defensive position or to eliminate the source of that fear. Contentment leads one to preserve the satisfying conditions.

Felt emotions can be inappropriate.[40] They convey information based on our understanding of a particular situation, so if we get the facts wrong, our emotions may be unsuitable to the occasion. The patient who is afraid to sign a surgical consent because he fears certain complications may be reassured to learn that his fears are misplaced. The patient who fears that his nurses may not have time to watch him closely after an operation may be reassured to learn that he will be transferred to the intensive care unit after surgery. The acquisition of facts can change fear to relief. Felt emotions, then, signify much about the nature of situations, and move us to respond accordingly. In the terms of competence, we must be able to receive emotions, recognize them as relevant information, and remember their relationship to past states of affairs. Persons relate present and preferred states of affairs to their well-being by paying attention to felt emotions and identifying whether or not those are preferred. If present felt emotions are not desired, they motivate persons to change their circumstances so as to acquire preferred felt emotions.

The next category of feelings, cognitive emotions, differ from felt emotions primarily in their source. They are felt emotions produced by the search for knowledge or attempts at problem solving, and they indicate success or failure of these searches or attempts. We feel frustration when a solution eludes us, surprise or annoyance when our answers are wrong. We experience delight, satisfaction, or relief when we solve a problem. Cognitive emotions, as with other felt emotions, elicit particular sorts of action. Frustration, surprise, or annoyance stimulate further efforts to acquire adequate information; delight, satisfaction, or relief signal an end to problem-solving efforts.[41] In the terms of competence, cognitive emotions must also be received and recognized as relevant information. In addition, patients must also be able to remember the relationship of cognitive emotions to particular sorts of situations to recognize those that indicate decision-making success and failure.[42] Furthermore, cognitive emotions relate a person's present and preferred affective states, and motivate persons to reason about how best to achieve the latter when they are absent.

The third and final category of emotions as conveyers of knowledge contains expressions. Expressions of emotion carry knowledge of feelings, though the knower is not the feeler, but another. If a person displays fear, as manifest by wide eyes, quivering jaw, and pallor, other persons who encounter this expression are moved to inquire what is wrong. Expressions function as signals to others. Thus, the patient who displays signs of fear is telling HCPs that he needs help. Expressions, like the preceding affective states, should motivate perceivers to behave in certain ways—for example, to investigate the causes of, and ways to relieve, that fear.

So far, we have said that persons need to be aware of or receive their feelings, recognize that feelings carry valuable information about the situation in which they find themselves, and remember, during the process of making a decision, the feelings that attend it. In other words, a person must pay attention to felt and cognitive emotions. Where cognitive competence involved abilities to relate to and reason about alternatives, cognitive emotions indicate the extent to which cognitive competence has been successful. The feelings that accompany the decision-making process indicate how efficient cognition has been in identifying the best option, for one's present situation (including one's values and desires). Feelings of frustration, surprise, or annoyance indicate that further consideration is called for; feelings of delight, satisfaction, or relief signal that a good decision has been made. Expressions of emotion are public displays of one's progress.

In keeping with the analogy to cognitive competence, resolution and resigning oneself to one's choices continue to play a role on the affective side. Resolution does not mean that persons will always be happy about their situations or choices. They must, however, monitor the emotional responses that accompany their choices. The felt and cognitive emotions of satisfaction or resignation tell people that they have made the best choices, all things considered, and indicate that the decision-making process is complete. The felt and cognitive emotions can also indicate satisfaction with the ranking of one's options. Conversely, felt and cognitive emotions of frustration or dissatisfaction indicate that more effort is required.

Finally, the affectively competent person will be able to recount the affective process by which he arrived at his decision. That is, the affectively competent person will be able to indicate the role emotions played in his choice. Ideally a patient can retrace the progression of felt and cognitive emotions from the onset of the decision-making process to its completion; but at least, the patient must be able to state his final felt and cognitive emotions.

One last analysis is necessary to demonstrate the relevance of affect to competence to consent. All the preceding analogies between affective and cognitive data analyses would be irrelevant if affect contributed nothing to the person's well-being. Its contributions are, however, immense.

In attempting to understand the role of affect in promoting well-being, the concepts of "first-order" and "second-order" desires (Frankfurt, 1971) are helpful.[43] First-order desires are desires for something (e.g., the desire for a "hit" of cocaine). All sentient creatures have first-order desires (e.g., the desire for food). Second-order desires, or the desires to have (or not have) certain kinds of first-order desires (e.g., the second-order desire not to have the first-order desire to use cocaine), are present only in rational beings who have the ability to envision how their lives would be if they had different first-order desires, and who prefer that their lives be one way rather than another.

Most persons have a multitude of first-order desires, including the common first-order desire that their lives go as well as possible. This desire can only be realized if persons have some concept of what will make their lives go well or poorly. The "what" that makes a good life possible is the person's goals, values, and interests—that is, the "what" is a person's value structure.

Common first-order desires take certain general forms. In addition to the subsistence desires for security and sustenance, persons have first-order desires for activities, objects, or relationships. Activity desires include involvement in certain activities, such as desires to work, participate in hobbies, or see good movies. People also desire objects—art, jewels, cars, or chocolate, for example. Lastly, people desire relationships—family, friends, colleagues. These desires give rise to other first-order, qualitative, desires. Persons desire to practice their professions *well*, to accumulate *fine* paintings, to spend time with friends, and so forth. Finally, persons have first-order procedural desires that help them achieve their other first-order desires, for example, to keep up with professional reading to maintain professional competence. We must note that one special desire—the desire for decision-making authority—is usually both independently and instrumentally valuable. People value and desire decisional authority for itself and as a means to other desires.

What has all this to do with affective competence? Many emotions signify the compatibility or incompatibility of various first-order desires. People have so many first-order desires that on occasion they come into conflict. When we experience conflict, we have negative felt emotions, e.g., anger, frustration, dismay. Their emergence signals a problem in need of solution. Consider a student who desires never to leave his sick father alone at night. If this same student also desires to be a physician, conflict arises. The student, knowing that physicians must often be away from home in the evening, cannot reconcile these desires. Even specializing in a field where emergencies are rare cannot guarantee that none will arise. Not surprisingly, the student feels dismay, anger, and frustration.

The first step in resolving conflicting first-order desires is to see which desires are less congruous with one's value structure. Does the student value his father's security and peace of mind more than a career as a physician, or vice versa? In other words, is one first-order desire more compelling? Can one be eliminated altogether? Appealing to second-order desires allows people to evaluate conflicting first-order desires, select those that are most compatible with their value structures, and, thus, resolve dilemmas. If the student has as a second-order desire that he does not want any desires that compromise his commitment to his father, he will work to obliterate the desire for a medical career. Conflicts generate negative felt and cognitive emotions and signal the need for problem solving. Successful resolution generates positive felt and cognitive emotions (satisfaction or, perhaps, resignation). In short, emotions signal both the need for and the success or failure of decision-making efforts.

The relevance of affective competence to consent to health care is evident. Affectively competent patients can recognize incompatible first-order desires as an impediment to their well-being and, consequently, as the source of negative felt and cognitive emotions. This recognition can motivate them to revise or rank their desires in order to promote their welfare and restore affective harmony. Moreover, throughout the process, they can monitor their emotions to assess whether their actions are restoring first-order equilibrium. When negative cognitive emotions are replaced by positive or neutral feelings, the problem has been resolved. We should, however, acknowledge that certain negative felt (but not cognitive) emotions can persist as a response to one's rotten luck. For example, the would-be Olympic athlete may have a cognitive emotion of resignation to having surgery a week before tryouts, yet still be angry that the accident negates years of training and hope. Negative felt emotions can be a side effect of one's situation. Because felt emotions result from circumstances rather than inadequate decision making, negative felt emotions can peacefully co-exist with positive cognitive emotions (though probably not the reverse).

In addition to its use in motivating and indicating the success of problem solving, affect can be a useful indicator of decision-making incompetence. Patients who embrace incompatible desires generally experience cognitive dissonance and negative felt emotions. Those in whom incompatible desires fail to provoke negative responses are rightly suspected of failing to appreciate their situations. HCPs should investigate unexpected equanimity to ascertain if a reasonable explanation exists. If a sensible explanation is not forthcoming, the patient's level of information and understanding should be reassessed. Recall Ms. B, the patient who wanted to go on living, but also desired not to have surgery for her cervical cancer. Her equilibrium in the face of incompatible desires made it impossible for her to protect and promote her own well-being, and justified decision-making intervention by others. Their assistance enabled Mrs. B to invoke second-order desires to determine that her desire to live was stronger than her desire to retain her uterus. A consideration of the implications of these distinctions for professional practice and their applications to some cases should help clarify their role in the consent settings.

## Implications

Since HCPs routinely assume that their patients have the first-order desires for a long, healthy life, they are in good position to point out potential sources of negative cognitive emotions. When patients choose in ways that fail to take these desires seriously, or act in ways that fail to promote them, HCPs must point out the potential risks to their well-being. (Such choices are not always inappropriate, but they often are. As such they trigger suspicions of incompetence, and should be more fully investigated.) When HCPs take seriously their patients' cognitive and affective efforts, they encourage patients to receive and to recognize both facts and feelings as information. Clinicians should remind patients that affective as well as cognitive information participates in the decision-making process. Thus patients will remember all meaningful elements of their choices. As HCPs indicate probable outcomes, so they should emphasize that patients should examine how they will feel about different results; thus patients will be better able to relate information to themselves in terms of their personal value structures. As HCPs provide data on risks, burdens, and benefits, and on the relation of different choices to different prognoses, so should they remind patients that different results may provoke different feelings; thus patients can reason about the efficiency of their cognitive processes and their felt and cognitive emotions, and use the resulting "good reasons" to rank their choices.

Patients need to resolve their decision-making situations in terms of cognitive and affective data. Cognitively and affectively they will actually choose the best options; affectively they will resign themselves to and be motivated to pursue them. If resignation seems inappropriate, patients can be urged to move their considerations to the level of second-order desires, in order to determine which first-order desires are best retained and which are best abandoned. Lastly, HCPs may want to hear patients recount not only their cognitive but their affective processes, especially in cases where the patient's choice is worrisome. Recounting one's decision-making process gives clinicians another opportunity to correct misconceptions and, again, to point out potential sources of negative felt and cognitive emotions. Recounting can also serve to satisfy HCPs that a choice does actually promote a patient's well-being, partly because it is the choice about which the patient feels best. It also provides an opportunity for patients to demonstrate why their first-order desires are not incompatible. Consider some examples.

> *CASE VI:* Ms. F, a 46-year-old research chemist, has just been admitted to the hospital for a biopsy and frozen section of a lump in her left breast. Because both her mother and sister died during operative procedures (one during a mastectomy), she has an enormous fear of surgery and strongly wishes to avoid any operative procedure that is not required to save her life. She is apprehensive, not only about what the biopsy will reveal, but about the fact that her surgeon has recommended a modified radical mastectomy should the frozen section reveal a malignancy. The surgeon was clearly upset by her decision to consent only to a biopsy and a lumpectomy, although Ms. F indicated that following recovery from the procedure she plans to undergo radiation therapy if necessary.
>
> At the time of her decision, there are no five-year data comparing outcomes between the two approaches, but preliminary results suggest that they will not be radically disparate. However, her surgeon has had good results with modified radical mastectomies. He is not confident that radiation therapy will provide the same disease-free outcome. Ms. F understands this. She adds that, even were the outcomes significantly different, she would rather take her chances with radiation therapy than subject herself to the overwhelmingly frightening (to her) experience of mastectomy. She admits that many people would find her choice indefensible, but she is not bothered by that fact. She notes that it is her choice and she willingly accepts its consequences. She acknowledges her fear and is resigned to incorporating it into her decisions.
>
> *CASE VII:* Mr. G is a 42-year-old computer programmer who was brought against his will to the hospital. His mother admitted him with a high fever, intractable vomiting for two days, and a distended and rigid abdomen. A diagnosis of acute bowel obstruction is made. At the time of his admission, he is extremely depressed.

His wife had died ten days earlier from amyotrophic lateral sclerosis (Lou Gehrig's disease), and his only child had been killed eight months ago in a motorcycle accident. Since that time Mr. G, normally an active problem-solver for both his family and his community, has withdrawn from his usual professional and personal activities. He has told family and friends that life is no longer worth living, now that the two people dearest to him are dead. When told he must have surgery immediately to relieve the obstruction or he quite likely will die from a ruptured bowel followed by peritonitis, he refuses the surgery. His only other remark is that this illness will spare him the trouble of taking his own life.

*CASE VIII:* Ms. H is a 58-year-old gerontology nurse diagnosed with Dementia, Alzheimer's Type (DAT) She works at a large teaching hospital that has an active DAT research program. Many of her patients have participated in this program, and she is quite familiar with its procedures. She and the research personnel have mutual respect and affection for each other and their joint patients. Moreover, her normal ebullience, sunny disposition, and optimistic outlook have made her a favorite of her patients and their families. When her diagnosis is confirmed, she is offered an opportunity to enroll in a research protocol for a new drug which is the most promising to date for halting the progression of the disease. She is reminded of all the relevant information, including the projected prognosis and side effects. She then assesses her options. If she takes no treatment, she will continue to deteriorate; If she takes the experimental drug, she has an estimated 40 percent chance of longer survival with fewer symptoms.

Her cognitive assessment of the data is flawless and methodical—no doubt because she has assisted her patients many times in the same sort of analysis—but she is affectively detached from the procedure. Ultimately she decides to enroll in the experiment. She informs the research staff that she has no feelings one way or another but given that there is some chance of a longer and better life, that seems the reasonable thing to do. The researchers, given their personal as well as professional concerns about her, are pleased. They wonder, however, if she is competent. Since their other patients have enthusiastically embraced the protocol, the HCPs are concerned that Ms. H's lack of emotion might invalidate her consent.

The common salient feature of these situations is that they exemplify patients in decision-making situations where affective capacities have great import. In addition, each illustrates concerns that relate directly to affective competence. Ms. H seems not to be using her affective system at all, while Mr. G seems to be using his affective system exclusively; and Ms. F is, at least according to her surgeon, using hers excessively. Such cases raise two key questions: (1) Is it ever permissible to completely shut out the affective system? and (2) Is it ever permissible to completely shut out the cognitive system?

A purely cognitive approach to decision making might be defensible. Since most people do prefer life to death, health to illness, and pain to pleasure, options that maximize life and health and minimize pain are to be preferred, other things being equal. Such options would be "rational" choices, but other things are never equal. Because patients have unique value structures, they consider factors and evaluate options differently. As a result, it might be impossible to defend the "rational" choice as best for any particular patient. Therefore, in spite of our intellectual appreciation of rational patients, real patients like Ms. H worry us. People who have no feelings about their care raise concerns that their affective systems are malfunctioning. In truth, total absence of affect often triggers suspicions that patients are not competent.

What are we to make of a total absence of affective response? There are two possible explanations. Perhaps the patient has felt and cognitive emotions, but is masking them. This possibility is easy enough to ascertain: ask the patient what he is feeling. If he reports felt and cognitive emotions, HCPs can conclude that he is suppressing their expression but is nonetheless affectively involved. That involvement can then be evaluated. On the other hand, perhaps the patient actually has no felt or cognitive emotions. Again, one can ascertain this possibility by asking, but how can a negative response be interpreted? The question is important because some people keep their emotions under such rigid control that they do not consciously intrude into decision making. The crucial question is, are such people competent? The answer is, yes and no.

There certainly are unemotional people in the world, persons who never let feelings get in the way. The quintessential rational person does not express emotions because he does not allow himself to experience them. If this is his typical pattern of behavior, he is competent. That the person is very much and very typically "in control" and moving ahead with decision making testifies to the involvement of at least part of the affective system, namely, the motivation to resolve the problem at hand. In such cases, patients either have no incompatible first-order desires, or have appealed to second-order desires to resolve the incompatibility. Moreover, the person who has always squelched (or discounted) emotions cannot be expected to change under duress. Stress often precludes any response other than those which are habitual. We should be able to ascertain if the unemotional approach is typical by asking the person. To override a person's typical response fails to respect him.

On the other hand, a person who usually both perceives and attends to his emotions but in a particular situation is doing neither, is not competent. First, the person is operating without important relevant information. As we would not accept a person's decision if he did not have the relevant cognitive facts, so we cannot accept a person's decision if he does not have the relevant affective facts because he is omitting a normal aspect of his decision-making system. If he does not know how he feels now, he is not fully informed. He cannot say if he has first-order incompatibility that requires resolution. Second, in such cases it is not possible to fully inform the patient. If the patient has shut himself off from certain sorts of information—namely, how he feels about his current predicament—he is incapable of even beginning the process of competent decision making because he cannot receive important information. Third, while appearing "in control" the person is, in fact, out of control. Instead of giving customary attention to his feelings, he has cut himself off from an important source of information. His typical response has been overridden. Letting a patient make decisions without the evaluations he normally considers important and worthy of attention permits him to go astray from the structuring or restructuring of his life plans. To accept his decision under such circumstances is to run the risk of honoring a choice that will not promote his well-being; it fails to respect him by permitting him to make an inautonomous decision. Thus, to determine Ms. F's and Ms. H's competence requires some history about their usual decision-making methods.

Thus, the person who shows too much reason or not enough emotion may be competent if that approach is habitual, but incompetent if such an approach is atypical. Total absence of affective expression is only superficially problematic; total absence of affective ability will make one incompetent to consent. This observation leads us to wonder about the reverse: is the person who displays too much affect or not enough reason competent?

To begin, strong emotions do not, in and of themselves, signify incompetence. As we have seen, strong emotions can be powerful signals that incompatible first-order desires are impeding efforts to promote or protect one's well-being. Thus, the worry is not that strong emotions exist, but that they may completely overpower the cognitive system. What should be said about unusually strong emotional responses? Four answers come to mind: One, the patient is competent, even though her dramatic emotional expressions suggest otherwise. Two, the patient is incompetent, because her emotions are impeding the cognitive process, but she is attempting to regain cognitive control. Three, the patient earlier made an autonomous choice to renounce cognitive attempts and just go along with her feelings. Four, the patient can control neither the cognitive nor the affective process, and the loss of control is not intentional. Questioning the patient should clarify which description applies. But what do the different replies mean?

In fact, an appeal to second-order desires allows us to diagnose competence in the first category and incompetence in the second and fourth. In the second category, emotion has overpowered cognition, and absence of cognitive ability justifies a diagnosis of incompetence. In the fourth category, the absence of second-order desires to regain control indicates that the patient has lost at least some of the abilities that competence to consent requires—specifically, the capacity to reason about the values that provide the rationale for choices. But we still must consider whether the third patient, who has chosen to consider only affective data, is competent to consent. Such cases are important because there are people who make important decisions by responding to their "gut level feelings." [44] Again, the crucial question is, are such people competent? And, again, the answer is, yes and no.

There surely are emotional decision makers, those who count on their feelings to point the way. As with the paradigmatic rational person, so with the paradigmatic emotional person: If the person typically behaves this way, she is competent to consent, and for the same reasons. Although the person seems to be out of control, going with her feelings is, in fact, a technique that she has previously adopted as part of her decision-making style. We can ascertain if the emotional approach is customary, by asking the person. Moreover, we can inquire about second-order desires. Is there a second-order desire to attend only to affect? If so, the person may be able to indicate that in times of stress she puts cognition "on hold" and, as such, is acting in character. The emotional decision maker cannot be expected, under stress, to suddenly become a cognitive chooser. Her typical approach is to feel rather than reason, a fact that is unsettling to her HCPs, but not out of the ordinary. In times of stress habitual responses are often more reliable. So long as she is moving ahead with the decision-making process (here, resolving the problem at hand by appealing to feelings), she is competent for her. To override a *typical* affective response fails to respect persons, just as if one had overridden a *typical* cognitive response.

On the other hand, a person who usually perceives and attends to cognitive facts but in a particular situation is doing neither is not competent. First, he is operating without complete information. We would not accept a person's decision if he had none of the affective facts. Similarly, we cannot accept a person's decision if he has none of the cognitive facts, because he is ignoring a key factor that is normally an aspect of his decision-making system (unless he can explicitly appeal to a second-order desire to eschew cognitive consideration of this situation). If he does not know what he thinks now, he is not adequately informed. Second, in such cases it is not possible to adequately inform the patient. If the patient has shut himself off from certain sorts of information—namely, what he thinks—he is incapable of even beginning the process of competent decision making because he cannot receive information. Third, in such cases a person is out of control. Instead of giving attention to rational analysis, as he usually does, he is cutting himself off from an important source of information. His typical response has been inhibited. To permit him to make decisions without the advice he would normally consider permits him to make inautonomous choices that may cause him harm. To accept his decision under such circumstances is to run the risk of honoring a choice that will not, because based on incomplete information, promote his well-being. As such, this is failing to respect him as a person by permitting what is, for him, incompetent behavior.

The person who shows too much affect or not enough reason is competent if that approach is habitual, but incompetent if the approach is atypical. Total absence of cognitive ability will make one incompetent to consent.

Like it or not, affective components must be incorporated into decision making. Moreover, a dual analysis of competence allows us to make sense of the different evaluations regarding the cases of Ms. F (who, because of her fear of surgery, is refusing a radical mastectomy), Mr. G (who, because he considers his life is no longer worth living, is refusing resection of his acute bowel obstruction), and Ms. H (who has no strong feelings about entering a research protocol with a very real chance to halt the progression of Alzheimer's Disease). Ms. F demonstrates the cognitive capacities that competence requires. She can receive data about her options (mastectomy vs. radiation), recognize their relevance, and relate them to her future well-being. She understands that the HCPs are less certain her choice will cure the cancer. She can reason about the different prognoses and rank the options. (Following her assessment of burdens and benefits of surgery vs. radiation and her willingness to risk not having the mastectomy, she indicates that she is willing to assume the burden of reduced certainty in return for the benefit of its being a nonsurgical option.) She has resolved her situation and has recounted the reasons for her choice. In addition to Ms. F's cognitive competence, she is affectively competent. She has received and recognized relevant affective data. She remembers her long-standing fear of surgery, relates it to her present situation, and reasons about it. The fear provides the rationale for preferring radiation, and her affective preferences enable her to rank her options and justify her decision to herself and to others. Affective facts (fear), coupled with cognitive facts (e.g., preliminary results suggest radiation will not produce markedly worse outcomes) provide her with valuable information that motivates her to choose radiation therapy over a mastectomy.

In terms of desires we may describe Ms. F as having at least four first-order desires: the desire to promote her own welfare, the desire to minimize her fear, the desire not to have surgery, and the desire to have radiation therapy. In addition, she has a second-order desire: the desire to act as directed by her fear. This second-order desire both justifies her choice and indicates why there is no first-order incompatibility. She could ignore or override her fear, but she sees it as an important indicator both of what she values—psychological and physical well-being—and of the appropriate means—no surgery—by which to maximize those values. The psychological cost of ignoring her fear of and desire to avoid surgery are not outweighed by the potential benefits of doing so. Consequently, she does not see acting in concert with the fear as failing to promote her own welfare. Since the five-year mortality rates do not indicate that she is clearly wrong about this, there is no good reason to dispute her assessment. Since her first-order desires are not swamping her capacity for second-order desires, and since she cognitively and affectively accepts her first-order desires, her first- and second-order desires are compatible. Her cognitive emotion of satisfaction with her choice is appropriate. In short, she is dually competent and her choice should be respected.

HCPs may find the discussion of Ms. F unsatisfying, especially since Ms. F demonstrates a common decision-making dilemma. Patients often choose on the basis of unshared or idiosyncratic values or goals. If their choices are sufficiently troubling, their competence may be questioned. In attempting (usually by way of a psychiatric consult) to determine if the patient is able to make decisions, the primary issue is whether the patient knows what he is doing. In the process of evaluating worrisome patients, HCPs generally seek evidence that patients appreciate how likely it is that their choices will promote their own well-being, and that their choices make sense in terms of their desires, goals, and interests. But this is just another way of saying that no incompatibility exists between first-order or between first- and second-order desires. As long as patients are able to relate their choices to their well-being, and there is no first-order incompatibility that is willfully being ignored, the concerns about competence are assuaged (though HCPs may still think the choice is a bad one).

Now, what about Mr. G (who, because he considers his life no longer worth living, is refusing resection of his acute bowel obstruction)? In avoiding the use of reason, Mr. G may be competent if—*but only if*—this avoidance is habitual. However, given what we know about the emotional impact of death, his refusal bears further investigation. If he normally appeals to reason alone, or to both reason and emotion, he is presently incompetent because he is not receiving all pertinent information.

We may describe Mr. G as having at least three first-order desires: the desire to promote his own welfare, the desire to die, and the desire not to have surgery. Unlike Ms. F, Mr. G has no second-order desires that justify his choice and indicate the absence of first-order incompatibility. True, if refusing surgery does promote his death and, thereby, his welfare, there is no first-order incompatibility, but his cognitive inactivity suggests that there has been no analysis to this effect. Affective responses that are cognitively incapacitating provide good reason to question his competence. If he is not dually competent, his cognitive emotion of resignation is inappropriate, and his choice should not be honored.

Mr. G could refute a claim of incompetence in three ways. He could demonstrate that there never was any first-order incompatibility, that he has already resolved any first-order incompatibility, or that his second-order desires require him to choose affectively. He could demonstrate that he has resolved the incompatibility by choosing to have the surgery. In that case his seemingly incompatible desires—to promote his own welfare and to avoid surgery—are resolved by appealing to a second-order desire that resolves the conflict. Since he has not done this, we need to consider his other options. A decision to choose affectively might be better accepted if this is his traditional decision-making approach. Since it is not, it triggers further investigation. If he explicitly invoked a second-order desire to this effect, he could be competent. Again, since this is not what he is doing, we are left with the most troubling option. Mr. G is claiming that he has abandoned the desire for a long healthy life and no longer desires to live at all. His desire for nontreatment is compatible with his other desires.

Mr. G's first-order desires admit two possible interpretations. First, he has autonomously reconsidered his values and goals and, on the basis of those considerations, has revised his value structure. If—and it is a big if—he has autonomously renounced his previous goals, values, and interests, or has autonomously determined that they will be impossible to realize, because of his personal tragedy, then his decision to forgo treatment is his (and quite possibly his last) autonomous choice and must be respected. His history suggests, however, that there was no autonomous reconsideration, but rather that his capacity for cognitive consideration of his goals, values, and interests has been overpowered by a depression. His overwhelming sadness in response to his personal tragedy has precluded his normal, cognitive approach, and his ability to appeal to second-order desires has been swamped by circumstances. As such, he cannot adjudicate between his previous autonomously adopted values and his changed circumstances. He is motivated by negative felt emotions that he has not, because he is not able to, cognitively considered and by values that he has not autonomously chosen. As such, he is incompetent.

Ms. H (who has no strong feelings about entering a research protocol with a very real chance to halt the progression of Alzheimer's Disease) raises similar worries, not because she is noncognitive, but because she is, quite literally, unaffected. In suppressing her feelings, she is competent only if this is her usual approach and either there is no first-order desire incompatibility or she has resolved it with appropriate second-order desires. However, based on what we know about responses to traumatic diagnoses, her consent bears further investigation. If she normally appeals to emotion alone or to reason and emotion, she is presently incompetent because not fully informed. Let us assume that she does normally appeal to both reason and emotion, and see if this particular choice is competent.

Ms. H has at least three first-order desires: the desire to promote her own welfare, the desire to take advantage of the experimental protocol, and the desire to suppress her emotions. If her choice is competent, Ms. H should have a second-order desire that justifies her choice and indicates the absence of first-order incompatibility. That second-order desire could take many forms, but would likely be a desire that, in this case she wishes explicitly to give no voice to her feelings. She may have many reasons for doing this. One of the more common is that giving any attention to emotions puts one at risk of being swamped by them. If this is so, then the desires to promote her welfare and to ignore her emotions are not incompatible. In this instance, they work together to promote her welfare and there is no good reason to force her emotional involvement or to dispute her choice. Because she is using reason to control emotion, she is dually competent. It is not that she has no felt emotions, but that she is consciously suppressing their expression. Just like Mr. G, Ms. H could demonstrate her competence in three ways. She could demonstrate that there actually is no first-order incompatibility, that she has already resolved any incompatibility, or that she has made a second-order decision to choose cognitively. The description just given could apply to both the first and third options. Her efforts to control her emotions do function to promote her welfare by promoting her compatible desires.

Including noncognitive aspects in the decision-making process is imperative. Such states as fear, anxiety, depression, pain, fatigue—all present to some degree in illness—have been thought to inhibit cognition. Therefore, many patients will have some reduction in cognitive function. If competence correlates only with cognitive functioning, the noxious circumstances under which many patients are evaluated will undoubtedly result in many of them being inappropriately labelled incompetent. And this mistake will occur in situations where those same factors—i.e., felt and cognitive emotions—are legitimate sources of input that ought to be factored into any decision about further treatment. The recognition that the affective components of competence can compensate for cognitive deficits serves to mitigate concerns regarding cognitive slack, so long as cognition is not entirely absent.

Thus we find that the correct definition is:

P is C to $D_n$ for this T if P possesses to $D_n$ the requisite cognitive and affective capacities for decision making (i.e., if P can to $D_n$ acquire cognitive and affective information about options, cognitively and affectively consider their probabilities of achieving chosen aims, choose on the basis of those considerations, and recount the cognitive and affective decision-making processes).

### Summary

We find that persons worthy of respect are persons who reason, to be sure, but who also experience and express their feelings. This being so, we understand that, while cognitive capacities are necessary, they are not sufficient. Just as acting from emotion without the benefit of reason is usually inappropriate, so acting from reason without counsel from affect is usually unacceptable. In addition, because we respect persons in virtue of all their capacities, affective as well as cognitive, we insist that both systems be recognized in competence assessments. Both can be more or less functional, but both must be present to some extent for a person to be considered competent.

### SUMMARY

Where does this leave us with regard to the concept of competence? Are we better off, or worse, after considering all the above? Probably both, for although our understanding of the concept of competence to consent is richer, the problems of incorporating all four components has enormously expanded the difficulties surrounding its application. Yet because each addresses an aspect of competence that the others leave untouched, a complete conceptual analysis of competence cannot afford to omit any of the options. A brief review should make this clear.

First, competence has been determined to be a specific notion. General assessments of competence may provide evidence as to what a person has been like in the past. As such, they give HCPs a rough standard against which to compare the patient's current behavior, and may trigger suspicions of incompetence if current behavior deviates greatly from past decision-making approaches. But competence to consent must be determined from the point of view of a particular situation because this approach best protects and promotes autonomy and beneficence. The practice of informed consent, which was established to protect these values, requires that a patient be competent for a *particular* decision. This tells us that *the context* for competence is *particular decision-making situations*. Thus we get:

P is C for *this* decision.

Second, competence is a matter of degree. DC better protects autonomy, beneficence, and decisional authority. Because people can be more or less competent, and because TC is both artificial and practically impossible to implement, attempts to define competence in terms of a threshold are misdirected. This tells us that the standard—that is, the capacities required for competence—can be present to varying degrees. Thus, the definition evolves to:

P is C *to* $D_n$ for *this* decision.

While the capacities for competence are variably present, there is a strong argument for omitting consequences from the logic of competence. Competence does not vary in terms of consequences, because such appeals stand in opposition to respecting persons' idiosyncratic or potentially tragic choices. Since competence is consequence-independent, the considerations of CIC vs. CDC do not change the definition.

Finally, both cognitive and affective capacities are necessarily included in competence. The arguments of the last section made clear that both are integral to evaluations of competence that respect patients' autonomous choices and promote their well-being. This dual conception has significant implications, since affective components have not traditionally played a positive role in competence assessments. Thus the final definition is:

P is C to $D_n$ for this T because P possesses to $D_n$ the requisite cognitive and affective capacities for decision making (i.e., P can to $D_n$ acquire cognitive and affective information about options, cognitively and affectively consider their probabilities of achieving chosen aims, choose on the basis of those considerations, and recount the cognitive and affective decision-making processes).

Competence is much more complex than has been previously recognized, and what has been thought to be a single-faceted issue is now seen to be multifaceted. We turn now to justifying the individual capacities that define competence to consent.

## NOTES

1. If decisions that fail to conform to one's value structure or promote one's own best interests are not to count as evidence of incompetence, they should be fairly infrequent. When persons regularly make choices that are at odds with their stated values or work against their own well-being, something is amiss. Perhaps the person has changed her value structure or revised her interests, but such decisions are at least cause for further investigation of the person's decision-making process. For further discussion about the relation of "bad" choices to competence and rationality, see Culver and Gert, 1982, especially Chapter Three.

2. See, for example, Appelbaum and Grisso, 1988; Buchanan, 1985; Buchanan and Brock, 1986, 1989; Carnerie, 1987; Culver and Gert, 1982; Morreim, 1991; and Pincoffs, 1991.

3. Abernethy refers to "global" rather than "general" competence. Although I believe she and I use these different terms to mean the same thing, I worry that "global" might be interpreted to mean "completely" or "always" competent. Since by "generally competent" I mean "usually competent" or "competent as a general rule," I have chosen to speak of "general" rather than "global" competence.

4. One can simultaneously be generally competent and an incompetent decision maker, so long as one's everyday life includes very little decision making. One example might be a moderately mentally retarded worker whose job requires only that he repeat a particular task (e.g., tying straws in a broom). He is competent to complete most daily activities, including the rote task his job requires, without being competent to make decisions.

5. If decision-making competence refers to historical decision-making abilities, a person's inability to decide under present conditions would not count against his competence. If the four criteria have usually been met in the past, a person is considered competent even when he appears to be incapable of choosing here and now. On this interpretation historical abilities transfer to the present, even though the necessary capacities are not now present (or are present but diminished). However a person can also be a generally competent

decision maker if he is able to make most of the decisions facing him at a particular time. Current decision-making competence need not say anything about past decision-making performance. On this interpretation historical abilities would provide evidence of what we may expect a person to be able to do, but would not count toward an assessment of his current competence.

We do not have to settle this issue now. As will be shown, competence applies to particular situations. As such, a patient's history is germane in that it provides a yardstick against which to compare his current abilities. Thus, HCPs should not be surprised (nor overly dismayed and concerned) when a patient who has been chronically unable to make decisions cannot make the one he now faces. On the other hand, patients who have not been but are now incapacitated warrant further investigation to determine the cause of current deficits and to correct or compensate for them, if possible.

6. Some specific consents must be less precise. Advance directives (e.g., natural death acts, living wills, or Durable Powers of Attorney for Health Care) must omit reference to particular practitioners, places, and times. They may or may not omit reference to particular treatments (e.g., "No CPR"), though presumably they will designate particular conditions (e.g., being terminally ill, or that death be imminent). See also Hackler et al., 1989.

7. Of course, if the decision need not be made immediately, that one will be informable at a later date is not only relevant but important for determining *when* the decision should be made. Carnerie (1987) gives an excellent argument for delayed decision making, especially for patients with chronic or recurring illness.

8. In truth this position is less pure than it may appear. Persons who have been competent but are no longer are not usually allowed decision-making freedom. They would probably not, for example, be allowed to handle their financial affairs or enter into contracts. Persons who anticipate their future incompetence may instruct others regarding their wishes as to how their affairs are to be managed, either through a durable power of attorney for health care or, in a more limited way, through a Ulysses contract (cf. Dresser, 1984). These mechanisms are not the same thing, however, as being allowed to make decisions at the time of incompetence.

9. Various accounts of why this would is so are in Abernethy, 1991; Buchanan, 1978; Buchanan, 1985; Baumgarten, 1980; Capron, 1974; Dresser, 1986; Lesser, 1983; Morreim, 1991; Mayo, 1986; Rennie, 1980; and Rosoff and Gottlieb, 1987. Hahn (1982) notes that assuming a "patient knows best" stance is the best way to assure that particular cultural backgrounds and biases are admitted to decision contexts.

10. One might wonder whether the value structure itself must be rational for the person to command respect. Speaking theoretically, one can make sense of an autonomous person autonomously adopting a nonrational value structure—that is, a set of values, goals, and interests for which there

are no (or very few) compelling reasons that command intersubjective support, as well as beliefs about which there is no or little intersubjective agreement. (Note that a nonrational value structure is not an irrational value structure [i.e., one in which the person sacrifices her own well-being without good reason].) I might, for example, autonomously choose to believe in Martians or Rigelians in the same way that others choose to believe in God. In addition, I might value harmonious relations with Martians and Rigelians and have intergalactic peace as a goal, and I might act autonomously on that belief from time to time. For example, I might take out newspaper advertisements encouraging people to plan for the arrival of Martians and urge that when they appear that they be treated courteously.

In theory, this value structure is no less bizarre than most religious sects. So there is no in-principle reason not to honor it. In practice, however, nonrational value structures are more worrisome. The patient who refuses surgery so as not to exhaust health care services that may be needed by Martians in the event of their crash landing appropriately triggers the suspicions of his HCPs that he may not be (fully) competent. Should examinations determine that he is competent, consistency demands that his wishes be respected. (See in this regard Freedman's discussion (1981) about "relevant reasons.") As a matter of fact, genuinely nonrational beliefs are often accompanied by cognitive or affective impairments that themselves demand the transfer of decision-making authority to a surrogate.

11. Regarding the importance of freedom to undertake risky behaviors, see Buchanan and Brock, 1986, 1989; Eth, 1985; Mill, 1982; Pincoffs, 1991; Sen, 1986; and Wikler, 1979. Moreover, some persons believe that controlling one's own life is intrinsically valuable, independent of any assessment of consequences.

12. Of course, whatever action one undertakes in attempting to respect a particular person in a particular situation, one must recognize that one is acting on a probabilistic best guess. The best estimates may be beset by bad luck, while the worst estimates may, through sheer good fortune, succeed in protecting a person's self-stated goals and interests. This possibility ought to make HCPs especially wary of imposing their own demands on patients who have strong conflicting preferences.

13. Surrogate decision makers can acquire that status formally or informally. If formally, the surrogate decision maker is appointed by the courts and the appointment carries such legal rights and responsibilities as the decision specifies. More commonly in the health care setting, family members step in when patients are unable to make their own decisions. The assumption is that family members best know the patient's values and will act to protect and promote them. They are presumed to be most likely and best able to decide as the patient himself would and, so, best able to function as surrogate decision maker.

Any or all of these assumptions may be erroneous in particular cases. The nuclear family with shared values is considerably less common than in previous times. Nonetheless, to rely on the already overburdened judicial system to assume decision-making responsibility for patients whose inabilities may be minimal, intermittent, or brief would be so burdensome that the informal method, while not unproblematic and without risk, seems preferable. For further discussions of surrogate decision making, see Appelbaum et al., 1987; Buchanan and Brock, 1986, 1989; Pellegrino, 1991; and The President's Commission, 1982b.

**14.** For any decision persons are competent to a particular degree. Because they may possess different degrees of the required capacities for different situations, they may be competent to different degrees for different tasks or for different decisions.

**15.** A degree definition of competence is compatible with a general notion of competence. One can envision persons who are, on a degree definition, 100 percent incompetent (e.g., the permanently comatose). While there could be, at least in theory, persons who are always 100 percent competent, these are somewhat harder to imagine. As common sense attests, persons are likely to be more or less competent decision makers, depending on the person and the decision. At any rate, if people are more or less competent for given decisions, they can be generally competent so long as they are more competent than not for most decisions. Conversely, if they are generally incompetent, they are less competent than not for most decisions. The notion of generally competent but to varying degrees for particular decisions is a fair description of most autonomous persons.

**16.** Beauchamp, 1991; Beauchamp and McCullough, 1984; Buchanan, 1985; Green, 1941; and Wikler, 1979 discuss thresholds as convenient fictions for designating genuine competence.

**17.** One might wonder whether CDC would make mandatory any or all expensive care in patients with terminal illnesses or, conversely, forbid it because it threatens the financial welfare of one's survivors. More radically, might CDC require euthanasia as a means of maximizing good financial outcomes? Cost-benefit analyses play an important role in evaluating health care, especially publicly funded health care. As long as funding is limited, not all medically useful care can be provided. As a result, policies will likely incorporate costs and benefits in an attempt to get the most bang for the public buck. Care that costs much while benefitting little (or few) will, other things being equal, be eschewed in favor of care that costs less and benefits more. In any case, since policy consequential analyses precede assessments of competence, care with negative cost-benefit ratios may not be available to patients, competent or otherwise, whose care is publicly funded. Determinations of cost-efficacy apply to policy, not personal, decision making. (I am grateful to Edmund Erde for drawing this issue to my attention.)

**18.** Edmund Erde, following Freedman, argues that these particular differences need not thwart autonomous decision making so long as patients give "recognizable reasons" for their choices. Such reasons may not persuade persons with different beliefs or values, but nonetheless would be recognized even by those persons as relevant to the decision at hand (Erde, 1991, pp. 241–243). Thus, even those who do not share the belief that one is "polluted" by accepting a blood transfusion from another person recognize the relevance of this belief for the Jehovah's Witness.

**19.** I cannot do justice here to the role of competing values in decision-making contexts. For further discussion of this important issue, and suggestions regarding adjudication of noncommensurate, competing values, see Abernethy, 1991; Beauchamp, 1991; Brody, 1982, 1988; In re Brophy, 1986; Buchanan, 1985; Buchanan and Brock, 1986, 1989; Caplan, 1988; Carnerie, 1987; Drane, 1984, 1985; Dresser, 1984; Gaylin, 1982; Mayo, 1986; Miller and Germain, 1988; Moutsopoulos, 1984; National Conference of Commissioners on Uniform State Laws, 1982; Pavlo et al., 1987; Pellegrino, 1991; Robertson, 1991; Roth et al., 1977; Sen, 1982, 1986; Sherlock, 1983; U.S. Law Week, 1984; and Wikler, 1979.

**20.** Note that doing something to a person is not necessarily the same thing as doing something for a person. The former implies a manipulation. The latter implies providing a benefit. Clinicians often do things to patients that do not provide benefits—especially when viewed from the perspective of the patient's own value structure.

**21.** In fact patients' specific and clearly articulated preferences or instructions are commonly ignored (Appelbaum and Roth, 1983, 1984; Buchanan and Brock, 1986; Caplan, 1988; Lesser, 1983; Robertson, 1991; Roth et al., 1982a; and Sherlock, 1983), especially when the patient makes a choice with which his HCPs disagree (Abernethy, 1991; Buchanan and Brock, 1986, 1989; Burch and Andrews, 1987; Eth, 1985; Robertson, 1991; and Roth et al., 1977).

**22.** In spite of a host of theoretical and logistical problems, appeals to consequences in competence assessment continue to attract wide support. See, for example, Appelbaum and Roth, 1983; Buchanan, 1985; Buchanan and Brock, 1986, 1989; Drane 1984, 1985; Gaylin, 1982; Green, 1941; Owens et al., 1987; Pavlo et al, 1987; President's Commission, 1982a; Roth et al., 1977; and Wikler, 1979.

**23.** See, again, Erde, 1991, and Freedman, 1981.

**24.** The exception to this claim could be false positive or false negative determinations of competence. The incompetent patient who has been falsely labelled competent is thrust into a decision-making role for which he is ill-suited. Insofar as he is unable to reliably protect his values, goals, and interests, he is at risk for harm of varying degrees. The more serious the deliberation, the greater the risk of harm. Similarly, the competent patient who has been falsely labelled incompetent is precluded from making decisions for which he is best suited. Insofar as his surrogate decision makers fail to incorporate his values into health care decisions he is also at risk of harm, including the additional harm of having his decision-making authority usurped. Assuming a competent patient will fight to regain his rightful decision-making authority, he may be at less risk because he may be able to convince others that the label of incompetence is a false one, thus overturning it and regaining decisional control.

25. Lezak, 1983, p. 12ff.

26. The claim that cognition and affect are symbiotic is supported in Appelbaum and Roth, 1981; Beauchamp, 1991; Buchanan and Brock, 1986, 1989; Callahan, 1988; Capron, 1974; Carnerie, 1987; Drane, 1984; Folstein et al., 1975; Hart et al., 1987; Hinton and Withers, 1971; Jacobs, et al., 1977; Katz, 1984; Keller and Manschreck, 1979; Lesser, 1983; McCartney, 1986; Robertson, 1991; Sherlock, 1983; and Wear, 1991.

27. The effects of emotion on cognition are extensively documented. For representative discussions see Appelbaum and Roth, 1981; Brand and Jolles, 1987; Buchanan and Brock, 1986, 1989; Callahan, 1988; Carnerie, 1987; Folstein et al., 1975; Hahn, 1982; and Wear, 1991. Early studies on informed consent discovered that the stresses of illness and of the foreign hospital environment sometimes left patients who had no history of cognitive impairment with a drastically reduced ability to absorb the information necessary for giving consent (Katz, 1977; Ingelfinger, 1972; Lankton et al., 1977). Subsequent studies have suggested that stress can be compensated for if not overcome, making this less problematic than was first thought to be the case (cf. Carnerie, 1987; Leeb et al., 1976; and Katz, 1984, Chapter 5).

28. See Abernethy, 1991; Callahan, 1988; Carnerie, 1987; Drane, 1984; Faden et al., 1987; Ingelfinger, 1972; Leeb et al., 1976; and Lesser, 1983 for discussions of the role of affect in competent decision making.

29. There is a practical reason for preferring a cognitive definition: cognitive function is more easily assessed (measured). When a patient repeatedly misreports the date, the error is obvious. It is much harder to determine that someone's feelings are erroneous.

30. See especially Aristotle's *De Anima*, Book III, Chapters 10 and 11, where he describes the unique nature of humans in terms of their mental capacities, as well as this passage from the *Nichomachean Ethics*:

> . . . we are seeking what is peculiar to man. Let us exclude, therefore, the life of nutrition and growth. Next there would be a life of perception, but it also seems to be common even to the horse, the ox, and every animal. There remains . . . an active life of the element that has a rational principle. . . . Now we state the function of man to be a certain kind of life, and this to be an activity or actions of the soul implying a rational principle. . . (1098a, 1–15).

31. A contemporary account of what the world in general and morality in particular looks like from an impartial point of view can be found in Nagel, 1986. Implications for morality are discussed in Chapter 9.

**32.** It is impossible to do full justice to the works of Kant. Many scholars have devoted a lifetime to the analysis of his *Critique of Pure Reason*. The *Critique of Practical Reason* and the *Foundations of the Metaphysics of Morals* are somewhat more accessible to the lay reader, but still require careful attention.

**33.** For another contemporary account of respect based on rationality, see Michael Tooley's *Abortion and Infanticide* (1983, especially pp. 123–146). Although less straightforwardly rationalist, Tooley's account depends heavily on cognitive abilities and does not depend in any obvious way on affective abilities. On this account respect requires a person to have sometime had a concept of herself as a continuing entity. Tooley's argument, very briefly, is this: persons are bearers of rights; rights presuppose interests that the rights protect (i.e., the purpose of rights is to protect interests). Interests depend on desires (i.e., it is in one's interests to have one's desires satisfied); and desires are indications of what one wants in the future. Thus, for desires to make any sense at all requires one to understand that she will be around in the future and will be the same person then who is now having the desire. But that is just to say, that she must have a concept of herself as a continuing entity.

**34.** It is also impossible to do justice here to the richness of Engelhardt's position. For his discussion of the origin of respect for persons, see *The Foundations of Bioethics*, Chapters 3 and 4.

**35.** Interestingly, Engelhardt demonstrates that respect translates to honoring the autonomous choices of rational beings, and that these choices can vary dramatically in content. The exceptionless values and rules Kant thought reason would identify give way to a pluralism that he would be loathe to embrace.

**36.** Some worry that if HCPs recommend a particular option over others a patient might be subtly coerced by that recommendation. Upon hearing what HCPs endorse, patients may feel they have no choice but to choose according to the professionals' advice. While this may be true in some cases, part of giving the patient full information is giving one's own considered judgment about the best way to proceed. After all, professional expertise includes experience in problem solving, and a patient in a consent setting has a problem to be solved. One would not want to present a recommendation as the only or even as necessarily the best solution without explaining why one makes such a strong claim. Nor should one badger a patient into "accepting" a recommendation. Nonetheless, to withhold one's advice omits important information (c.f. Lidz et al., 1983, and Meisel and Roth, 1981).

**37.** In theory a patient could have, but be unable to recount, good reasons for his decision. This issue has more theoretical than practical interest, for if the patient could not communicate either his reasons or the process by which he came to his decision, how could anyone know either that the reasons existed, that they were good, or that the process was satisfactory? Of course the person might later be able to provide this information, but that would not help evaluate his competence at the time it is in question. Therefore, the inability to communicate these facts calls competence into question.

Even if the patient's competence is not suspect, HCPs are likely to want to hear a recounting if the patient is soliciting their cooperation for an odd or especially risky choice. Although democratic societies often defend persons' rights to share information only when they desire to do so, persons who require the assistance of others are well advised to offer an explanation or, at least, to indicate why they do not want to provide an account. Of course patients have a right to refuse to explain their decision-making processes, but those who exercise this right should not be surprised if help is not forthcoming. We recall that we need not honor even autonomous choices if they place others at risk of harm. HCPs who are concerned that harm may ensue have the right to refuse to participate if no good reasons are given that illustrate a professional responsibility to assist.

**38.** Perkins is not unique in claiming that feelings carry information. The same position is advocated by de Souza, 1980, pp. 130ff; Rorty, 1980b, p. 5; Gelatt, 1989, pp. 254–255; and Callahan, 1988, pp. 12–13.

**39.** Correlations between feelings and motivation are addressed in Perkins (1981, pp. 114–121). See also Gaylin, 1979, p. 7; Frank, 1988, pp. 52ff; Rorty, 1980a, pp. 105–107; de Souza,1980, pp. 134ff; Callahan, 1988, pp. 10–11; and Solomon, 1976, pp. 246ff. In the classical philosophical literature, the eighteenth-century Scottish philosopher, David Hume, gives a wonderful account in *A Treatise on Human Nature* (1977) where he claims: "Reason is, and ought only to be, the slave of the passions [feelings], and can never pretend to any other office than to serve and obey them" (pp. 127ff). By this he meant that passions alone move people to act; reason only identifies the most expeditious means to achieve desired goals.

**40.** See Rorty (1980a, notes 2 and 3, p. 123) on erroneous emotions.

**41.** See Scheffler (1977), for an extended discussion of the cognitive emotions.

**42.** The relationship of memory and affect is thought to be especially close. While HCPs often worry that emotions impede memory, de Souza argues (1980, pp. 134ff) that emotions serve in part to determine what is important and so to focus one's attention (cf., Leeb et al., 1976). In a similar vein, Sydney Callahan (1988) sees emotions and cognition as mutually corrective in the sense that each system can revise a plan of action suggested by the other.

**43.** Note that this approach is compatible with the desire-preference theory of the good.

**44.** The validity, usefulness, and efficacy of "gut-level feelings" are discussed in Capron, 1974; Drane, 1984; Fennell et al., 1987; Lesser, 1983; Lankton et al., 1984; Morreim, 1991; and Pincoffs, 1991.

# 5

# The Capacities that
# Define Competence to Consent

We turn now to the final step in the analysis of competence to consent: a detailed explanation of how the capacities enumerated in our preliminary definition actually participate in competence to consent. Because competence to perform any particular task requires possession of the capacities necessary for its completion, competence is defined in terms of capacities. Competence to consent, being no exception, is defined in terms of capacities required for decision making, of which free and informed consent is an example. The necessary capacities for competence to consent have been identified in the previous chapters. In this chapter we will demonstrate how and why these capacities jointly define competence to consent.

## THE NECESSARY CAPACITIES FOR COMPETENCE TO CONSENT

Recall that the nine individual criteria for competence to consent were assembled under four broad categories: informability, cognitive and affective capability, ability to choose, and ability to recount one's decision-making process. Informability consists of the capacities to (1) receive information, (2) recognize relevant information as information, and (3) remember information. Cognitive and affective capability includes the capacities to (4) relate situations to oneself, (5) reason about alternatives, and (6) rank alternatives. Choosing incorporates the abilities to (7) select an option and (8) resign oneself to the choice. Recounting one's decision-making process, alone among the broad capacities, is not a composite. The only ability here is (9) the ability to explain, by way of recognizable reasons, how one came to one's decision.[1]

Each of these capacities will now be considered more fully. First, each capacity will be defined. Second, each capacity will be correlated to decision making. Third, a discussion of the degrees of both cognitive and affective capacities will be presented. Finally, cases will be used to illustrate the varying degrees of the capacities and their application.

Before we begin, some clarifying remarks are in order. First, even after deliberating about degrees of competence, some ambiguity about individual cases may remain. The degree conception is an instance of the belief that persons possess certain characteristics in different measure, but it is often difficult to determine even a few of those levels with precision. Disagreement is bound to occur. The unease that one feels at such disagreement will vary with how uncomfortable one is with the thought that some assessments must be based on judgments rather than on precise measurements. The general messiness of the world extends into the health care setting in particularly unnerving ways. While this fact will give no one comfort, its recognition might at least avert futile searches for a single right answer.[2]

Second, because it is impossible to consider all possible degrees of competence, I will discuss only three: adequate, marginal, and inadequate competence to consent. An adequately competent person possesses all components to a high degree. The inadequately competent person is one in whom components are significantly diminished; when they are completely absent, the person is fully incompetent. The marginally competent person is one in whom the components are usually sufficiently present to enable her, with on-going assistance, to grasp and examine a basic core of salient facts—diagnosis, that treatment options carry differing prognoses and burden-benefit ratios, the HCPs' recommendation, and that she is expected to be the decision maker in this situation. The marginally competent person can usually, with on-going assistance, come to a conclusion that will (probably) promote her well-being.

The meaning of these distinctions for individual components of competence will become clearer as each is addressed; however, a few theoretical remarks to justify them are in order here. Since informed consent was developed to promote and protect autonomy and individual beneficence, the extent to which these values can be protected plays an important role in structuring the mechanisms by which those goals are reached. The fully autonomous individual has—and can share—a well-developed value structure in terms of which to organize his life. So long as this person continues to possess the ability to run his life with those values in mind, he is competent to make decisions. Although there are many degrees of this ability, all autonomous individuals share the common trait of clearly being adequate to the task of protecting autonomy and promoting well-being.

At the other end of the competence spectrum are persons who clearly lack the ability to run their lives in terms of autonomously specified value structures. These persons are incompetent decision makers. The causes of their incompetence are many and varied. They may be developmentally disabled, such that they cannot develop an autonomous value structure; they may have suffered cognitively disabling diseases (e.g., Alzheimer's Disease) that obliterate the abilities to relate present to past experiences and values. Again, there are many degrees of incompetence, but all render a person inadequate to the task of protecting autonomy and promoting well-being.

Many persons do not fall neatly into a designation of clearly competent or incompetent. To the extent that their ability to protect their autonomy and promote their own welfare is dynamic and ambiguous, they hover at the margin between competence and incompetence. These persons are especially worrisome to HCPs because clinicians are uncertain that their choices are autonomous or will actually promote their own welfare. Still, many such patients can make autonomous, prudential choices with assistance. These persons may, like adequately competent patients, retain an explicit—and expressed—interest in retaining decisional authority. Because this recognized, widely shared interest itself provides a benefit, marginally competent persons command the assistance of others as they strive for decisional adequacy. Still, their limited abilities will make this goal elusive for some decisions. In such cases, they fluctuate at a second margin—that which separates individual from general beneficence. The patient who cannot explicitly connect her present circumstances and options to her values, goals, and interests cannot reliably protect the latter. Thus she slips across the margin separating idiosyncratic notions of welfare from general notions of beneficence.

In short, the varying abilities of patients to choose autonomously in ways that protect their own welfare result from their varying decisional competence. Patients whose abilities fall between clearly adequate and clearly inadequate evoke concerns that they may not be competent to protect their own values. To respect their choices is to put them at, rather than rescue them from, risk of harm. For the majority of choices they can only achieve decisional competence with much assistance. For complex choices their inabilities are especially inadequate and they may slip across the margin into incompetence (and general beneficence).

## INFORMABILITY AND DECISION MAKING

Each component of informability is important to decision making because these capacities jointly enable a person to acquire the information on which an autonomous consent depends.

### The capacity to receive information

#### Its meaning

The capacity to receive information is the ability to acquire facts about the world. This most basic capacity requires the functioning of certain physiological and psychological systems. The ability to procure data presupposes that a person can see, hear, or feel, and that his central nervous system can receive stimuli. He is conscious (potentially aware of the stimuli) and his mind is not blocking information. To be able to receive information means that cognitive and affective facts can "get in."

#### Its relationship to decision making

The relationship of the ability to receive information to decision making is straightforward. Decisions are choices. Choices—at least autonomous choices—are based on an analysis of relevant information. If one cannot receive information, one cannot analyze it. If one cannot analyze information, one cannot make an autonomous decision. One can arbitrarily select an option and hope for the best, but absence of information significantly reduces the likelihood that the choice will promote one's well-being (which, we recall, is why people are choosing). The more one knows about one's environment, the better one can resolve a situation so as to increase the possibility of achieving one's goals. But, of course, one can only know about environments if one can acquire information about them. Thus, the ability to receive information is one of the criteria for competence to consent.

#### Its degrees and applications

How can a person be adequately, marginally, or inadequately informable? Since informability depends on physiological and psychological integrity, these degrees will be discussed with reference to these systems.

The physiological prerequisites are dispatched with relative ease: one is competent if one is conscious and if one's capacities for sight, hearing, or touch are present and functioning normally (naturally, or because they have been functionally corrected, e.g., eyeglasses). For purposes of consent, the appropriate focus for cognitive competence is on sight and hearing because the data HCPs provide come in the form of explanations. Since these explanations are given orally or in writing, patients must be able to hear or read them; they cannot be deaf and blind (unless the explanation can be provided in Braille and the patient's sense of touch is intact).[3] One cannot be competent if none of these senses is working. The person who is deaf, blind, and unable to feel has no way of getting the information required for autonomous consent. Any serious discussion of decision making necessarily presumes the presence of some sensory capacity through which information can enter the decision maker's consciousness.

In addition, the adequately competent person has no profound, untreated neuropsychological deficits that impede the flow of information from the external world into the central nervous system data processing centers (e.g., autism), or the actual processing of acquired information (e.g., advanced Alzheimer's Disease). An adequately competent information receiver must also have access to his felt and cognitive emotions. This requires not only physiological but also psychological integrity.

The marginally competent person has cognitive capacities that are diminished, or affective capacities that are diminished or exaggerated. With cognitive deficits, the person can still be competent if he can acquire and consider the core cognitive data and his felt and cognitive emotions. Affective excess raises concerns that cognitive efforts will be undercut. However, even exaggerated feelings can help direct decision making as long as they do not preclude effective cognitive activity. Marginally competent patients can still obtain cognitive facts, though they require on-going assistance to do so. They often need help from others to keep cognitive data present to their consciousness (e.g., frequent reminders regarding the core data), so that powerful emotions do not push them from the decisional arena. With affective deficiency, patients' feelings are weaker and at risk of being unrecognized or discounted. Information carried by felt and cognitive emotions may be missed. These patients must make a conscious effort to acknowledge the information provided by these weaker emotions.

Consideration of both felt and cognitive emotions can, again, be stimulated by reminding patients to take note of them and to incorporate them into the decision-making process.

The point is that the more effective system can partially compensate for its less efficient counterpart. Because marginally competent patients suffer impairments that generate factual deficits, they require greater assistance from others in their decision-making efforts. Still, they can usually consent if on-going, explicit efforts are made to help them reach that end. Of course, all patients require some assistance; they depend, for example, on HCPs to provide and explain the nature of diagnoses and treatments, among other things. Marginally competent patients, however, require support beyond the typical provision or clarification of information on a few occasions. A need for ongoing, active assistance is the hallmark of the marginally competent patient.

The inadequately competent patient will be unable to acquire sufficient data, cognitively or affectively. If a person's cognitive capacities are impaired, cognitive facts either cannot be received or cannot be efficiently processed (e.g., clinical depression).[4] If feelings are being suppressed (e.g., post-traumatic shock), there will be no relevant felt emotions.

Let us relate this analysis to previous examples. Mr. D, the pharmacist with terminal AIDS, exemplifies adequate competence. He is able to receive explanations. He is aware of and able to express his felt and cognitive emotions. He can relate them to his value structure, and they motivate his actions. Mr. C, the homeless man with the decubitus, is marginally competent. He is able to receive enough factual information about his diagnosis and prognosis to relate them to his overall value structure. Moreover, he is keenly aware of and motivated by his feelings about his future: he is unhappy being institutionalized, wants to be discharged, and says so repeatedly. Ms. H, the nurse with early Alzheimer's, is affectively incapacitated. Since she is denying access to feelings she would normally consider, she is failing to receive relevant information.

To demonstrate cognitive incapacity with affective ability, consider:

*CASE VIII:* Ms. I is a 68-year-old female who was placed in a skilled nursing facility (SNF) 2 weeks ago. Her past medical history is uneventful, except for increasing forgetfulness and loss of cognitive function. For the last several months, Ms. I's behavior has been increasingly unsettling. She leaves the water running in the bathroom, leaves the stove on, and puts her clothes in the trash. Worst of all, she has repeatedly wandered away from home. On one occasion, she was struck by a car (though not seriously injured) when she stepped into traffic. Prior to her admission, she lived at home with her sisters, aged 61 and 63.

The three sisters have had a long-standing agreement that they will care for each other. All three have long been adamantly against "putting anyone we love in a nursing home." After much soul-searching, her sisters have finally concluded that they can no longer care for Ms. I at home, and that to continue to do so endangers her—and their—well-being. Repeated efforts by her HCPs and family to get Ms. I to understand the need for her SNF placement have consistently failed. She cries much of the day, and accuses her sisters of breaking their promise. She refuses to cooperate with the SNF personnel. Two days ago, she stopped eating. Her only remark is, "If I have to die in this awful place, I'd rather it be sooner than later."

Ms. I, uninformed (because uninformable) of the relevant cognitive data about her case, is cognitively incompetent. She neither has, nor is able to acquire for consideration the cognitive facts (e.g., her sisters' inability to care for her, the jeopardy to her life). She is considering cognitive facts from the past (e.g., the promise), but her attempts to use old facts to manage her current situation are doomed to fail, because the old facts do not apply to her current situation. She is, however, assimilating affective facts from the present, which she is expressing. In addition, her affective state is consistently motivating her. In short, she is affectively competent, but cognitively incompetent.

People try to manage their lives to promote their well-being. To succeed, they need to know something about their environments. They can know something about their environments only if they are at least marginally competent to receive information. They must, that is, be able to receive both cognitive and affective information.

### The capacity to recognize relevant information as information

#### Its meaning

The capacity to recognize relevant information as information is the ability to screen out "noise" from salient data. Not all stimuli need to be incorporated into the decision-making process. At each moment we are subject to what philosopher William James called a "blooming, buzzing confusion." The richness of the world, internal and external, must be attended to selectively to permit any management of it at all. Decision makers must identify and focus on stimuli that are relevant. They must separate what is important (information) from what is immaterial (noise). This ability to separate useful from irrelevant data is what is meant by the capacity to recognize relevant information as information.

### Its relationship to decision making

Again, the relation of this capacity to decision making is straightforward. Just as having no information makes it impossible to decide, having the wrong information makes it impossible (or at least very unlikely) to make choices that will promote one's well-being. Again, the more one knows, the better one can achieve one's goals. (I am not advocating information overload of patients, but reminding HCPs that certain core data must be available to patients.) In sum, one only can know something if one can acquire correct information. The ability to recognize relevant information as information is important—it allows one to attend to appropriate facts, thus maximizing the chances for satisfactory decision making.

Toward that end one must be able to sort out from among the plethora of stimuli the information that genuinely informs the choice at hand. Since only facts that are useful to making the decision count as information, these facts must be identified. Trivia that impede decision making must be screened out. If irrelevancies or excess information intrude on the calculations, they may delay appropriate, or lead to inappropriate, decisions.

### Its degrees and applications

What does it mean to be adequately, marginally, or inadequately competent to recognize relevant information as information? Adequately competent information recognizers realize that their situations call for choice. They are able to identify and attend selectively to data that apply to the choice to be made (e.g., diagnosis, treatment alternatives, prognosis). They understand the content of incoming data, and are able to pay close attention to those that help them choose so as to promote their own well-being. Moreover, they recognize the information as relevant to their lives—that is, they recognize that the data are information for and about them. In addition to this cognitive capacity, they display affective ability to recognize current felt and cognitive emotions as generated by the present situation. They recognize felt emotions as pleasant or noxious, and cognitive emotions as related to the desirability of and progress toward changing the present situation—and they accomplish these tasks independently. Having received information, they work through the process unassisted.

Marginally competent information recognizers understand that they are expected to make a choice, but are unable to identify relevant data without on-going assistance. Once the key facts are pointed out, they recognize their applicability. They generally understand the content of incoming data, but have difficulty discriminating relevant from irrelevant facts. Thus they are unable, without persistent guidance, to understand which facts apply to the choice at hand or to appreciate how this choice is important to their welfare.

Affectively, marginally competent persons recognize felt emotions, but may have difficulty relating them to the current situation. They are likely to be inept in relating present to future felt emotions, so as to plan behavior. Cognitive emotions may be slow in appearing, or ambiguous, since some of the decision-making process is undertaken by others. Again, they require on-going aid to recognize and appreciate the relevance of these emotions to their continued well-being.

The primary differences between adequately and marginally competent persons are the extent of their abilities and, as a result, the degree of independence with which activities are carried out. Marginally competent persons depend on others to identify, organize, and appreciate relevant information, as well as to direct attention to decisional components. Once these have been specified, marginally competent persons perceive their importance. They are then motivated (reminded, perhaps) to consider these aspects. Marginally competent persons cannot work through the process unassisted, but they can understand and appreciate information once others indicate its importance. The adequately competent person can independently complete these tasks. I do not mean to imply that the adequately competent person has no assistance; only that his assistance primarily takes the form of a provision or clarification of information—the sort of medical detail with which nonprofessionals have little or no familiarity. Of course, many (perhaps, most) adequately competent persons enlist the aid of others in making important decisions. They glean suggestions, opinions, and analyses from others, and use others as a sounding board. The difference is that the adequately competent person could reach a decision independently of such assistance, were it unavailable. The marginally competent person could not.

Inadequately competent information recognizers are unable to understand the content of incoming data or to see the relevance of the data even when others identify their importance. They may be unable to understand how cognitive or affective facts pertain to the present circumstances. They cannot relate them to their lives as a whole. Unlike marginally competent persons who appreciate facts with assistance, inadequately competent persons cannot realize their significance, even with help.

Consider again Mr. D, the pharmacist dying from AIDS. He recognizes that he must choose between hospitalization and home care. He can screen out irrelevant material (e.g., the high cost of hospitalization, since that is an option he wishes to forgo). He can locate his situation within his life as a whole (e.g., he desires to spend his remaining time with his friends rather than in a hospital). His cognitive emotion of resolution to his imminent death (as opposed to, say, frustration) signals a choice that is synchronous with his values.

Contrast Mr. D with Mrs. B, who initially refused a hysterectomy for cancer of the cervix because she wanted to be a surrogate mother. She recognized that she had to make a choice, but was unable to rule out important data (e.g., that her post-menopausal status precluded her being a surrogate mother). Nor was she initially able to see the relevance of the life-threatening nature of her disease. Nonetheless with persistent help she came to understand explanations about her disease and its prognosis. Repeated educational efforts by her son and HCPs helped her to see that her disease threatened her life. Ultimately, her felt emotion of indignation turned to concern for her future well-being. Interestingly, she was able to locate her decision within her life plan. She realized that a hysterectomy made her goal of surrogacy impossible, but with on-going assistance came to appreciate the importance of this choice for her continued physical health and well-being.

Inadequately competent patients cannot recognize data—cognitive or affective—as important to the current situation. Because Ms. I, the sorrowful SNF patient, cannot acquire or recognize information pertaining to her future, she receives no new information. Thus, she is cognitively incapacitated. Ms. H (who has no strong feelings about entering a research protocol with a very real chance to halt the progression of Alzheimer's Disease), in denying her feelings, is affectively disabled.

The differences in the degrees of competence experienced by these patients stem from qualitative and quantitative differences. Mr. D and Mrs. B have the same abilities, though Mr. D has them to a greater extent and can exercise them independently. Ms. H has cognitive but no affective capacities; Ms. I has affective but inadequate cognitive capacities.

Competence to manage their lives requires that people be able to make choices. Toward that end they must be able to recognize relevant data. They must be able to recognize that a choice is required, identify what counts as information, understand explanations about that choice, and correlate the choice with their lives as a whole. They may be able to do these things independently, in which case they are adequately competent. They may be able to do them with on-going assistance, in which case they are marginally competent. If they are unable to connect facts to feelings or choices, they are incompetent for decision making.

## Remembering information

### Its meaning

Most decisions are not made instantaneously but over time, so it is essential that persons have repeated access to material about pending decisions. Some material will have been acquired in the remote past (e.g., one's value structure). Some material will have been recently acquired (e.g., diagnosis, prognosis, treatment options). In both cases it is essential to be able to call up information to consider and reconsider its relevance to the choice at hand. This capacity to bring previously stored facts into consciousness is what is meant by remembering.

### Its relationship to decision making

Even if persons are able to receive and recognize pertinent facts, these facts are unhelpful if they cannot remember them. Most patients need to be able to mull over information, to consider it in various imagined scenarios, in order to fully understand its meaning and appreciate its gravity. Such scrutiny requires time. If persons cannot remember the facts, careful scrutiny is impossible. Moreover many persons need to reflect quietly on the nuances of situations they are expected to resolve. This is possible only if they can remember the details of the options about which they must deliver a verdict. In brief, no information; no decision. No memory; no information. This is why memory is important.

### Its degrees and applications

The temperamental nature of memory is an all-too-familiar, maddening fact of life. Moreover, memory often becomes less reliable with age. Memory is classified with reference to time: short-term memory, or memory for immediate (within the past hour) events; recent memory, or memory for events of the last few weeks or months; and long-term memory, or memory for anything that occurred prior to the last few months. Memory impairment that occurs with age is often selective: short-term and recent memory are often more impaired than long-term memory. This is problematic because people develop values and goals over a life time, but often have to make health care decisions on the basis of recently acquired data that are (or should be) stored in their short-term or recent memory banks. Thus the relevant data may be only variously available to them. For example, Ms. I (the elderly SNF patient who is refusing to eat) recalls from distant memory that she does not want to spend her remaining years in a nursing home. She is simultaneously unable to recall from recent memory that her condition requires such a facility.

What does this mean for adequate, marginal, and inadequate competence? Adequately competent patients are able to retrieve salient facts from all three memory banks. As they have access to nearly all applicable memories, they can recall data important to the decision at hand. They are able to remember details regarding diagnosis, prognosis, risks, and benefits. The ability to recall felt and cognitive emotions from previous situations enables them to relate feelings to projected outcomes. They are able to recall and use their value structures for evaluating projected outcomes. Their access is largely independent of others' prompting. They can recall the facts at will and examine them at their leisure and convenience.

Marginally competent persons have a less facile but still functional memory. They may require frequent repetition of data to compensate for deficits in short-term or recent memory. They may also require reminders of how they felt about similar situations in the past.

In addition, reminders may be the only mechanism by which to relate current events to their values and, thereby, to their lives as a whole. Oft-repeated reminders will help to overcome memory ineptitude, either by exercising the pathways needed for information retrieval (and thereby facilitating unassisted memory) or by helping them to relate present situations to past choices.

Some incapacitated patients are able to remember some data, but their memory is so erratic and unreliable that meaningful consideration of relevant cognitive data is impossible. If recent memory is significantly impaired, comparison between past and present felt emotions and the stimuli that elicit them will be largely impossible. Even frequent reminders will not keep pertinent current information before the mind's eye.

Without memory it would be difficult to make any genuine choice or live any sort of integrated life. Ms. F (whose fear of surgery prompts her to refuse radical mastectomy) exemplifies adequately competent memory. She can recall the just-learned facts about her case, as well as the previous negative experiences that motivate her to refuse any surgery that is not immediately life-saving. Her recent memories regarding prognosis, risks and benefits, and her memories of past felt emotions associated with surgery lead her to reject further occasions for such feelings.

Compare Ms. F to Mr. A, whose "voices" prompted his repeated repeal of consent for a cisternal tap. Only a psychiatrist's repeated prompting enabled Mr. A to remember the auditory hallucinations that led him to refuse the cisternal tap. With prompting he was able to relate his intraoperative apprehension to the hallucinations, and to remember more positive felt emotions—pleasure and the absence of pain—that treatment would allow him to enjoy again. With help, he is marginally competent. Ms. I, unable to remember new facts, is incompetent.

The difference between these patients again lies partly in the degree of assistance required in the exercise of memory. But additional qualitative and quantitative differences in the nature and extent of their recollections are present as well. Patients who must make choices within a health care setting need to consider the different burdens that attend different options—their nature, their likelihood, their impact upon lifestyle. This takes time and requires that they be able to recall the details stored in their short-term and recent memory. Long-term memory must also be functioning, to permit the person to locate this situation in his life as a whole, to determine how this choice will fit with his previously espoused value structure. The adequately competent person will have easy, independent access to all three memory banks; the marginally competent person will have access to these banks with assistance (or perhaps will have an assistant who functions as the patient's recent memory). The incapacitated patient will have only random, unreliable memory access (or no access at all).

## Summary

The criterion of informability is crucial to consent because its component capacities enable persons to acquire, identify, and consider the information upon which free and informed consent is based. Informability is, however, only the first set of capacities on which competence to consent depends. We turn now to the analysis of the second major criterion, cognitive and affective capability.

## COGNITIVE AND AFFECTIVE CAPABILITY

The components of cognitive and affective capability are the capacities to relate current situations to one's life as a whole, to reason about the various possible courses of action, and to rank options. Each of these is important to decision making because these faculties enable patients to consider the wisdom of pursuing different alternatives, and to correlate past, present, and future aspects of their lives, and to organize their lives in terms of their value structures.

### Relating Situations to Oneself

#### Its meaning

Just as we are besieged with many stimuli, so we face many choices. Since pursuit of every possible opportunity is impossible, we must choose those in which to participate and those to avoid. Persons must be able to determine which options are most desirable, given their particular circumstances and values. The ability to evaluate situations in terms of one's own welfare is the capacity to relate situations to oneself.

#### Its relationship to decision making

Possibilities are evaluated as more or less acceptable on the basis of one's previously espoused value structure. Regulating one's life in an on-going, satisfactory manner requires an ability to distinguish (probably) helpful from (probably) harmful options. The ability to relate options to oneself requires that persons be able to identify opportunities with which they are faced and values that are at stake, and to perceive which actions (or inactions) will most likely promote those values and goals (including the production of desired felt emotions). Those promoting them will be pursued; those obstructing them will be avoided. Only thus can persons promote their welfare.

### Its degrees and applications

How, then, do adequately, marginally, or inadequately competent persons relate information to themselves? Adequately competent persons are able to identify which opportunities will promote and which will inhibit their goals and values. They are able to distinguish which options will affect which values. They can postulate different affective states that will attend different outcomes, and can relate projected to past felt emotions so as to understand which future state they would affectively prefer or which one would most likely maximize their well-being. Adequately competent persons can undertake these evaluations independently.

Marginally competent persons are able to complete such evaluations with on-going assistance. They need help correlating options to values, or in associating past felt emotions to present options and projected prognoses. Inadequately competent persons are unable to complete the evaluation process, either because they are unable to identify or understand the relevant options, or because they are unable to relate them to their value structures, felt emotions, or lives as a whole.

Recall Ms. E, the diabetic who refused a kidney transplant and plans to discontinue dialysis. She has identified three options: transplantation, continuing dialysis, and no further treatment. She has identified two values: altruism, by which her failure to accept the kidney makes it available to "a younger person who has more time"; and a certain quality of life (which her disease precludes) below which life is not worth living. She understands the relationship between her options and her values: if she accepts the kidney, she forgoes an opportunity for altruism; if she continues dialysis, she forgoes the quality of life she desires; if she forgoes treatment, she honors her values of altruism and her commitment to a particular quality of life. She foresees that physical discomfort will accompany her death, but she also expects to experience greater psychological satisfaction from this choice than from the other. Her thorough understanding of these factors and their interrelationship makes her adequately competent.

Mrs. B exemplifies marginal competence. As a result of on-going assistance in the analysis of her situation, she has come to understand that she has two options for her cervical cancer: a hysterectomy and no treatment. Persistent coaching by her son and primary nurse have enabled her to recognize that two important, incompatible values are involved: her desire to be a surrogate mother and her continued existence. She has come to realize that her continued existence requires her to forfeit her (imagined) opportunities for being a surrogate mother. Her anticipated future pleasure in her continued existence overrides her (imagined) future pleasure at being able to help childless women.

Ms. I (the elderly SNF patient who is refusing to eat) is cognitively incompetent to relate her current situation to her value structure. Insofar as she thinks of the two, she sees them as totally unrelated. As a result, she is unwilling to entertain any thoughts of future therapeutic options. Ms. H (who has no strong feelings about entering a research protocol with a very real chance to halt the progression of Alzheimer's Disease) exemplifies the other side of the coin. Having cut herself off from her affective realm, she has no feelings to relate to her current situation.

It is crucial to distinguish the patient who cannot relate a situation to herself and her value structure from the patient who will not do so. The former is incompetent; the latter is uncooperative—quite possibly for good reasons, at least by her own lights. Consider:

*CASE IX:* Ms. J is a 28-year-old weaver who has been quadriplegic since a boating accident 18 months ago. She requires complete assistance in activities of daily living. For the first several months, she was cautiously optimistic about her prognosis (in spite of repeated kind, but firm, declarations by her HCPs that she would regain no function). She was eager to hear all about her treatments and to participate in evaluations of her responses to them. For the last year, however, she has recognized that her paralysis is complete and permanent. A brilliant and nationally acclaimed artist who ran her own studio, she has not adjusted emotionally to the fact that she will never again be able to practice her craft. She is tearful during most of her waking hours.

Months of antidepressants and psychotherapy have failed to reduce her grief. She continues to express the sentiment that her loss is too great to be borne. Rarely she smiles and has a warm conversation with her companion of 12 years; but even with her Ms. J is usually sad. She repeatedly expresses her sorrow and her wish that someone would help her end her life. She sees her future as worthless and refuses to be involved in choices about her care. Now when her HCPs try to discuss her treatments or responses, she stops them. She states that nothing matters to her any more; if she has to go on living, she does not care what happens to her during that life. From her HCPs she wants only that they take her life. She has no interest in anything else they might do to her. The HCPs want Ms. J declared legally incompetent and a guardian appointed to make treatment decisions.

Ms. J poses an interesting problem. She is not incompetent, although she is—by choice—uninformed about therapeutic regimens. What should her HCPs do about her? Suppose Frankfurt is right about second-order desires. Then, we can imagine that Ms. J has reasoned thus:

I can no longer live what I have defined as a worthwhile life.  My HCPs tell me that if I work at it I can acquire and learn to enjoy different goals, interests, and values. That is, I can erect a new value structure that will generate new first-order desires. However, my current second-order desires are relevant to that: I desire to be the person I used to be with the desires I used to (and continue to) have; I do not want to become the sort of person who will come to have a new value structure or those new first-order desires; if, by some quirk of fate, I did acquire those new first-order desires, I know myself well enough to know I would have second-order desires that I not have them. So the best option and the one I desire most of all is my death now. Since I cannot take my own life, my most pressing first-order desire is that my HCPs cause my death.

Had that reasoning been accepted, Ms. J would not currently be in a position to have her competence questioned. Her HCPs would have recognized that she was cognitively competent—having initially received information about her condition, recognized it as information, and remembered it. Now, in relating it to herself, she realizes that the self which was the foundation for her value structure has largely ceased to be effective. The self to which all future therapeutic endeavors will apply is a self that is not related to her in any meaningful way. As a result, she has no motivation to be in any way involved in its future. Who should have decision-making authority for Ms. J is still a problem, of course; but it does not arise because she is incompetent. In fact, Ms. J may be no different from patients who instruct their HCPs to "do what you think is best." True, Ms. J's reason—that she does not care what happens to her if she has to go on living—differs from patients whose reason is the belief that their HCPs know best. But practically, no difference exists.

In sum, competent decision makers must be able to relate their current circumstances to their values and goals. They must be able to identify pertinent options and their possible effects, know how different decisions will influence different values, and explore how they feel about possible outcomes.

## Reasoning About Alternatives

### Its meaning

Reasoning about alternatives is evaluating options. This capacity is the ability to examine disparate outcomes, to predict the likelihood of each, to estimate how each would influence one's life, to consider these factors from a variety of perspectives, to recognize how one would feel about different possible futures, and to make choices based on these considerations. Assuming that one can successfully receive relevant information, recognize its pertinence to the current state of affairs, remember it, and relate it to one's life as a whole, one then needs to be able to assess the sundry burden to benefit ratios and respective probabilities of each option. To be able to do this is to be able to reason about alternatives.

There is clearly some overlap between this capacity and that of relating situations to oneself. In practice distinguishing between the two is difficult, if not impossible, since both involve evaluating actual and potential situations with an eye to how they will influence the course of one's life. There is, however, at least this theoretical distinction: the former requires a person to recognize that a choice must be made and why; the latter requires one to recognize that different choices will change her life in different ways, and to determine which of those changes she would prefer, and why.

### Its relationship to decision making

These activities, coupled with the assessment of the relationship of various options to one's life as a whole, allow persons to make predictions about the meaning of different choices. Most people want their lives to go as well as possible. Facility in reasoning about alternatives helps to achieve that goal. The process begins when one identifies the different outcomes that might ensue from one's current situation. Then, having identified x, y, and z as legitimate options, one assesses the differing burden to benefit ratios that attend each, and postulates the various impacts (including affective states) of each option on one's life as a whole. This necessarily includes the chances that each option provides for achieving desired outcomes, as well as how one's options would change in case of failure. The outcome of this process is a rough guide to the value and likelihood of the options—x has two moderate benefits, two minor burdens, and a 50 percent chance of realizing predicted outcomes; y has three major and four minor benefits, three major burdens, and a 60 percent chance of realizing its predicted outcomes, and so on.

Most people do not go through this process in so formal or structured a fashion. In fact, since detailed data are lacking for many treatment modalities, even HCPs must often settle for anecdotal evidence and best guesses. Still, patients and professionals alike do make lists of pros and cons for various options, and often discount a longer list of pros in favor of a shorter one when the chances of success are higher for the latter than for the former. That is, some patients choose lesser benefits that are virtually assured over greater benefits whose realization is unlikely, or lesser benefits that carry with them fewer or less onerous burdens. For example, some patients choose coronary artery by-pass grafting over changes in lifestyle. It is not that they prefer surgery per se, but that they believe symptomatic relief is more likely with surgery because they doubt their abilities to change their lifestyles (e.g., diet, exercise); or they may believe they can change their lifestyles, but that the burdens of doing so are too great.

The whole process of reasoning about alternatives is somewhat messy. Moreover, only rarely is a single outcome and route toward realizing it acceptable. Rather, the entire undertaking will likely require tradeoffs. For example, Mr. D, the pharmacist dying from AIDS, will have to compare an early death at home that may greatly distress his friends to a longer but more constrained life, some of which is spent in the more restrictive hospital setting. Each option has its own burden to benefit ratio. Each has, in fact, different burdens (distress of loved ones in the former, loss of freedom in the latter) and different benefits (better quality of last days of life in the former, possible longer life in the latter).

Toting up factors, while never easy, is important to decision making because this activity leads decision makers to genuinely appreciate their options. HCPs can provide details about diagnosis, treatment alternatives, medical risks and benefits of the options, and estimates of prognosis. They cannot, however, provide information about the acceptability of each of these to individual patients. Patients alone, after examining data in light of their own values, can make those assessments. They can best project how they will feel in each of the possible outcomes.

At this point in the decision-making process, persons must consider their own personal and idiosyncratic beliefs. Recall Ms. E, the diabetic who has chosen to discontinue renal dialysis. If the only data factored into the estimates were the medical risks and benefits, the only acceptable outcome would be to have a kidney transplant, for this route would offer the best chance of minimizing (or at least reducing) the pathological effects of her diabetes. She would no longer suffer from end stage renal disease. The untoward, distressing symptoms—nausea, malaise, hypertension, and prostration—that attend renal failure would most likely be reduced. Moreover, the transplant would restore much of her independence; she would no longer be required to restrict her diet and her fluid intake, nor schedule her life around dialysis treatments (although she would be required to take expensive immunosuppressants).

What the medical burden to benefit ratio fails to take into account is Ms. E's other, personal values. Medical estimates do not acknowledge circumstances unrelated to her health problems—her altruistic desires, the diminished value to her of her life. They do not take account of her felt emotions. Idiosyncratic values that the patient brings to the bargaining table enable patients to make decisions that are best for them, all things considered. Without both medical and personal evaluations, patients operate in a partial information vacuum which, if not corrected, jeopardizes the very values that people seek to protect through medical interventions. Reasoning about alternatives is important for decision making: it maximizes decision-making success for the person, considered as a whole.

### Its degrees and applications

Adequately competent persons are able to complete the calculations of burdens and benefits, determine future outcomes and their probabilities, evaluate how they would feel in each case, project how the different choices would promote their well-being, and speculate on the effects each option would have on their lives, all things considered. Having received information about medical risks, benefits, and probabilities, they can work through the remaining calculations on their own. Mr. D (the pharmacist dying from AIDS), Ms. E (the diabetic who has chosen to discontinue renal dialysis), and Ms. F (whose fear of surgery prompts her to refuse radical mastectomy) display such capacities.

Marginally competent persons are also able to complete the appropriate calculations but, again, will require on-going assistance. They may, for example, be unable to weigh burdens and benefits or assign probabilities independently. This ineptitude may result from a difficulty with the mathematical concepts themselves or because they are unable to integrate this information into their own systems of goals and values. Or they may suffer from an inability to project themselves into the future, to imagine what their lives would be like as a result of choosing one option over another. They may be unable to relate past feelings to present options and future outcomes.

There is, additionally, the problem that certain false beliefs may interfere with the decision-making process. Patients may misunderstand information. When this happens, efforts to correct these misconceptions should allow the process to move forward in a satisfactory fashion. On the other hand, persons who suffer from fixed inappropriate beliefs need a different kind of assistance. Mr. A, for example, believes there is one overriding risk—that his physicians are trying to kill him. Were this true, he would be foolish to submit to their interventions. Since it is not, his persistence in granting it absolute decisional weight renders him incompetent, partly because the risk he identifies is non-existent and partly because his singleness of focus causes him to fail to recognize that—in terms of his own values—he can profit from the diagnostic procedure.

So long as marginally competent persons have assistants who can help them perform these necessary assessments, they will be able to understand the actual or anticipated scenarios and come to appreciate how certain choices will better promote their values. They differ from adequately competent persons, then, in the ability for independent decision making based on appraisals of burden to benefit ratios and predictions of success. Mrs. B whose desire to be a surrogate mother prompted her refusal of a hysterectomy for cervical cancer, displays such characteristics.

Inadequately competent persons are unable to complete the process. They are unable to perform some or all of the required calculations or to understand that there is a choice to be made and that life will go differently, depending on which option they select. They may also be unable to realize that their values are at stake or the importance of this decision to their welfare. Felt emotions may get in the way (as with Mr. G who, because he considers his life is no longer worth living, is refusing resection of his acute bowel obstruction). Cognitive or affective deficits may make data manipulation impossible, as in the cases of Ms. I (the elderly SNF patient) and Ms. H (who has no strong feelings about entering a research protocol), respectively.

In sum, the capacity to reason about alternatives is the ability to construct personalized burden to benefit ratios for each option, to assess the probability that each will occur, and to foresee how one's life would be variously changed and one's values variously promoted by each possible action.

## Ranking Alternatives

### Its meaning

The person who has the capacity to rank alternatives can make a list. Using the sort of reasoning discussed in the preceding section, a decision maker should be able to come up with at least a rough hierarchy of choices, to say, "I choose y, then x, then z, in that order." This means that y is the preferred solution. If for some reason y becomes unavailable, the person then endorses x. But another person may embrace only y and count all other options unacceptable. Then, if y is not available, he may see inaction as his only acceptable alternative, choosing thereby not to act on x or z. The ability to order options according to one's preferences is what is meant by the capacity to rank alternatives.

### Its relationship to decision making

The goal of decision making is, tautologically, making a decision. This means that one alternative is adopted and the others forgone.

Selecting one option and committing to one course of action signal the end of the process. Therefore, persons must be able to determine that one option is the best (or least worse). This does not mean that persons cannot reconsider their decisions or that they cannot have second thoughts or worries. What it does mean is that they can bring closure to the process, even if that closure is attended by some uneasiness and even if there is recognition that such closure may be temporary. This progress results from being able to rank opportunities. Once persons can identify their first choice, they can proceed accordingly. The ability to rank alternatives moves the decision-making process toward completion.

### Its degrees and applications

Adequately competent persons are able to place options along a continuum. They see one act as being optimal, given their values and circumstances. They see other options as being less likely to promote their welfare (though, to the extent that they may do so, they are permissible), and see some as being either unlikely to do so or, for other reasons, as being absolutely unacceptable. Further, they are able to make these determinations without assistance. Mr. D (the pharmacist dying from AIDS), Ms. E (the diabetic who has chosen to discontinue renal dialysis), Ms. F (whose fear of surgery prompts her to refuse radical mastectomy), and Ms. J (the quadriplegic weaver who wants her HCPs to take her life) demonstrate this capacity.

Marginally competent persons have some difficulty constructing a hierarchy of choices. This problem may result from the difficulties they have in relating alternatives to themselves, or with reasoning about alternatives. Or perhaps they cannot make the precise distinctions that differentiate similar options. They should, however, be able to distinguish between classes of actions, that is, to assign actions to either "acceptable" or "unacceptable" categories. Then the final choice can be made by someone else. Their families may determine which option from the "acceptable" class will best promote their interests, all things considered. Or perhaps their HCPs can choose, again from the "acceptable" group, the action with the best medical burden to benefit statistics. As before, marginally competent decision makers—Mr. A (whose "voices" prompted his repeated repeal of consent for a cisternal tap), Mrs. B (whose desire to be a surrogate mother prompted her refusal of a hysterectomy), and Mr. C (the street person with the coccygeal ulceration)—require assistance to complete the process.

Inadequately competent persons are unable to organize their options in a fashion that promotes their well-being. They may be unable to construct general groupings or to relate options to themselves or to reason about options. This incapacitation will persist, in spite of attempts on the part of others to help them organize choices on the basis of their values.

Thus, the capacity to rank alternatives is the final step in the evaluation process that attends decision making. Ranking requires that persons be able to organize options, recognizing their burden to benefit ratios and their various probabilities for promoting and protecting one's values. The degree of success with which persons are able to compose a prudent hierarchy of preferences separates the adequate, marginal, and incompetent decision maker.

## Summary

The criterion of cognitive and affective capability is crucial to competence to consent because it enables persons to correlate facts about the world with how their lives will go. Cognitive and affective capability is necessary for persons to successfully integrate their past, present, and future lives, and to protect and promote values through time. Without these skills no self-interested decisions could be made, because data could not be considered from unique personal perspectives. It is cognitive and affective competence that makes personal evaluation possible.

## RESOLUTION AND RESIGNATION IN DECISION MAKING

### Resolution

#### Its meaning

Resolution means choosing one of the available options in an informed, affectively and cognitively capable fashion. It means making a choice.

#### Its relationship to decision making

Resolution settles the question of what to do; it aims persons at particular courses of action and ends the vacillation that attends a panoply of choices. Resolution is the successful culmination of the decision-making process.

### Its degrees and applications

Adequately competent persons make independent choices. Others may provide information or other episodic assistance throughout the process, but analysis and choice are largely (and potentially exclusively) independent ventures. Felt and cognitive emotions reflect satisfaction at having completed the process, and patients express their wishes.

Marginally competent persons also make a choice. Their consideration of relevant information and their ultimate decisions are greatly guided by others. They may be less completely informed, or may be expressly ambivalent, both cognitively and affectively. Ultimately, however, they express their choices—which may be to cooperate with an option selected by others.

Inadequately competent persons are never able to come to a decision. They fail to see their situations as requiring decisions, or vacillate between options, permanently unable to commit to one, either cognitively or affectively. Others must determine the course of action for them. Once a choice is made, incompetent persons may still be unable to halt the process in their own minds. This inability may derive from inabilities in affective and cognitive capacities, but it may also be an independent incapacitation; that is, they may simply be unable to make a lasting choice, as was Mr. A (whose "voices" prompted his repeated repeal of consent for a cisternal tap).[5]

In sum, resolution is the ability to reach a conclusion. As choosing brings closure to the decision-making process, the absence of this capacity can lead to the failure of the entire project.

## Resignation

### Its meaning

People rarely face situations in which there is one, and only one, perfect choice. Rather, they must usually make "the best choice, all things considered." They may, therefore, harbor doubts that their choices really were the best ones. Their cognitive emotions may be in flux and their felt emotions may include ambivalence, and if their choices are unpopular, others may repeatedly attempt to persuade them to reconsider. A choice commits one to a course of action. Sometimes the chooser himself is not enthusiastic about his choice, but sees it as the best option available. Nonetheless to proceed with the tasks ahead, he must persevere in his choice. Persistence in one's decision, both publicly and privately, is necessary for all parties to get on with what needs to be done. This persistence is particularly difficult if the ensuing course is in any way onerous, because it will require him to undergo disagreeable experiences. Such choices are best undertaken with a sense of purpose and commitment to the designated end. Persons are more likely to succeed if they can dedicate themselves to a course of action. Their perseverance, especially in the face of uncertainty or dismay at what may follow, is what is meant by resignation.

Note that resignation does not commit people to being happy about their choices. Many people wish other choices had been available. In all cases, patients undoubtedly wish that they did not have to make health care choices at all, that their lives had not included serious illness. Beyond that fact, many—perhaps most—wish their circumstances had been qualitatively different in other important ways. Ms. E, among our previous examples, wished her opportunity for transplantation had come when she was younger. Ms. F would have preferred to have information available on the comparative long-term morbidity and mortality rates of lumpectomy with radiation vs. radical mastectomy.

### Its relationship to decision making

Many choices are only one among several possibilities. Often estimates of burden to benefit ratios and probabilities are uncertain; often the database is incomplete. There is, therefore, a certain amount of hesitation about the correctness of any serious decision. Insofar as possible, information deficits ought to be corrected; but it is probably never possible to eliminate them completely. Ultimately it becomes necessary to proceed in spite of these limitations. That one makes a choice does not, in and of itself, erase the concerns that attend it. As a result, persons may find themselves in the position of having to reassure themselves on an on-going basis about their choices.

The decision maker can usefully review the process that led to the decision, recalling the factors that told both for and against the ultimate choice. (Clearly, this review will require the same capacities that went into making the decision in the first place.) Resignation to a plan allows decision makers to undertake the tasks required for its successful completion. The relationship of resignation to decision making, then, is that this capacity empowers persons to act on their decisions. Persisting in one's choice allows its implementation and, hence, the promotion or preservation of the values that are the aim of the decision.

## Its degrees and applications

Competent persons proceed with their decisions; incompetent persons are unable to do so. This capacity seems not to admit of degrees in the same ways that the others do, probably because there are really only the two outcomes: acting on one's decision and failing to do so. Possibly adequate and marginal competence differ in terms of how enthusiastically persons pursue a goal, or with how much dispatch. But, since part of the meaning of resignation is that one proceeds in spite of a lack of enthusiasm or in the face of outright distaste, this distinction seems unhelpful. The incompetent person (e.g., Mr. A, whose "voices" prompted his repeated repeal of consent for a cisternal tap) continues to change his mind, thereby forestalling action.

Resignation means that one can set aside one's own uncertainties about a choice and proceed with the actions it dictates. It is the courage of conviction without which people would be unable to act except when they were certain that they had absolutely all relevant information and had analyzed it correctly. Since these conditions rarely exist, decision makers must be able to move forward in the face of doubt. The competent person can do so; the incompetent person cannot.

## RECOUNTING ONE'S DECISION-MAKING PROCESS

### Its meaning

Insofar as other people will be affected by one's choices, those choices must be communicated to (and hopefully accepted by) them. For example, friends of Mr. D, the pharmacist dying from AIDS, will experience some distress and inconvenience as a result of his choice. As his primary care givers, they will have to participate in his experience with disease, disability, and death. If respect for autonomous decisions were the only relevant factor, free and informed consent by competent patients would suffice to preclude interference and insure cooperation. However, one's choices often impose demands on others who may be reluctant to help, and may even threaten to interfere with the patient's chosen course. Helpers—professional or lay—may need to be convinced of the wisdom of one's choice. The ability to recount one's decision-making process is the capacity to explain the factors—personal and medical—that generated a choice, and why it is personally preferable.

### Its relationship to decision making

In a theoretical sense, this capacity has less to do with making decisions than with engaging the support of others who may be better positioned to effect them. Even when others are affected unfavorably by our choices, we often expect them to help us realize our goals. Since they have the right to refuse, it becomes necessary to impart a sense of importance regarding those choices so that they can understand and be moved to help, or at least not hinder, one's efforts.[6] Part of respecting autonomous decisions is not having them ignored or thwarted. The ability to recount one's decision-making process in the face of others' dismay or disagreement can ameliorate their criticism and engage their assistance, or at least forestall their interference.

### Its degrees

Part of promoting autonomous decisions is persuading others to help us, even when they do not approve of our goals or the means to them. We must, therefore, be able to provide explanations that help them understand our choices. At best, this will mean sharing, in as articulate a fashion as possible, the process that led to the decision. We must be able to recount what factors were considered, how various alternatives were evaluated, and what personal values were pivotal to the process.

Adequately competent persons are able to recount the process by which they arrived at their decisions. They are able to argue persuasively about how decisions will promote their well-being and why they should be honored, even when others are reluctant to accept them. They may recount their burden to benefit calculations, their current felt and cognitive emotions, and their projected felt emotions. They may appeal to the considerable effort they have expended in making what, for them, are appropriate choices. They may also appeal to the moral propriety of respecting autonomous decisions. Regardless of whether others are persuaded, they will continue to embrace their decisions.

Sometimes so thorough a description will not be possible. Marginally competent persons are likely to be less articulate, either because they are not, by nature, very fluent; because, given the extensive participation by others, they may be unclear about the entire process; or because they cannot at that time muster the energy needed for a complete recapitulation. They may be able to state that the choices are very important to them. Or they may simply mutely persevere in spite of efforts to dissuade them or to interfere. They may be less adamant than adequately competent persons. At best they may only be able to assent or dissent to explanations suggested by others, or give a terse justification, perhaps a simple but firm "This is the best thing *for me.*"

Worse yet, decision makers may be totally at a loss to articulate justifications for their choices. They may not fully understand these themselves; they may be unable, for whatever reasons, to express anything to others or to behave as if they were committed to a course of action. Yet the importance of the choice to the decision maker may be signalled by her perseverance in that choice. The fact that in the face of persistent opposition she remains constant in her decision gives evidence of its gravity and of its worth to her as a person worthy of respect.

Nor can the distress she would suffer, were others to act against her best interests as she herself has defined them, be discounted. One way of showing respect for persons is to not subject them to pain and suffering to which they have not consented.[7] Decision makers may need to appeal to this value to enlist others to their cause. Absent the ability to coherently argue for protection of this value, their persistence in acting in concert with the choice will perhaps serve as an eloquent, if less articulate, expression of it.

The inadequately competent person fails to give any justification for her choice. She may state, but fail to persevere, either verbally or behaviorally, in her choice. She cannot explain her decision. She does not insist, nor act as if she believes, that it should be honored.

The importance of recounting the decision-making process, then, is that this capacity testifies to the importance of the decision to the well-being of the decision maker as he himself has defined it. In addition, it serves to engage the assistance of others who may be needed to operationalize one's choices. Because completion of most health care tasks almost always requires the participation or understanding of others—especially HCPs—the decision maker must be able to convey to others that his choice is important to him. Adequately competent persons will give both verbal and behavioral testimony to the worth of their decisions. Marginally competent persons will give some, albeit less compelling, evidence. Incompetent choosers will give neither.

## CONCLUSIONS

In this chapter competence has been described in terms of the capacities to receive information, recognize relevant information as information, remember information, relate information to oneself and one's values and circumstances, reason about alternatives, rank alternatives in order of preference, resolve situations, resign oneself to one's choices, and recount one's decision-making process. These abilities must be intact for a person to be adequately competent to give or refuse a consent that will be respected by other persons. The hallmark of the adequately competent person is the possession and independent exercise of these capacities. Absence of or inability to exercise these capacities renders a person incompetent to give or refuse consent. Decisions regarding the incompetent person will necessarily be made by others.

Between adequate and inadequate competence lies marginal competence. Marginally competent persons differ from the former in that they require the assistance of others to reach a decision. They differ from the latter in that, given time and assistance, they can usually reach (or agree with) a decision.

Persons who make autonomous decisions should generally have them respected. This is because autonomous choices are, in and of themselves, worthy of respect. In addition, autonomous decisions help to insure that persons' lives go the way they want them to go. Competence is the first criterion for autonomous decision making. The analyses in this and the preceding chapter identify the structure of and the necessary capacities for competence to consent.

## NOTES

1. The concept of recognizable reasons is more fully discussed in Erde (1991), and Freedman (1981).

2. Three scholars who reach a similar conclusion are Aristotle, Sir David Ross, and Baruch Brody. They argue that appropriate actions are always defined, in part, by the circumstances in which the action is contemplated. Since circumstances are always, to some extent, imprecisely specified,

what one ought to do is always a judgment. Brody's discussion focuses explicitly on health care decision making (Brody, 1988, especially chapters 5–7). Similarly, Roth et al. (1977, p. 284) claim that the complexities of consent situations quite likely make the search for a single test for competence a "search for a holy grail."

3. While smell and taste also give humans interesting and useful information, they do not provide the sort of information required in the consent setting. Thus, only sight, hearing, and touch will be discussed.

4. Level of consciousness also correlates with degree of competence. Adequately competent persons are alert and attentive to explanations. Marginally competent persons may be lethargic and initially inattentive, but they can be stimulated to attend to factual explanations. Inadequately competent persons are obtunded or stuporous and, therefore, unable to attend to discussions.

5. In cases of pathological indecision persons are quite unable to make a choice, even if they have been able to construct burden to benefit ratios, assign probabilities, and relate options to their own well-being. Part of the pathology in such cases seems to be an unusually strong concern that important data may have been overlooked and, hence, that any decision will be made on the basis of incomplete evidence. Any choice that eliminates any opportunity from further consideration provokes fear that one has made the wrong choice. If choice commits one to any sort of "irreversible" action, the person worries about missed opportunities, or fears his life may be irretrievably ruined.

6. Even HCPs, whose Codes of Ethics commit them to promoting the patient's welfare, can withdraw from the care of patients whose requests, if honored, would require the HCP to sacrifice her own personal or moral values. Abortion and euthanasia are common examples of such a conflict.

7. Persons can, of course, elect to undergo misery (and, sometimes, a great deal of it) to accomplish goals that they have chosen. Willfully to undertake suffering for the sake of a chosen purpose is not, however, the same thing as suffering for others' choices.

# 6

# Implications and
# Anticipated Criticisms

Because of the increased complexity of the concept of competence, the role it plays in the clinical arena is undergoing important changes that will probably be evolutionary in nature. That is, the benefits of an expanded definition will only unfold as HCPs and courts come to appreciate its implications and become increasingly adept at applying it in the day-to-day provision of health care. Some general predictions can, however, be made here.

## IMPLICATIONS OF A NEW UNDERSTANDING OF COMPETENCE TO CONSENT

The definition of competence to consent has the potential to alter health care practice in several interesting ways. First, HCPs' traditional appeals to medical consequences will be reduced. If I am right about the relationship of respect for autonomy and beneficence to the concept of competence, then invoking consequences as grounds for a declaration of incompetence must be rejected. One might, of course, make such appeals in conversation to persuade competent persons to reevaluate choices that do not seem to promote their well-being. However, further appeals to outcomes are prohibited. From a practical aspect, the threat of really noxious consequences may serve as a mandate to further investigate a patient's database, to make certain he has all relevant information and genuinely understands the ramifications of his choice. But if a person is competent, appeals to any horrible results that might follow from his choice are forestalled (at least insofar as competence is concerned). Thus, HCPs may find themselves participating in therapeutic regimens they find distasteful.

The goal of health care has long been to promote the welfare of patients. Traditionally this good has been defined (almost) solely according to the guidelines for successful professional practice. (In the crassest sort of way, this philosophy is recognized in the old saw: "The operation was a success, but the patient died.") The justification for such an approach was often based on claims that patients were, if not incompetent, at least suffering from a reduction in competence. Disproving such claims has been difficult and, in the absence (although sometimes in the presence as well) of strenuous resistance on the patient's part, the recommendations of the HCPs were generally followed even when the patient expressed reticence or dissatisfaction. Such scenarios ought to disappear with a reliable and thorough definition of competence to consent. Insofar as competence can be determined, its presence in a person will make her the court of last appeal in the decision-making process. The competent patient is the best authority of what will, in fact, promote her well-being. The definition of competence should more reliably enable HCPs to attain long-cherished professional goals.

This reflection leads to the second crucial implication: the need for a valid and reliable test for competence is critical. With a definition in place, the absence of reliable methods for testing will no longer be theoretically defensible. Although this work has not attempted to formulate a test for competence, from the clinician's perspective, testing is arguably the most important aspect of competence to consent. Located in the day-to-day demands of health care, in which the practice of informed consent requires that a person's competence be established, clinicians need a tool by which to determine who can and cannot give valid consent. As noted throughout, there is currently no dependable test for competence, because one cannot construct a reliable test without knowing what to look for. With a definition of competence in place, this important task can begin, for now there are guidelines to steer its undertaking. The list of requisite capacities provides a direction that HCPs interested in constructing a test for competence can follow.

Moreover, for patients identified as incompetent, the definition and the tests it will engender help HCPs locate more precisely the source of a patient's incompetence. HCPs can hone in on the exact capacity (or capacities) that generate the decision-making inability. Attention can then be paid to resolving the particular difficulties. Attempts at rehabilitation will be better focused.

A third general implication of this project would be the application of these concepts to children. One problem that has plagued pediatrics is the competence of young people. The law, of course, is quite clear: anyone below the age of majority is not an adult, and therefore may not have the rights (e.g., decision-making authority) that adults possess. But the question of competence, turning as it does on the possession of capacities, ought not be decided by fiat in medical settings. Given that the moral justification for informed consent appeals to respecting autonomy and producing the best consequences, there may be good moral reasons for extending decision-making authority to children who possess the relevant capacities. At the very least, since the cooperation of children is often essential for successful completion of particular health care ventures, understanding how competence applies to children in these settings will be useful. In addition, designations of competence are especially important for resolving cases in which children and their parents or guardians strongly disagree about how best to proceed in managing the child's illness.

In a broad sense this extension of competence to children is part of the project of constructing a test for competence. Children who pass the test may be considered competent decision makers. But there will be more to this investigation: it requires that we determine who precisely is the appropriate decision maker in a health care setting. And this determination will have interesting sociological, philosophical, and legal implications for children and adults (e.g., in deciding when children are competent enough to override their parents and construct their own plans of care).

Another theoretical question that attends free and informed consent is this: What counts, within the practice, as a voluntary consent. Recall that a valid consent is voluntarily as well as competently given. The same concerns that attend determinations of competence attend determinations of voluntariness. For the practice of informed consent to stand on solid foundations, this concept must also be examined.

My sense is that many of the capacities that inform determinations of competence—most notably informability and cognitive and affective capability—also inform determinations of voluntariness. The practice of informed consent can profit from further analysis in this area, and the analysis of competence may be able to suggest a structure for that project.

## ANTICIPATING THE CRITIC

HCPs will probably find (at least) three causes for concern with this approach. First, they will claim that there are not enough hours in the day to carry out such complex determinations. Second, HCPs will note that under certain conditions—namely, those in which life and health are at stake—patients may desire to abandon their previous value structures, if they ever had them in the first place. To hold such patients hostage to "out-dated" values is inappropriate. Third, some HCPs will no doubt claim that decision-making authority is not settled by the question of competence alone. Do these criticisms undermine the approach just developed?

### So Many Patients, So Little Time

First, assessments of competence will initially be more difficult than in the past. Part of the difficulty, of course, lies in the simple fact that many capacities will have to be explicitly assessed. Evaluations will be more complex, and it will be more difficult to say with certainty that persons are or are not competent. Such difficulties attend any venture that requires procedural changes in professional practice. For the following reasons, I think this complexity will not pose insurmountable problems.

First, as noted in earlier chapters, in most patients, competence can be assumed. The vast majority of patients are competent upon entering the health care system, give no evidence to suggest otherwise, are rightly assumed to be competent, and are treated as such. Thus, the occasions for using this approach are infrequent, making the time constraints less worrisome.

However, when a patient's behavior triggers a suspicion of incompetence, will HCPs have time to fully consider all the issues? Again, as noted earlier, the procedure described here seems to capture much of what HCPs currently consider when evaluating patients' decision-making ability. If so, HCPs are not being asked to do anything radically different, but to think about their activities within a new conceptual framework.

Even if the proposed approach is completely foreign to HCPs, it is, in that respect, like any other procedural change. HCPs are or should be accustomed to revising patient care procedures when the advantages for patient care indicate that revisions are appropriate. As with any new procedure, competence consideration will be cumbersome at first. But again as with any new procedure, HCPs will get better (and swifter) with practice.

Most importantly, insofar as competence is an important aspect for appropriate decision-making authority, and insofar as it promotes patient welfare, its accurate determination is an important mechanism by which HCPs can achieve the moral and professional goals of protecting patient autonomy and well-being. These goals are presumably worth some inconvenience.

## Must Patients Be "Authentic"?

The justification for a more complex approach to competence is largely based on the notion that competence is a means of promoting patient welfare in terms of previously established goals, values, and interests. A common objection is that when patients are faced with serious life- or health-threatening illnesses, their goals, values, and interests can—or should—change. This objection is a powerful one that needs careful consideration.

Does morality insist that value structures be immune to revision? Such an approach would seriously jeopardize persons' welfare. Imagine what would happen if Olympic hopefuls were not allowed to revise their goals or values after repeatedly failing to make the team. These athletes would be doomed to continue their efforts long after they had lost interest in the goal and long after they possessed the abilities to reach it. Such a fixation cannot be in their best interests. In fact, people often revise or rescind their goals, values, and interests. The reconsideration of one's value structure is part of life, so to hold persons hostage to outdated goals fails to promote or protect autonomy and beneficence. From the moral point of view, persons must have latitude to edit their value structures.

Does morality insist that value structure revisions be permitted by anyone at anytime for any reasons? This approach also seriously jeopardizes persons' welfare. Renouncing one's values, goals, and interests without giving the act serious consideration also fails to promote or protect autonomy or beneficence. The same Olympic hopeful who suffers a fractured ankle in an automobile accident, but who drunkenly refuses surgery cannot be taken seriously. The request is not autonomous and cannot genuinely be supposed to promote the patient's welfare. By fully ignoring values, goals, and interests that have provided direction to her life, she (and her HCPs, if they go along with her) risks grievous harm.

The only option remaining is that some patients at some time in some circumstances may legitimately revise their value structures. The questions are who, when, and why. Who is straightforward: any autonomous decision maker. Why is because the previous goals and values have become impossible or are no longer compelling. Thus, the Olympic hopeful who suffers an injury that prevents further competition has good reason to set new goals. Likewise, the young athlete who, after consideration, decides he is no longer interested in international competition (and there may be countless reasons why different athletes lose interest), can restructure his aims. Thus the when follows the why. The key point here is that there is a connection between past, present, and future value structures. In the absence of any connection, there is no way to know what actions will promote a patient's welfare. The persons concerned must have some sense of these relationships—it is how they answer the why and when questions.

Health care conditions not uncommonly motivate patients to reconsider their values, goals, beliefs, and interests. Like the athlete who loses interest and ability by natural attrition, patients often lose interests or abilities though disease, disability, or injury. When the profession is unable to cure a disease, repair an injury, or reverse a disability, patients may be forced to rethink what they count as important, as well as appropriate means to their goals. Patients who take their original value structures as their starting points and revise in light of their altered circumstances maintain their authenticity.

### None of My Patients Has an Autonomously Developed Value Structure

A related, potentially devastating claim is the criticism that most people have not and never will consciously undertake the construction of a value structure. Even those who actually have a structure in place rarely know it, may understand it poorly, and may be unable to articulate it. Thus, the concept of a value structure cannot bear the weight of this concept of competence to consent. What are we to make of this charge?

If the critic means that most people cannot defend their choices in terms used by HCPs or bioethicists, I agree. If the meaning is that most people do not have values or goals that provide decision-making guidance, I disagree. While it is true that most persons/patients do not defend their choices by referring to autonomously developed value structures, they do defend their choices in terms of goals, values, and interests (although they rarely use those terms either). What they do say, however, can be readily understood in terms of those concepts. The hypertensive patient who says, "If you make me exercise, I have less time for work," is indicating something about his goals and interests. Likewise, the woman with ovarian cysts facing an exploratory laparotomy who insists that one ovary be preserved because she wishes to have children is reporting a goal. The post-myocardial infarction patient who hesitates to give up his beer and cigarettes, because "on Saturday night me and the boys celebrate gettin' through another week," is saying something about his interests and values. Eventually, these patients may get around to revising these values, goals, and interests. But they often fight hard to avoid it, not because they enjoy giving their caregivers a hard time, but because the activities in question are part of who they are, what they want to be or do, and what is important to them. In sum, they have value structures even when they fail to realize it. And the protection of their values is important to their welfare—even if only as a starting point for revision.

## There is More to Moral Decision Making than Competence

There are two schools of thought as to whether designations of competence settle the issue of decision-making authority. For simplicity's sake, I will call these the libertarian and communitarian schools. Libertarians take personal freedom as their foundational moral value. Once the person's competence has been established, the person is given the facts and presented with the choices. He makes his choice and others abide by it, usually with varying degrees of enthusiasm. The communitarian, however, takes freedom to be one among many, equally important, values. True, the competent person has decision-making authority, but other questions are also germane. Will the person's choice do unintentional or incidental harm to others? For example, the person who chooses to forgo treatment and die sooner than he would with therapy is often charged with exposing his family and friends to extra grief. Some will count this extra grief as a reason against respecting the decision, even though the decision maker is competent, and even though he is free to refuse treatment.

These philosophies are poles apart, subject to enormous dialogue in contemporary literature, and far from resolution. For our purposes, we need only note that in both cases competence plays an important role. For the libertarian, only competent persons can appropriately claim freedom from interference. For the communitarian, respecting autonomous decisions is an important, if not the only, moral value. Thus, whichever approach is preferred, competence needs to be determined.

**Try It. You'll Like It.**

The definition of competence developed here should enable HCPs to make important progress toward ensuring their patients' ability to give morally valid consents to or refusals of treatment. To those who are intrigued by the approach, as well as those who are skeptical, I urge that you give it a try. If it helps you to make sense of your tough cases, you and your patients will be better off. If not, perhaps your experience will lead to new theoretical efforts that will be more fruitful.

In either case, it is my hope that this work will contribute to both the theoretical dialogue and the practical process that enhance HCPs' ability to respect patients' autonomy and promote their well-being.

# Bibliography

Abernethy, V. 1984. "Compassion, Control, and Decisions about Competency." *American Journal of Psychiatry* 141:53–60.
_____. 1991. "Judgments about Patient Competence: Cultural and Eco-
nomic Antecedents." In M. A. G. Cutter and E. E. Shelp, eds., *Competency:
A Study of Informal Competency Determinations in Primary Care.* Kluwer
Academic Publishers, Dordrecht, The Netherlands.
Alfidi, R. J. 1971. "Informed Consent: A Study of Patient Reaction." *Journal of
the American Medical Association* 216:1325–29.
American Medical Association Council on Ethical and Judicial Affairs. 1989.
*Current Opinions.* American Medical Association, Chicago.
American Nurses' Association. 1973. "Code for Nurses with Interpretive
Statements." *Perspectives on the Code for Nurses.* American Nurses' Associ-
ation, Kansas City.
Anthony, J. C., et al. 1982. "Limits of the "Mini-Mental State" As a Screening
Test for Dementia and Delirium among Hospital Patients." *Psychological
Medicine* 12:397–408.
Appelbaum, P. S., and T. Grisso. 1988. "Assessing Patients' Capacities to Con-
sent to Treatment." *New England Journal of Medicine* 319:1635–38.
Appelbaum, P. S., and L. H. Roth. 1981. "Clinical Issues in the Assessment of
Competency." *American Journal of Psychiatry* 138:1462–67.
_____. 1984. "Involuntary Treatment in Medicine and Psychiatry." *Ameri-
can Journal of Psychiatry* 141:202–5.
_____. 1983. "Patients Who Refuse Treatment in Medical Hospitals." *Jour-
nal of the American Medical Association* 250:1296–1301.
Appelbaum, P. S., et al. 1987. *Informed Consent: Legal Theory and Clinical Prac-
tice.* Oxford University Press, New York.
Aristotle. 1973. *De Anima* and *Nichomachean Ethics.* In R. McKeon, trans. and
ed. *Introduction to Aristotle.* The University of Chicago Press, Chicago.
Baron, J., and J. C. Hershey. 1988. "Outcome Bias in Decision Evaluation."
*Journal of Personality and Social Psychology* 54:569–79.
Baumgarten, E. 1980. 'The Concept of 'Competence' in Medical Ethics." *Jour-
nal of Medical Ethics* 6:180–84.
Beauchamp, T. 1991. "Competence." In M. A. G. Cutter and E. E. Shelp, eds.
*Competency: A Study of Informal Competency Determinations in Primary
Care.* Kluwer Academic Publishers, Dordrecht, The Netherlands.

Beauchamp, T. L., and L. B. McCullough. 1984. *Medical Ethics: The Moral Responsibilities of Physicians.* Prentice-Hall, Inc., Englewood Cliffs.

Bentham, J. 1948. *An Introduction to the Principles of Morals and Legislation.* Hafner Publishing Company, New York.

Black, F. W., and R. L. Strub. 1986. "Memory Assessment Using the Strub-Black Mental Status Examination and the Wechsler Memory Scale." *Journal of Clinical Psychology* 42:147–55.

Bloom, J. D., and L. R. Faulkner. 1987. "Competency Determinations in Civil Commitment." *American Journal of Psychiatry* 144:193–96.

Brand, N., and J. Jolles. 1987. "Information Processing in Depression and Anxiety." *Psychological Medicine* 17:145–53.

Brandt, R. B. 1982. "Two Concepts of Utility." In H. B. Miller and W. H. Williams, eds. *The Limits of Utilitarianism.* University of Minnesota Press, Minneapolis.

Brody, B. A. 1982. "Towards a Theory of Respect for Persons." In O. H. Green, ed., *Respect for Persons: Tulane Studies in Philosophy,* Tulane University, New Orleans.

———. 1988. *Life and Death Decision Making.* Oxford University Press, New York.

Brophy v. New England Sinai Hospital, Inc. 398 Mass. 417, N.E. 2d 626 (1986).

Buchanan, A. 1978. "Medical Paternalism." *Philosophy and Public Affairs* 7:370–90.

———. 1985. *Surrogate Decisionmaking for Elderly Individuals Who are Incompetent or of Questionable Competence.* Government Printing Office, Washington, D.C.

Buchanan, A., and D. Brock. 1986. "Deciding for Others." *Milbank Memorial Quarterly* 64:17–94.

———. 1989. *Deciding for Others: The Ethics of Surrogate Decision Making.* Cambridge University Press, Cambridge, Massachusetts.

Burch, E. A., and S. R. Andrews. 1987. "Cognitive Dysfunction in Psychiatric Consultation Subgroups: Use of Two Screening Tests." *Southern Medical Journal* 80:1079–82.

Callahan, S. 1988. "The Role of Emotion in Ethical Decision Making." *Hastings Center Report* 18:9–14.

Caplan, A. L. 1988. "Informed Consent and Provider-Patient Relationships in Rehabilitation Medicine." *Archives of Physical Medicine and Rehabilitation* 69:312–17.

Capron, A. M. 1974. "Informed Consent in Catastrophic Disease Research and Treatment." *University of Pennsylvania Law Review* 123:340–438.

Carnerie, F. 1987. "Crisis and Informed Consent: Analysis of a Law-Medicine Malocclusion." *American Journal of Law and Medicine* 12:55–97.

Conroy, 486 A. 2d 1209 (N.J. 1985).

Cruzan v. Director, Missouri Department of Health, 110 S.Ct. 2841 (1990).

Cullen, D.J., et al. 1974. "Therapeutic Intervention Scoring System: A Method for Quantitative Comparison of Patient Care." *Critical Care Medicine* 2:57–60.

Culver, C. M., and B. Gert. 1982. *Philosophy in Medicine.* Oxford University Press, New York.

Cutter, M. A. G. and E. E. Shelp, eds. 1991. *Competency: A Study of Informal Competency Determinations in Primary Care.* Kluwer Academic Press, Dordrecht, Holland.

de Souza, R. 1980. "The Rationality of Emotions." In A. Rorty, ed., *Explaining Emotions,* University of California Press, Berkeley.

Devine, P. 1978. *The Ethics of Homicide.* Cornell University Press, Ithaca, New York.

Dodd, M. J., and D. W. Mood. 1981. "Chemotherapy: Helping Patients to Know the Drugs They Are Receiving and Their Possible Side Effects." *Cancer Nursing,* 311–18.

Drane, J. F. 1984. "Competency to Give an Informed Consent: A Model for Making Clinical Assessments." *Journal of the American Medical Association* 252:925–27.

_____. 1985. "The Many Faces of Competency." *The Hastings Center Report* 15:17–21.

Dresser, R. 1984. "Bound to Treatment: The Ulysses Contract." *Hastings Center Report* 14:13–16.

_____. 1986. "Life, Death, and Incompetent Patients: Conceptual Infirmities and Hidden Values in the Law." *Arizona Law Review* 28:373–405.

Dworkin, G. 1982. "Autonomy and Informed Consent." In President's Commission for the Study of Ethical Problems in Medicine and Biomedical and Behavioral Research, *Making Health Care Decisions: A Report on the Ethical and Legal Implications of Informed Consent in the Patient-Practitioner Relationship, Volume Three: Appendices, Studies on the Foundations of Informed Consent,* U.S. Government Printing Office, Washington, D.C.

Dworkin, R. 1977. *Taking Rights Seriously.* Harvard University Press, Cambridge, MA.

Edwards, W. 1954. "The Theory of Decision Making." *Psychological Bulletin* 51:380–417.

Elster, J. 1982. "Sour Grapes—Utilitarianism and the Genesis of Wants." In A. Sen and B. Williams eds., *Utilitarianism and Beyond.* Cambridge University Press, Cambridge.

Engelhardt, H. T., Jr. 1986. *The Foundations of Bioethics.* Oxford University Press, New York.

Erde, E. L. 1991. "Breaking Up the Shell Game of Consequentialism: Incompetence—Concept and Ethics." In M.A.G. Cutter, and E.E.Shelp, eds., *Competency: A Study of Informal Competency Determinations in Primary Care.* Kluwer Academic Publishers, Dordrecht, The Netherlands.

Erickson, R. C., and M. L. Scott. 1977. "Clinical Memory Testing: A Review." *Psychological Bulletin* 84:1130–49.

Eth, S. 1985. "Competency and Consent to Treatment." *Journal of the American Medical Association* 253:778–79.

Faden, R. R., and T. L. Beauchamp. 1986. *A History and Theory of Informed Consent.* Oxford University Press, New York.

Faden, R., et al. 1981. "Disclosure of Information to Patients in Medical Care." *Medical Care* 19:718–33.

Fennell, M. J., et al. 1987. "Distraction in Neurotic and Endogenous Depression: An Investigation of Negative Thinking in Major Depressive Disorder." *Psychological Medicine* 17:441–52.

Folstein, M. F., et al. 1975. "'Mini-Mental State': A Practical Method for Grading the Cognitive State of Patients for the Clinician." *Journal of Psychiatric Research* 12:189–98.

Frank, R. H. 1988. *Passions within Reason: The Strategic Role of the Emotions.* W. W. Norton & Company, New York.

Frankena, W. 1973. *Ethics*, 2d ed., Prentice-Hall, Inc., Englewood Cliffs, NJ.

Frankfurt, H. 1971. "Freedom of the Will and the Concept of a Person." *Journal of Philosophy* 68:5–20.

Freedman, B. 1981. "Competence, Marginal and Otherwise." *International Journal of Law and Psychiatry* 4:53–72.

Gaylin, W. 1979. *Feelings: Our Vital Signs.* Harper & Row Publishers, New York.

_____. 1982. "The Competence of Children: No Longer All or None." *Hastings Center Report* 12:33–38.

Gelatt, H. B. 1989. "Positive Uncertainty: A New Decision-Making Framework for Counseling." *Journal of Counseling Psychology* 36:252–56.

Gert, B., and K. D. Clouser. 1986. "Rationality in Medicine: An Explication." *Journal of Medicine and Philosophy* 11:185–205.

Ginsberg, G. L. 1985. "Psychiatric History and Mental Status Examination." In H. I. Kaplan and B. J. Sadock, eds., *Comprehensive Textbook of Psychiatry,* Vol. 1. 4th ed. Williams & Wilkins, Baltimore.

Green, M. D. 1941. "Judicial Tests of Mental Incompetency." *Missouri Law Review* 6:141–65.

Hackler, C., et al., eds. 1989. *Advance Directives in Medicine.* Praeger, New York.

Hahn, R. A. 1982. "Culture and Informed Consent: An Anthropological Perspective," in President's Commission for the Study of Ethical Problems in Medicine and Biomedical and Behavioral Research, *Making Health Care Decisions: A Report on the Ethical and Legal Implications of Informed Consent in the Patient-Practitioner Relationship. Vol 3: Appendices, Studies on the Foundations of Informed Consent,* U.S. Government Printing Office, Washington, D.C.

Hart, R. P., J. A. Kwentus, J. R. Taylor, and S. W. Harkins. 1987. "Rate of Forgetting in Dementia and Depression." *Journal of Consulting and Clinical Psychology* 55:101–5.

Hinton, J., and E. Withers. 1971. "The Usefulness of the Clinical Tests of the Sensorium." *British Journal of Psychiatry* 119:9–18.

Hume, D. 1966. *Enquiries Concerning the Human Understanding* and *Concerning the Principles of Morals.* L. A. Selby-Bigge, ed., Oxford at the Clarendon Press, London.

_____. 1977. *A Treatise on Human Nature.* Dutton, New York.

Ingelfinger, F. J. 1972. "Informed (But Uneducated) Consent." *New England Journal of Medicine* 287:465–66.

Jacobs, J. W., M. R. Bernhard, A. Delgado, and J. J. Strain. 1977. "Screening for Organic Mental Syndromes in the Medically Ill." *Annals of Internal Medicine* 86:40–46.

Kant, I. 1959. *Foundations of the Metaphysics of Morals.* trans. L. W. Beck. The Bobbs-Merrill Company, Inc., Indianapolis.

——. 1965. *Critique of Pure Reason.* trans. N. K. Smith. St. Martin's Press, New York.

——. 1983. *Critique of Practical Reason.* trans. L. W. Beck. Bobbs-Merrill Educational Publishing, Indianapolis.

Katz, J. 1984. *The Silent World of Doctor and Patient.* The Free Press, New York.

Katz, R. L. 1977. "Informed Consent: Is It Bad Medicine?" *The Western Journal of Medicine* 126:426–28.

Keene, A. R., and D. J. Cullen. 1983. Therapeutic Intervention Scoring System: Update 1983." *Critical Care Medicine* 11:1–3.

Keller, M. B., and T. C. Manschreck. 1979. "The Biologic Mental Status Examination: Higher Intellectual Functioning." In A. Lazare, ed., *Outpatient Psychiatry: Diagnosis and Treatment,* The Williams and Wilkins Company, Baltimore.

Kendell, R. E. 1968. "An Important Source of Bias Affecting Ratings Made by Psychiatrists." *Journal of Psychiatric Research* 6:135–41.

Kiernan, R. J., et al. 1987. "The Neurobehavioral Cognitive Status Examination: A Brief but Differentiated Approach to Cognitive Assessment." *Annals of Internal Medicine* 107:481–85.

King, N., and A. Cross. 1989. "Children As Decision Makers: Guidelines for Pediatricians." *The Journal of Pediatrics* 115:10–16.

Knaus, W. A., et al. 1985. "APACHE II: A Severity of Disease Classification System." *Critical Care Medicine* 13:818–29.

Lankton, J. W., et al. 1977. "Emotional Responses to Detailed Risk Disclosure for Anesthesia: A Prospective, Randomized Study." *Anesthesiology* 46:294–96.

Leeb, D., et al. 1976. "Observations on the Myth of 'Informed Consent'." *Plastic and Reconstructive Surgery* 58:280–82.

LeGall, J. R. et al. 1984. "A Simplified Acute Physiology Score for ICU Patients." *Critical Care Medicine* 12:975–77.

Leikin, S. L. 1982. "Minors' Assent or Dissent to Medical Treatment." In President's Commission for the Study of Ethical Problems in Medicine and Biomedical and Behavioral Research, *Making Health Care Decisions: A Report on the Ethical and Legal Implications of Informed Consent in the Patient-Practitioner Relationship, Volume Three: Appendices, Studies on the Foundations of Informed Consent,* U.S. Government Printing Office, Washington, D.C.

Lemeshow, S., D. Teres, H. Pastides, J. S. Avrunin, and J. S. Steinbrub. 1985. "A Method for Predicting Survival and Mortality of ICU Patients Using Objectively Derived Weights." *Critical Care Medicine* 13:519–25.

Lemeshow, S., D. Teres, J. S. Avrunin, and H. Pastides. 1987. "A Comparison of Methods to Predict Mortality of Intensive Care Unit Patients." *Critical Care Medicine* 15:715–18.

Lesser, H. 1983. "Consent, Competency and ECT: A Philosopher's Comment." *Journal of Medical Ethics* 9:144–45.

Lezak, M. D. 1983. *Neuropsychological Assessment.* 2d ed. Oxford University Press, New York.

Lidz, C., and A. Meisel. 1982. "Informed Consent and the Structure of Medical Care." In President's Commission for the Study of Ethical Problems in Medicine and Biomedical and Behavioral Research, *Making Health Care Decisions: A Report on the Ethical and Legal Implications of Informed Consent in the Patient-Practitioner Relationship, Volume Two: Appendices, Empirical Studies of Informed Consent,* U.S. Government Printing Office, Washington, D.C.

Lidz, C. W., A. Meisel, M. Osterweis, J. L. Holden, J. H. Marx, and M. R. Munetz. 1983. "Barriers to Informed Consent." *Annals of Internal Medicine* 99:539–43.

Lidz, C. W., A. Meisel, E. Zerubavel, M. Carter, R. M. Sestak, and L. H. Roth. 1984. *Informed Consent: A Study of Decisionmaking in Psychiatry.* The Guilford Press, New York.

Lynn, J. 1988. "Conflicts of Interest in Medical Decision-Making." *Journal of the American Geriatric Society* 36:945–50.

McCartney, J. R. 1986. "Physicians' Assessment of Cognitive Capacity: Failure to Meet the Needs of the Elderly." *Archives of Internal Medicine* 146:177–78.

McCartney, J. R., and L. M. Palmateer. 1985. "Assessment of Cognitive Deficit in Geriatric Patients: A Study of Physician Behavior." *Journal of the American Geriatrics Society* 33:467–71.

MacIntyre, A. 1981. *After Virtue: A Study in Moral Theory.* University of Notre Dame Press, Notre Dame, Indiana.

Mack, E. 1988. "Moral Rights and Causal Casuistry." In B. A. Brody, ed., *Moral Theory and Moral Judgments in Medical Ethics,* Kluwer Academic Publishers, Dordrecht, The Netherlands.

MacKinnon, R. A., and S. C. Yudofsky. 1986. *The Psychiatric Evaluation in Clinical Practice.* J. B. Lippincott Company, Philadelphia.

Mayo, D.J. 1986. "The Concept of Rational Suicide." *Journal of Medicine and Philosophy* 11:143–55.

Meisel, A., and L. H. Roth. 1981. "What We Do and Do Not Know about Informed Consent." *Journal of the American Medical Association* 246:2473–77.

Meisel, A., L. H. Roth, and C. W. Lidz. 1977. "Toward a Model of the Legal Doctrine of Informed Consent." *American Journal of Psychiatry* 134:285–89.

Mill, J. 1924. *Autobiography of John Stuart Mill.* Columbia University Press, New York.

———. 1975. *Utilitarianism.* Bobbs-Merrill Educational Publishing, Indianapolis.

———. 1982. *On Liberty,* Bobbs-Merrill Educational Publishing, Indianapolis.

Miller, B. L. 1981. "Autonomy and the Refusal of Lifesaving Treatment." *Hastings Center Report* 11:22–28.

Miller, R. D., and E. J. Germain. 1988. "The Retrospective Evaluation of Competency to Stand Trial." *Journal of Law and Psychiatry* 11:113–25.

Moore, G. E. 1978. *Ethics.* Oxford University Press, London.

Morreim, E. H. 1991. "Competence: At the Intersection of Law, Medicine, and Philosophy." In M. A. G. Cutter and E. E. Shelp, eds., *Competency: A Study of Informal Competency Determinations in Primary Care*, Kluwer Academic Publishers, Dordrecht, The Netherlands.

Moutsopoulos, L. 1984. "Truth-Telling to Patients." *Medicine and Law* 3:237–51.

Nagel, T. 1986. *The View from Nowhere*. Oxford University Press, New York.

National Conference of Commissioners on Uniform State Laws: 1982. "Uniform Law Commissioners' Model Health-Care Consent Act." National Conference of Commissioners on Uniform State Laws, Chicago.

Nelson, A., et al. 1986. "Bedside Cognitive Screening Instruments: A Critical Assessment." *The Journal of Nervous and Mental Disease* 174:73–83.

Owens, H., et al. 1987. "The Judge's View of Competence Evaluations II." *Bulletin of American Academy of Psychiatry and Law* 15:381–89.

Parfit, D. 1984. *Reasons and Persons*. Clarendon Press, Oxford.

Pavlo, A., et al. 1987. "Christian Science and Competence to Make Treatment Choices: Clinical Challenges in Assessing Values." *International Journal of Law and Psychiatry* 10:395–401.

Pellegrino, E. D. 1991. "Informal Judgments of Competence and Incompetence." In M. A. G. Cutter and E. E. Shelp, eds., *Competency: A Study of Informal Competency Determinations in Primary Care*, Kluwer Academic Publishers, Dordrecht, The Netherlands.

Perkins, D. N. 1981. *The Mind's Best Work*. Harvard University Press, Cambridge, Massachusetts.

Perl, M. 1991. "Competency Judgments: Case Studies from the Psychiatrist's Perspective." In M. A. G. Cutter and E. E. Shelp, eds., *Competency: A Study of Informal Competency Determinations in Primary Care*, Kluwer Academic Publishers, Dordrecht, The Netherlands.

Pfeiffer, E. 1975. "A Short Portable Mental Status Questionnaire for the Assessment of Organic Brain Deficit in Elderly Patients." *American Geriatrics Society* 23:433–41.

Pincoffs, E. L. 1991. "Judgments of Incompetence and Their Moral Presuppositions." In M. A. G. Cutter and E. E. Shelp, eds., *Competency: A Study of Informal Competency Determinations in Primary Care*, Kluwer Academic Publishers, Dordrecht, The Netherlands.

Pollay, R. W. 1970. "A Model of Decision Times in Difficult Situations." *Psychological Bulletin* 77: 274–81.

President's Commission for the Study of Ethical Problems in Medicine and Biomedical and Behavioral Research. 1982a. *Making Health Care Decisions: A Report on the Ethical and Legal Implications of Informed Consent in the Patient-Practitioner Relationship. Volume One: Report.* U.S. Government Printing Office, Washington, D.C.

————. 1982b. *Making Health Care Decisions: A Report on the Ethical and Legal Implications of Informed Consent in the Patient-Practitioner Relationship, Volume Three: Appendices, Studies on the Foundations of Informed Consent,* U.S. Government Printing Office, Washington, D.C.

Rawls, J. 1955. "Two Concepts of Rules." *Philosophical Review* 64:3–32.

Reitan, R. M., and D. Wolfson. 1985. *The Halstead-Reitan Neuropsychological Test Battery: Theory and Clinical Interpretation.* Neuropsychology Press, Tucson.

Rennie, D. 1980. "Informed Consent by 'Well-Nigh Abject' Adults." *The New England Journal of Medicine* 302:917–18.

Robertson, J. A. 1991. "The Geography of Competency." In M. A. G. Cutter and E. E. Shelp, eds., *Competency: A Study of Informal Competency Determinations in Primary Care*, Kluwer Academic Publishers, Dordrecht, The Netherlands.

Roe, P. F. 1982. "Prognostic Value of the Abbreviated Mental Status Questionnaire." *Gerontology* 28:252–57.

Rorty, A., ed. 1980. *Explaining Emotions.* University of California Press, Berkeley.

————. 1980. "Explaining Emotions" and "Introduction." In A. Rorty, ed. *Explaining Emotions.* University of California Press, Berkeley.

Rosoff, A. J., and G. L. Gottlieb. 1987. "Preserving Personal Autonomy for the Elderly." *Journal of Legal Medicine* 8:1–47.

Ross, W. D. 1963. *The Right and the Good.* Oxford University Press, New York.

Roth, L. H. 1979. "A Commitment Law for Patients, Doctors, and Lawyers." *American Journal of Psychiatry* 136:1121–27.

Roth, L. H., A. Meisel, and C. W. Lidz. 1977. "Tests of Competency to Consent to Treatment." *American Journal of Psychiatry* 134:279–84.

Roth, L. H., P. S. Appelbaum, R. Sallee, C. F. Reynolds, III, and G. Huber. 1982a. "The Dilemma of Denial in the Assessment of Competency to Refuse Treatment." *American Journal of Psychiatry* 139:910–13.

Roth, L. H., C. W. Lidz, A. Meisel, P. H. Soloff, K. Kaufman, D. G. Spiker, and F. G. Foster. 1982b. "Competency to Decide about Treatment or Research: An Overview of Some Empirical Data." *International Journal of Law and Psychiatry* 5:29–50.

Schaffner, K. F. 1991. "Competency: A Triaxial Concept." In M. A. G. Cutter and E. E. Shelp, eds., *Competency: A Study of Informal Competency Determinations in Primary Care*, Kluwer Academic Publishers, Dordrecht, The Netherlands.

Scheffler, I. 1977. "In Praise of the Cognitive Emotions." *Teachers College Record* 79:171–86.

Schwamm, L. H., et al. 1987. "The Neurobehavioral Cognitive Status Examination: Comparison with the Cognitive Capacity Screening Examination and the Mini-Mental State Examination in a Neurosurgical Population." *Annals of Internal Medicine* 107:486–91.

Sen, A. K. 1977. "Rational Fools: A Critique of the Behavioral Foundations of Economic Theory." *Philosophy and Public Affairs* 6:317–44.

————. 1982. "Rights and Agency." *Philosophy and Public Affairs* 11:3–39.

————. 1986. "The Right to Take Personal Risks." In D. MacLean, ed., *Values at Risk*, Rowman and Allenheld, Totowa.

Sherlock, R. 1983. "Consent, Competency, and ECT: Some Critical Suggestions." *Journal of Medical Ethics* 9:141–43.

Sidgwick, H. 1981. *The Methods of Ethics.* Hackett Publishing Company, Inc., Indianapolis.

Smith, A. 1967. "The Serial Sevens Subtraction Test." *Archives of Neurology* 17:78–80.

Smith, D. 1986. "Legal Recognition of Neocortical Death." *Cornell Law Review*

71:850–88.
Solomon, R. C. 1976. *The Passions: The Myth and Nature of Human Emotion.* Anchor Press/Doubleday, Garden City, New York.
Stanley, B., et al. 1984. "The Elderly Patient and Informed Consent." *Journal of the American Medical Association* 252:1302–6.
Stone, A. A. 1976. "Competency to Stand Trial." In *Mental Health and Law: A System in Transition,* U.S. Government Printing Office, Washington, D.C.
Strub, R. L., and F. W. Black. 1985. *The Mental Status Examination in Neurology.* 2d Edition. F. A. Davis Company, Philadelphia.
Sumner, L. 1981. *Abortion and Moral Theory.* Princeton University Press, Princeton.
Tancredi, L. 1982. "Competency for Informed Consent: Conceptual Limits of Empirical Data." *International Journal of Law and Psychiatry* 5:51–63.
Tancredi, L. R. 1987. "The Mental Status Examination: Its Meaning and Validity in Caring for the Elderly." *Generations* 11:14–31.
Taylor, A., et al. 1980. "Cognitive Tasks in the Mental Status Examination." *The Journal of Nervous and Mental Disease* 168:167–70.
Taylor, P. J. 1983. "Consent, Competency, and ECT: A Psychiatrist's View." *Journal of Medical Ethics* 9:146–51.
Thompson, William C. 1982. "Psychological Issues in Informed Consent." In President's Commission for the Study of Ethical Problems in Medicine and Biomedical and Behavioral Research, *Making Health Care Decisions: A Report on the Ethical and Legal Implications of Informed Consent in the Patient-Practitioner Relationship, Volume Three: Appendices, Studies on the Foundations of Informed Consent,* U.S. Government Printing Office, Washington, D.C.
Tooley, M. 1983. *Abortion and Infanticide.* Oxford University Press, New York.
Toombs, S. K., 1992. *The Meaning of Illness: A Phenomenological Account of the Different Perspectives of Physician and Patient.* Kluwer Academic Publishers, Dordrecht, The Netherlands.
Tversky, A., and D. Kahneman. 1974. "Judgment under Uncertainty: Heuristics and Biases." *Science* 185:1124–31.
————. 1981. "The Framing of Decisions and the Psychology of Choice." *Science* 211:453–58.
United States Law Week 1984. "Mental Health." *United States Law Week* 52:2357–58.
Wear, S. 1991. "Patient Freedom and Competence in Health Care." In M.A.G. Cutter and E.E. Shelp, eds., *Competency: A Study of Informal Competency Determinations in Primary Care,* Kluwer Academic Publishers, Dordrecht, The Netherlands.
Wear, S. 1993. *Informed Consent: Patient Autonomy and Physician Beneficence within Clinical Medicine.* Kluwer Academic Press, Dordrecht, Holland.
Weinstock, R., et al. 1984. "Competence to Give Informed Consent for Medical Procedures." *Bulletin of the American Academy of Psychiatry and Law* 12:117–25.
Wikler, D. 1979. "Paternalism and the Mildly Retarded." *Philosophy and Public Affairs* 8:377–92.

# Index